The Public Policy Theory Primer

The Public Policy Theory Primer

Kevin B. Smith
University of Nebraska, Lincoln

Christopher W. Larimer
University of Northern Iowa

Westview Press
A Member of the Perseus Books Group

Every effort has been made to secure required permissions to use all images, maps, and other art included in this volume.

Westview Press books are available at special discounts for bulk purchases in the United States by corporations, institutions, and other organizations. For more information, please contact the Special Markets Department at the Perseus Books Group, 2300 Chestnut Street, Suite 200, Philadelphia, PA 19103, or call (800) 810-4145, x5000, or e-mail special.markets@perseusbooks.com.

Designed by Pauline Brown
Set in 10.5-point Minion by the Perseus Books Group

Library of Congress Cataloging-in-Publication Data

Smith, Kevin B.
  The public policy theory primer / Kevin B. Smith, Christopher W. Larimer.
    p. cm.
  Includes bibliographical references and index.
  ISBN 978-0-8133-4381-5 (alk. paper)
  1. Policy sciences. 2. Political planning. I. Larimer, Christopher W. (Christopher Wesley) II. Title.

  H97.S58 2009
  320.601—dc22

                                                            2008045540

10 9 8 7 6 5 4 3 2 1

CONTENTS

Preface   vii

1   Public Policy as a Concept and a Field (or Fields) of Study   1

2   Does Politics Cause Policy? Does Policy Cause Politics?   27

3   Who Makes Decisions? How Do They Make Decisions?
    Actors and Institutions   49

4   Where Does Policy Come From? The Policy Process   75

5   What Should We Do? The Field of Policy Analysis   101

6   What Have We Done? Impact Analysis and
    Program Evaluation   129

7   How Does It Work? Policy Implementation   155

8   Whose Values? Policy Design   181

9   New Directions in Policy Research   209

10 Do the Policy Sciences Exist?   231

    References   249
    Index   269

PREFACE

This book has its origins in the challenges of introducing upper-division undergraduates and beginning graduate students to the field of policy studies. Advanced survey courses in public policy are a standard curricular component of graduate programs in political science, public administration, and other fields, and similar courses are increasingly common for upper-division undergraduates. The field of public policy, however, is so broad, diffuse, and balkanized that imposing order on it from an instructor's perspective—let alone from a student's perspective—can be a difficult and frustrating undertaking.

In facing this challenge in our own classes, we came to the realization that the real challenge was not simply the logistical and organizational demands of putting together a coherent syllabus. What lay beneath was a fundamental question, perhaps *the* fundamental question, of the field of public policy studies: does such a field really exist? Comparing syllabi with colleagues rapidly revealed a widely divergent approach to introducing students to the study of public policy. The differences ranged across methodology, epistemology, theory, and specific policy subject matter. These are not just differences related to teaching style but differences in the substance of what is being taught. In viewing the fractured nature of the field of policy studies, we came to the conclusion that it is not possible to provide a comprehensive and coherent introductory survey of the field until those of us who study public policy come up with some coherent notion of what that field is.

This book has two primary aims. First, we seek to provide an integrationist vision of the field of policy studies. In short, we mount an argument for what is at the core of the study of public policy. Our approach is to define the key research questions in the field and use these to organize policy studies into coherent and related subfields that bear on those questions. Second, we seek to provide a coherent and organized introduction to the field of public policy studies. In other words, we see our table of contents as a reasonable outline for a generic survey course on public policy.

Our broader academic goal was inseparable from our pedagogical goal in that the latter is a direct outgrowth of the former. However, we also tried very hard to ensure that the latter is useful and practical even to those less concerned with the former. In what follows we claim to contribute to, rather than just report on, the professional academic public policy research. We are fully cognizant that our integrationist argument is going to meet skepticism, and perhaps even outright opposition, from some quarters. Rationalists and post-positivists, for example, will find plenty to damn and praise in equal measure. We recognize the scope for disagreement and encourage readers to make up their own minds rather than simply accept or reject our argument. Regardless of the level of agreement or disagreement on our more theoretical goals, however, what springs from our attempt to seriously engage and answer the question of "What is the field of policy studies?" is what we believe to be a coherent and logically organized survey of the field itself. Regardless of one's conclusions about our integrationist vision of the field, we believe the resulting organizational structure can be practically adopted and adapted to virtually any advanced survey course on public policy.

A book is rarely the product of the authors acknowledged on the cover; they simply get the credit for what is very much a team effort. Thanks are due to many people for making this book possible. These include former editor Steve Catalano, who aggressively nurtured the original idea, brought us to the good folks at Westview Press, and helped translate the idea into reality. Thanks also to Brooke Kush, who shepherded the book through rewrites, revisions, and the inevitable delays that come with working with academic authors. Kevin Smith would like to thank Catherine Smith and Brian Smith for providing pleasant distractions from writing (Catherine with star turns in *Macbeth*, Brian for being one of the best U12 midfielders in the state of Nebraska), and also Kelly Smith (who put up with her husband disappearing for lengthy weekend writing sessions because he'd spent too much time watching Shakespeare productions and youth soccer during the week). Chris Larimer would like to thank Drew Larimer for providing joy at all hours of the day *and* night (his birth also provided a nice deadline for finishing the first draft of the book), and Danielle Larimer for showing remarkable patience for her husband's irregular hours and recurring injuries.

CHAPTER ONE

Public Policy as a Concept and a Field (or Fields) of Study

A common criticism of the academic field of public policy studies is that no such thing exists. The study of public policy is concentrated in no single academic discipline, has no defining research question, is oriented toward no fundamental problem, has no unifying theory or conceptual framework, and has no unique methods or analytical tools. As the introduction to *The Oxford Handbook of Public Policy* puts it, the study of public policy is "a mood more than a science, a loosely organized body of precepts and positions rather than a tightly integrated body of systematic knowledge, more art and craft than a genuine 'science'" (Goodin, Rein, and Moran 2006, 5).

Yet despite the vagueness associated with the field of policy studies, there is no doubt that a lot of people *are* studying public policy. Undergraduate and graduate public policy courses are part of the curriculum in fields such as political science, public administration, and economics. In fact, for many, public policy is treated as an independent academic discipline in its own right: prestigious institutions such as Harvard University's Kennedy School of Government and the University of Michigan's Gerald R. Ford School of Public Policy offer PhD programs in policy studies. There are professional societies for the study of public policy (the Policy Studies Organization, the Society for the Policy Sciences) and entire academic journals devoted to promoting and disseminating the best of academic public policy scholarship (e.g., *Policy Studies Journal, Policy Science, Journal of Policy Analysis and Management*). Outside of academics, professional students of public policy—typically called policy analysts—are scattered throughout all levels of government, with staffers in the Congressional Budget Office, the Government Accountability Office, state-level legislative reference bureaus (not to mention various executive agency policy shops), all constituting a considerable industry dedicated to producing policy studies, reports, and recommendations. Outside of government, there are plenty of think tanks, interest groups, nongovernmental organizations (NGOs), and private sector consulting firms producing cost-benefit analyses, program evaluations, decision-making methods, and alternate public policy options on everything from watersheds in Colorado to counterterrorism strategies in the Middle East.

Is there anything that ties all of this together? Is there some common thread that unites such a varied group of people and activities? In short, is there really such a thing as a distinct and definable field that can be called public policy studies? This book seeks an answer to this question. We seek to provide readers not just with an overview of how policy is studied and why, nor simply to provide a tour of the major conceptual models and methodologies commonly employed in the study of public policy, though we hope to squarely address these goals in what follows. The core of our effort, however, and the true goal of this book, is to help readers to draw a reasoned conclusion about the nature, and future, of the field of public policy studies.

A central difficulty for the beginning (and often the experienced) student of public policy is gaining just this sort of coherent perspective and orientation to the field. It is so all-encompassing, both in terms of its potential subject matter and in its promiscuous attachments to wildly different academic disciplines, that it seems less a noun (I study policy) and more an adjective (I am a policy economist, or I am a policy political scientist). Rather than the focus of scholarly study, it is the modifier, a derivative of the main scholarly enterprise. Studying public policy takes so many forms from so many different perspectives that stitching its constituents into an overall systematic pattern may seem a daunting task. Nonetheless, that is the goal of this book. In what follows, we claim it is possible to integrate the many strands into a coherent whole and to present a systematic picture of a field that is at least as much a science as it is an art or a craft.

Defining Public Policy

A logical place as any to begin such an effort is to try to come to grips with what the field of public policy studies is actually studying. This is not an easy task. Public policy is like pornography. U.S. Supreme Court Justice Potter Stewart famously commented in his concurring opinion in *Jacobellis v. Ohio* (1964) that it was unlikely he could ever intelligibly define hard-core pornography, "but I know it when I see it." Public policy is like that; an intuitive concept that is maddeningly difficult to precisely define.

A small academic industry is dedicated to defining public policy. Some definitions are broad. Policy is "whatever governments choose to do or not to do" (Dye 1987, 1); "the relationship of governmental unit to its environment" (Eysestone 1971, 18); or "the actions, objectives, and pronouncements of governments on particular matters, the steps they take (or fail to take) to implement them, and the explanations they give for what happens (or does not happen)" (Wilson 2006, 154). Such definitions are accurate in the sense that they cover pretty much everything that could conceivably be considered public policy, but they are so general that they do little to convey any idea of what makes policy studies different from political science, welfare economics, or public administration. They convey no clear boundary that isolates the intellectual quarry of the policy scholar and differentiates it from, say, the political scientist who studies institutions or even voting behavior (what elected governments choose to do or not to do is, after all, ultimately tied to the ballot box).

Others' definitions are narrower. James Anderson's widely used undergraduate textbook, for example, defines policy as a "purposive course of action or inaction undertaken by an actor or set of actors in dealing with a problem or matter of concern" (1994, 5). This definition implies a distinguishing set of characteristics for public policy. Policy is not random but purposive and goal oriented; public policy is made by public authorities;

public policy consists of patterns of actions taken over time; public policy is a product of demand, a government-directed course of action in response to pressure about some perceived problem; public policy can be positive (a deliberately purposive action) or negative (a deliberately purposive decision not to take action). Others seek to extract common characteristics by isolating common elements of broader definitions. Theodoulou (1995, 1–9) used this approach and ended up with a list that overlaps considerably with Anderson's, but she also added that public policy has distinct purposes: resolving conflict over scarce resources, regulating behavior, motivating collective action, protecting rights, and directing benefits toward the public interest.

Defining public policy, as Anderson and Theodoulou have, by trying to distill a set of characteristics core to the underlying concept is no doubt a useful exercise. However, these sorts of approaches are vulnerable to the criticism that they simply take a different route to end up at the same conceptual destination of the more succinct "it's what government does." The list of characteristics becomes so long that taken together they still add up to the "everything and nothing" approach captured more succinctly by Dye and Eyestone. A purposive course of action or inaction to address a problem or matter of concern covers a lot of ground.

The bottom line is that there is no precise and universal definition of public policy, nor is it likely that such a definition will be conceived in the foreseeable future. Instead, there is general agreement that public policy includes the process of making choices and the outcomes or actions of particular decisions; that what makes public policy "public" is that these choices or actions are backed by the coercive powers of the state; and that, at its core, public policy is a response to a perceived problem (Birkland 2001).

Consensus on such generalities, though, does not lead easily to conceptual specifics. This lack of a general agreement on what policy scholars are actually studying is a key reason why the field is so intellectually fractured. As Bobrow and Dryzek (1987, 4) put it, the field of policy studies is "a babel of tongues in which participants talk past rather than to one another." This is not so surprising. If a group cannot agree on what it is studying, it is hard to talk about it coherently. Just because we cannot define the concept beyond generalities, however, does not mean we cannot define the field (or fields) of policy studies.

Defining the Field(s) of Public Policy Studies

Lacking a general definition of public policy means the various disciplines with policy orientations can adopt their own definitions and not worry that other supposed policy scholars seem to be studying something very different, and for very different reasons. From this perspective there is not a *field* of public policy studies, there are *fields*—plural—of public policy studies. This plurality is not necessarily such a bad thing. For one thing, it frees the study of public policy from the insular intellectual silos that constitute traditional academic disciplines. Policy scholars are free to jump fences, picking whatever pasture seems most suited to the issue or question at hand.

Rather than defining a single concept as the core focus of different activities, then, perhaps it is better to define the field (or fields) rather than the core concept. Some may argue this restates the definitional problem rather than solves it. The field of policy studies, for example, has been defined as "any research that relates to or promotes the public interest" (Palumbo 1981, 8). Such broad definitions make the field of policy studies as vague and nongeneral as the concept of public policy appears to be. Definitions for the "policy sciences"—for our purposes a synonym for "policy studies"— include the "application of knowledge and rationality to perceived social problems" (Dror 1968, 49) and "an umbrella term describing a broad-gauge intellectual approach applied to the examination of societally critical problems" (P. deLeon 1988, 219). From the field-level perspective, then, the study of public policy is about identifying important societal problems that presumably require government action to be effectively addressed, formulating solutions to those problems, and assessing the impact of those solutions on the target problem (P. deLeon 2006).

Under this general umbrella are a range of subfields that have developed quite independently of each other. These include policy evaluation, policy analysis, and policy process. Policy evaluation seeks to systematically assess "the consequences of what governments do and say" (Dubnick and Bardes 1983, 203). Policy evaluation is typically an *ex post* undertaking that uses a wide range of methods to identify and isolate a causal relationship between a policy or a program and an outcome of interest (Mohr 1995). The fundamental question in policy evaluation is empirical: what have we done?

Whereas policy evaluation is largely an empirical exercise, policy analysis is more normative. Policy analysis focuses on *ex ante* questions. The most fundamental of these is: what should we do? The object is to determine the best policy for public authorities to adopt to address a given problem or issue of concern. The challenge for policy analysis is coming up with some comparative yardstick to serve as a decision rule for "best." Efficiency and effectiveness, for example, are both defensible criteria for judging what is, or is not, the best policy to address a particular problem or issue of concern. Yet the most efficient policy is not necessarily the most effective, and vice versa.

If policy evaluation asks questions about what have we done, and policy analysis asks questions about what should we do, policy process research is focused on the how and why of policymaking. Those who study policy process are interested in finding out why governments pay attention to some problems and not others (agenda-setting), why policy changes or remains stable across time, and where policy comes from.

Imposing organization and order onto the field of policy studies through a taxonomy of its constituent subfields such as policy analysis, policy evaluation, and policy process can in one sense lead us back to the definitional dead ends we found in trying to squeeze specificity and clarity out of the underlying concept of public policy. Most of these fields have an intellectual history that mimics the definitional struggles surrounding the concept of public policy. Policy analysis, for example, has been defined as "a means of synthesizing information including research results to produce a format for policy decisions" (Williams 1971, xi), and as "an applied social science discipline which uses multiple methods of inquiry to produce and transform policy-relevant information that may be utilized in political settings to resolve policy problems" (Dunn 1981, ix). Parsing out such definitions leads to either loopholes (shouldn't the definition say something about who is using the information and for what purposes? See Weimer and Vining 2005, 24), or to vacuous generalities (policy analysis covers everything dealing with government decision making).

This approach, however, does provide at least one clear advantage. *By carving the field into broad, multidisciplinary orientations such as policy or program evaluation, policy analysis, and policy process, it is possible to identify within each some roughly coherent framework.* If nothing else, this approach clarifies a series of research questions central to the field of public policy studies as a whole: how do public authorities decide what problems or issues to pay attention to? How does government decide what to do about those problems? What values should be used to determine the "best" government response to a particular problem or matter of concern? What do government actions intend to achieve? Have those goals been achieved? If so, to what extent? If not, why not? These questions systematically sort and organize different policy subfields such as policy process (the first two questions), policy analysis (the second two questions), and policy evaluation (the last questions). And within each of these particular orientations identifiable conceptual frameworks have been either constructed or appropriated to provide systematic answers to the underlying questions. Even accepting the difficulties with defining the concept of public policy, most would agree these are important questions and finding the answers is important, both as a means to improving the lot of society and to better understanding the human condition generally.

Although it is not immediately clear what connects, say, the work of a political scientist studying the formation of coalitions within a particular policy subsystem, to, say, a program evaluator running a randomized field trial on the effectiveness (or lack thereof) of a particular government activity, the connections definitely exist. For one thing, most (if not all) of the subfields under the policy studies umbrella trace to a common historical root. There may be fields (plural) of policy studies rather than a field (singular), but the original intent was to till all with a common intellectual plow.

The Policy Sciences: A Very Short History of the Field of Policy Studies

It is not hard to extend the history of policy studies back to antiquity: what governments do or do not do has occupied the attention and interest of humans ever since there were governments. All advisers who whispered in the ears of princes, and their rivals who assessed and countered the prince's decisions, were students of public policy. All were interested in answering the research questions listed just a few paragraphs ago. Using these questions as a means to define its intellectual heritage, policy studies can legitimately claim everyone from Plato (who laid out a lot of policy recommendations in *The Republic*) to Machiavelli (who in *The Prince* had some definite ideas on how policymaking power should be exercised) among their intellectual founders. Other political thinkers—Thomas Hobbes, John Locke, James Madison, Adam Smith, John Stuart Mill—qualify as policy scholars under this definition. They all were broadly concerned with what government does and does not do and were often interested in specific questions of what the government should do and how it should go about doing it as well as in assessing what impact the government has on various problems in society.

Most students of public policy, however, consider the field of policy studies a fairly new undertaking, at least as a distinct academic discipline. Public administration, economics, and political science consider their respective policy orientations to be no more than a century old. Many claim a lineage of less than half of that. Systematic policy analysis is sometimes attributed to the development and adoption of cost-benefit analyses by the federal government (mostly for water projects) in the 1930s (Fuguitt and Wilcox 1999, 1–5). Others trace the roots of policy analysis back no further than the 1960s (Radin 1997).

Whereas any claim to identify the absolute beginning of the field of public policy studies and its various subfields should rightly be taken with a grain of salt, most histories converge on a roughly common starting point. That starting point is Harold Lasswell, who laid down a grand vision of what he called the "policy sciences" in the middle years of the twentieth century. Even though his vision has been, at best, imperfectly realized, most of the various policy orientations discussed thus far share Lasswell as a common branch in their intellectual family tree, even as they branch off into very different directions elsewhere.

In some ways Lasswell's vision of the policy sciences was a vision of what political science should become (see Lasswell 1951a and 1956). Yet though Lasswell gave political science a central place in the policy sciences, his vision was anything but parochial. The policy sciences were to draw from all the social sciences, law, and other disciplines. The idea of the policy sciences was an outgrowth not just of Lasswell's academic interests but also his practical experience in government. Lasswell was one of a number of high-profile social scientists who helped government formulate policy during World War II (Lasswell was an expert on propaganda—he wrote his dissertation on the topic—and during the war he served as the chief of the Experimental Division for the Study of War-Time Communications). This experience helped solidify Lasswell's idea that a new field should be developed in order to better connect the knowledge and expertise of the social sciences to the practical world of politics and policymaking.

Lasswell's vision of the policy sciences, and of the policy scientist, was expanded and refined over a series of publications between the 1940s and his death in 1978. The foundational article, however, was "The Policy Orientation," an essay published in an edited volume in 1951. It was here that Lasswell attempted to lay out the goals, methods, and purposes of the policy sciences. Lasswell began with a clear(ish) notion of the concept of public policy. He viewed policy generically as "the most important choices made in organized or in private life" (1951b, 5). Public policy, then, was the response to the most important choices faced by government. The policy sciences would be the discipline that developed to clarify and inform those choices, and to assess their ultimate impact. Specifically, Lasswell laid out the following distinguishing characteristics of the policy sciences.

Problem Oriented. The policy sciences were oriented to the major problems and issues faced by government. These were not necessarily outcome focused; process is also a critical focus of the policy scientist. Under the umbrella of important problems were the formation and adoption, as well as the execution and assessment of, particular choices. The key focus of the policy scientist was not a particular stage of policymaking (analysis, evaluation, process) but rather an important problem faced by government (what should we do to best address the problem? How should we do it? How do we know what we've done?).

Multidisciplinary. Lasswell made clear that policy science and political science were not synonymous (1951b, 4). The policy sciences were to cut across all disciplines whose models, methods, and findings could contribute to addressing key problems faced by government.

Methodologically sophisticated. Lasswell recognized that many of the important contributions social science made to public policy during World War II were tied to their methodological sophistication. In his 1951 essay he specifically mentioned improvements in economic forecasting, psychometrics, and the measurement of attitudes. Advances in these areas helped government make more effective decisions on everything from allocating resources within the war economy to matching individual aptitudes with particular military specialties. Lasswell saw quantitative methods as "amply vindicated" and assumed any debate would not be about the development and worth of quantitative methods, but how they could be best applied to particular problems (1951b, 7).

Theoretically sophisticated. If the policy sciences were going to help effectively address important problems, they had to understand cause and effect in the real world. Understanding how social, economic, and political systems operated and interacted was absolutely critical if government was going to squarely address problems in those realms. This meant that policy scientists had a critical need for conceptual frameworks with enough explanatory horsepower to clarify how and why things happened in the larger world of human relations. How do institutions shape decision making? How can government best provide incentives for desirable behaviors? An effective policy science had to be able to credibly answer these sorts of questions, and to do so it would need sophisticated theoretical models.

Value oriented. Importantly, Lasswell did not just call for a development of the "policy sciences." He called for a development of the "policy sciences *of democracy.*" In other words, the policy sciences had a specific value orientation: their ultimate goal was to maximize democratic values. In Lasswell's words, "the special emphasis is on the policy sciences of democracy, in which the ultimate goal is the realization of human dignity in theory and fact" (1951b, 15).

Overall, Lasswell's vision of the policy sciences was of an applied social science, whose roving charge was to fill the gap between academically produced knowledge and the real world of politics and problems. The operating model was that of a law firm or of a doctor. The job of the policy scientist was to diagnose the ills of the body politic, understand the causes and implications of those ills, recommend treatment, and evaluate the impact of the treatment. Like a doctor, the policy scientist had to have a scientifically grounded training but would employ that knowledge to serve a larger value-oriented purpose. Though there was no suggested Hippocratic oath for the policy scientist, his or her expertise was supposed to be harnessed to the greater good and deployed for the public good and the general betterment of humanity.

This, then, was the original vision of the field of policy studies. It was not a field built around a core concept; it did not need a universal definition of public policy to function as an independent discipline. In

Laswell's vision policy studies (or as he would put it, the policy sciences) was a field analogous to medicine. Within the field were to be numerous subspecialties, not all of them necessarily tied together within a universal intellectual framework. What was to give the field its focus was its problem orientation. Yet while Lasswell gave policy studies a unifying focus in the problem orientation, his vision contained the seeds of its own demise.

The Fracturing of the Policy Sciences

Lasswell's vision of the policy sciences is breathtaking in its scope, and many still find it an attractive notion of what the field of policy studies *should* be. For good or for ill, though, this vision is not an accurate description of what the field of public policy studies *is*. Why? The short answer is that Lasswell's vision contains too many internal contradictions to support the broader project. Lasswell called for the training of a set of specialized experts to play a highly influential role in policymaking. Ceding such influence to technocrats smacks of elitism, not the more egalitarian ethos of democracy. Where does the citizen fit into democratic policymaking? In Lasswell's vision it is hard to discern much of a role for the citizen at all. The policy scientist as physician for the body politic might produce more effective or efficient policy, it might help solve problems, it might even produce policy that is viewed as in the public interest. It is hard, however, to see how it is democratic when it assigns the ultimate source of sovereign power—the citizen—to a passive and secondary role (P. deLeon 1997).

It is also hard to square the values underpinning science with the values that underpin politics. As an epistemology, science's fundamental values are not particularly democratic. Science values objectivity and believes in an objective world that is independent of those who observe it. Science is oriented toward that world, a place where disagreements and debates are amenable to empirical analysis. If one set of people hypothesize the sun moves around the earth, and another group the opposite, the different explanations of movement are ultimately resolved by careful observation and analysis of the actual universe that exists independently of either perspective. This universe operates in a certain way according to certain laws, and no amount of belief or ideology can make them work differently. It matters not a whit if one believes the sun revolves around the earth, the simple empirical fact of the matter is that the sun does no such thing. The earth-centric worldview is empirically falsified, and no degree of faith or belief will make it otherwise in the eyes of science.

As critics of the Lasswellian project point out, this is not a particularly accurate description of the world of politics. In the political world perception is everything. Indeed, these critics argue that perception in the social and political world *is* reality; no independent, universal world separate from our own social and mental constructions exists (see Fischer 2003). It is exactly one's faith or belief in a particular part of the world that creates political reality. For example, what constitutes a problem, let alone what constitutes the best response, is very much in the eye of the political beholder. Some view the lack of universal health care as a critical issue the government must face. Others believe it is not the government's role or responsibility to provide health care; these are services best left to and controlled by the market. What resolves that difference of perspectives? Whatever the answer, it is unlikely to be an objective, scientific one. Both sides have access to the facts, but it is how facts are filtered through particular belief systems that defines problems and suggests solutions. The answers, in other words, are value-based, and those are values held by particular individuals and groups—there is no independent, objective world with the "correct" set of values.

As a method of gaining knowledge, science has few equals, and its benefits have contributed enormously to the betterment of humankind and a deeper understanding of our world. Science, however, cannot make a political choice any less political. The difficulty of reconciling knowledge with politics, of fitting values into the objective, scientific approaches that came to dominate the social sciences, has never been resolved. Lasswell argued that facts would be put into the service of democratic values. He never seemed to fully recognize that facts and values could conflict, let alone that values might in some cases determine "facts."

These sorts of contradictions fractured and balkanized the field of policy studies from its inception. Lasswell's vision helped birth a new field but simultaneously crippled it with logical inconsistencies. As one assessment put it, "Lasswell's notion of the policy sciences of democracy combined description with prescription to create an oxymoron" (Farr, Hacker, and Kazee 2006). Rather than a coherent field, what emerged from Lasswell's vision was the range of orientations or subfields already discussed, in other words, policy evaluation studies, policy analysis, and policy process. Each of these picked up and advanced some elements of the policy sciences, but none came close to fulfilling the grander ambitions of Lasswell's call for a new field.

Across these different perspectives were some discernable commonalties rooted in the larger policy sciences project. The methodological aspects, for example, were enthusiastically embraced and pursued. It is all but impossible, at least in the United States, to study public policy in a sustained fashion without getting a heavy dose of quantitative training. Cost-benefit analysis; risk assessment; operations research; matrix analysis; just about everything in the econometric, statistical, and mathematical tool kit of the social sciences has been adapted to the study of public policymaking. The jury is out, however, on just how much that has gained for the study of public policy. The heroic assumptions required to make, say, cost-benefit analysis mathematically tractable (e.g., placing a dollar value on human life) justifiably raise questions about what the end product of all this rigorous quantitative analysis tells us. And, as critics of development of technocratic policy studies are quick to point out, the historical record of the most science-oriented aspects of policy research have a spotty historical record. Number-crunching policy scientists wielding complex causal models bombed (sometimes quite literally) in a series of big, broad-scale problems, such as the war in Vietnam, the War on Poverty in the 1960s, and the energy crisis of the 1970s (Fischer 2003, 5–11; P. deLeon 2006, 43–47).

Other aspects, however, were largely ignored. Lasswell's notion of the policy sciences was explicitly normative; it was the policy sciences *of democracy*. This created an internal tension within all disciplines with a policy orientation, a conflict between those who gave precedence to the values of science and those who gave precedence to the values of democracy (or at least to particular political values). Academics of a scientific bent are inherently suspicious of pursuing explicit normative agendas. Declaring a value-based preference or outcome tends to cast suspicion on a research project. Ideology or partisanship does not require science, and the latter would just as soon do without the former. With notable exceptions, academics have not been overly eager to build political portfolios because their aim is to further knowledge rather than a particular partisan policy agenda.[1]

Those who see their job as shaping policy in the name of the public good, on the other hand, may find themselves less than satisfied with a mathematically and theoretically complex approach to public policy. The technocratic orientation of the policy sciences can be especially frustrating to those with an advocacy bent; the very notion of reducing, say, universal health care to cost-benefit ratios strikes some as misleading, or even ludicrous. From this perspective, the real objective of policy study is not simply the production of knowledge. The more important questions center on values: do citizens in a given society have a right to universal health care? What is the proper place and influence of minority viewpoints in public policy decision making? How do we know if a policy process, decision, output, or outcome is truly democratic? The answers to such questions will not be found in a regression coefficient generated by a model that assumes an independent, value-free world. Values, like facts, are stubborn things.

Setting aside the problems of trying to get objectively grounded epistemologies to deal with normative values, coalescing the various academic policy orientations into the more coherent whole envisioned by Lasswell has also been bested by practical difficulties. Because policy scholars are, almost by definition, multidisciplinary, it can be hard to find a definite niche within a particular field. Political scientists who study American politics, for example, tend to study particular institutions (Congress, special interest groups, the media) or particular forms of political behavior or attitudes (voting, opinion). These provide neat subdisciplinary divisions and organize training, curriculum offerings, and not insignificantly job descriptions within the academic study of American politics. The problem for policy scholars is that they do not do any of these things; they do *all* of them—and quite a bit else besides—which tends to give them a jack-of-all-trades-master-of-none reputation (Sabatier 1991b). This in turn gives rise to a widespread view that policy scholars within political science are not pulling their weight, especially in terms of generating theories of how the social, political, and economic worlds work. Instead, they simply piggyback on the subfield specialties, borrowing liberally whatever bits of conceptual frameworks they find useful, but doing little in the way of reciprocation. As we shall see, this is a central criticism of policy studies generally, and one that must be creditably answered if policy studies is to make any credible claim to be an independent field of study.

The end result of the internal inconsistencies, the friction between science and democratic or other political values, the failure to generate conceptual or methodological coherence, has largely prevented Lasswell's vision of the policy sciences from taking root as an independent academic discipline. Rather than a single field, we have the multiple, multidisciplinary orientations already discussed. Taken on their own terms, each of these orientations can provide a good deal of clarity and systematic orientation toward important questions about what government does and why (a good deal of this book is devoted to making this point). But these different orientations do not seamlessly fit together and make for a poor vessel to hold Lasswell's vision. The gaps in the joints are so large, the policy sciences simply leak away.

Does this mean that we have managed to answer our key question before we have finished the first chapter? There really is no such thing as the field of policy studies, just a set of marginally related academic orientations cobbled together out of bits and pieces of different social sciences, each distinguishable only by the sorts of questions it's trying to answer? Not necessarily.

The research questions at the heart of the subdisciplines that make up the field of policy studies are big questions, with large, real-world consequences. We contend in this book that if there is such a thing as a field of policy studies, or if there is ever going to be such a thing as a field of policy studies, those important questions have to be pushed to the forefront and so do the broader conceptual frameworks created to answer them. It is not just core questions, in other words, that define a field. It is some systematic, core gyroscope that serves to orient those searching for the answers. In other words, a field—a distinct, defensible, coherent discipline—needs theory. And theory, according to critics and champions of public policy scholarship, is something that policy scholars have done pretty miserably for a very long time.

Why Build When You Can Beg, Borrow, and Steal?

There is no general theoretical framework tying together the study of public policy. So how is it possible to make sense of the complex world of public policy? Sabatier (1999a, 5) has argued there are two basic approaches. The first is to simplify and make sense of that complexity ad hoc: simply use what works in a given situation. Employ whatever particular lens brings focus to a particular issue or question at a particular time and place. Make whatever assumptions seem to make sense and make up whatever categories bring tractability to the analysis at hand. The second is science. This means trying to do in public policy what students of markets have done in economics. Specifically, it means making assumptions that underlying the highly complex world of public policymaking is a set of causal relationships. Just as assumptions about utility maximization and the law of supply and demand can explain a wide-ranging set of observed behaviors in markets, there are corollaries that explain how and why governments address some problems and not others. If these causal relationships can be identified, presumably they can be linked together logically to build overarching explanations of how the world works. These claims can be tested, the tests can be replicated, and the model can be refined into general propositions that hold across time and space. In other words, theories can be built.

The ad hoc approach has a good deal to recommend it. For one thing it provides policy scholars with a license to beg, borrow, or steal from the full range of conceptual frameworks developed across the social sciences. It also relieves policy scholars of the pressure to shoehorn conceptual frameworks onto an ill-fitting and messy reality. Analytic case studies can provide a wealth of information and detail about a particular policy or process, even if they are ad hoc in the sense that they have no grand conceptual framework proposing causal links to empirically verify. A good example is Pressman and Wildavsky's (1973) classic study of implementation, which has shaped virtually all implementation studies that followed. The big problem here is that it is hard to build cumulative and generalizable knowledge from what are essentially descriptive studies (implementation studies have struggled with this problem). Policy scholars are forever reinventing the wheel, and what is found to work in one circumstance is trapped there—the causal assumptions hold only for a particular place in a particular slice of time.

Such limitations, coupled with the policy field's penchant for poaching theories rather than producing them, have done much to sully the reputation of policy scholarship, especially in fields such as political science. Policy scholars are viewed as theory takers rather than theory makers. They swipe whatever is useful for them but rarely return a greater, more generalizable understanding of the world they study. In the eyes of many, this consigns the field of policy studies—whatever that field may or may not be—to a social science discipline of the second or third rank. It is hard to overstate this point: a central problem, perhaps *the* central problem, of policy studies is its perceived inability to contribute to a more general understanding of the human condition.

This general argument has wide currency and leads to no small amount of hand-wringing among policy scholars. Indeed, self-flagellating ourselves for our theory—or lack thereof—is a long-standing tradition in policy studies. Public policy "is an intellectual jungle swallowing up with unbounded voracity almost anything, but which it cannot give disciplined— by which I mean theoretically enlightened—attention" (Eulau 1977, 421). The policy studies literature, at least the political science end of it, "is remarkably devoid of theory" (Stone 1988, 3), with policy scholars making, at best, "modest contributions to developing reasonably clear, and empirically verified theories" (Sabatier 1991a, 145). This inability to provide coherent explanations of how policy is formulated, adopted, implemented, and evaluated leads to policy studies being "regarded by many political scientists, economists and sociologists as second-best research" (Dresang 1983, ix).

Some argue that the attempt to produce generalizable theories of public policy is not only pointless but hopeless. Political scientists seem to have all but given up on trying to construct systematic explanatory frameworks for policy implementation (though perhaps other disciplines are taking up the challenge; see Saetren 2005). Though everyone agrees implementation is a critical factor in determining policy success or failure, the sheer complexity of the subject defies general explanation. After spending thirty years struggling to distill parsimonious, systematic patterns in implementation, political scientists found themselves making little progress from the initial observations of Pressman and Wildavsky's (1973) classic study. Though there are periodic calls to reinvigorate this particular orientation, political scientists mostly seem content to let the study of implementation return to its origins: Many case studies, some of them very good, but not adding up to a comprehensive and general understanding of what's happening and why (P. deLeon 1999a).

Some scholars of public policy see the general failure of the project to construct "scientific" theories of public policy as a good thing, a hard lesson that has been finally been learned. From this perspective, the lack of good theory exposes notions of a positivist "science" of policy theory for what they actually are, i.e., Lasswellian pipe dreams. As Deborah Stone (2002, 7) put it, the scientific approach to public policy that has occupied the attention of so many social scientists is, in effect, a mission to rescue "public policy from the irrationalities and indignities of politics." The problem being, of course, that public policy is very political and not particularly scientific, so nobody should be surprised that science isn't much help in explaining the political world. Rather than pursue that "rationalistic" project (Stone's term) of building scientific theories, it's better to recognize the value-laden realities of public policy and embrace normative theories as the gyroscope of policy studies (P. deLeon 1997; Stone 2002; Fischer 2003). Normative theories (e.g., discourse theory, social constructivism) may not reveal universal truths—they assume there may not be any to reveal—but they can get us closer to understanding the different perspectives that underlie conflict in public policy arenas. This unabashedly political approach to organizing the study of public policy, argue its advocates, is more illuminating and ultimately more practical than quixotically tilting at scientific windmills.

There is considerable merit to such criticisms of the scientific approach (these are typically called post-positivist or post-empiricist approaches). Yet, as we shall see, it is not clear post-positivism can separate itself from the dichotomous choice laid down by Sabatier. Post-positivism may reject science, but it's not clear it can completely duck charges of being ad hoc. This is a debate we shall return to in some depth in later chapters. For now, let us say it is our view that much of the criticism of the scientific approach to policy theory is overblown, at least in the sense that it highlights problems unique to policy studies. The general failure of policy studies to produce generalizable theories to explain the world and unify the field is shared by a number of other social science disciplines. Public administration, for example, has long agonized over its lack of intellectual coherence (Frederickson and Smith 2003). And political scientists who criticize policy studies for its theoretical failings can in turn be held accountable for throwing rocks from glass houses. The last time we checked, our home discipline (both authors are political scientists) had no unifying conceptual framework, an observation that can be verified by a glance through any major political science journal. Policy scholars, as we intend to convincingly demonstrate in what follows, actually have constructed a remarkable array of conceptual frameworks, some of which have been disseminated within and across social science disciplines and are usefully employed to bring order to the study and understanding of the policy realm.[2]

Economics is a social science with a central, unifying conceptual framework and a well-developed set of methods to operationalize that framework and test its central claims. Notably, that framework has come to dominate considerable areas of public administration, political science, and policy studies (usually under the rubric of public choice). Such successful, if highly incomplete, colonization of other disciplines demonstrates the power of good theory. Because economic models spring from a largely coherent, general view of how the world works, they are applicable to a wide range of human interaction, even if it does not directly involve the exchange of goods and services.

It is exactly with this sort of operation that policy scholars are supposed to have done such a poor job. Beginning with the next chapter, we intend to begin making the argument that the study of public policy has actually done a lot more in this area than it is given credit for. For now, however, we freely concede that the field of policy studies has nothing remotely close to a general theory of policy comparable to mainstream models of economics.[3] While it doesn't have *a* theory (singular), we claim it has produced functional theories (plural) within a wide-ranging set of policy orientations such as policy process, policy evaluation, policy analysis, and policy design. Within each of these orientations are core research questions that have prompted the construction of robust conceptual frameworks that usefully guide the search for answers. Those frameworks can be pragmatically mined by advocates and others who are less interested in theory and more interested in making an impact in the real world of a particular policy issue. The real question for us is whether these policy orientations constitute a core foundation for a coherent field, or are so different in terms of questions, frameworks, and methods that they are best considered as adjuncts to other scholarly enterprises rather than an independent discipline.

Conclusion

Is there such a thing as a field or discipline of public policy studies? There is, no doubt, a strong claim for answering this question in the negative. Scholars in this field, after a half-century of trying, have yet to produce a general definition of the concept supposedly at the heart of their study. At a minimum, public policy has never been defined with a degree of specificity that clearly separates what a public policy scholar is studying from what, say, a political scientist or economist is studying. It may be that such a definition is impossible.[4]

Despite the lack of agreement on what public policy scholars are studying, there seems to be no lack of interest in the study of public policy. There are graduate programs, academic societies, and professional careers all supposedly dedicated to the specialist field of policy studies. Yet even a cursory inspection of these activities reveals more differences than similarities. Different questions, different methods used to produce answers, different audiences, and different purposes. How to make sense of this? What, if anything, connects all of this activity? Does it really add up to an independent and coherent field of study?

One way to bring the field of public policy into focus is to view it in the plural rather than the singular sense. Within a range of different orientations toward the study of public policy, it is possible to identify a rough and ready coherence. This starts with a central research question (or questions) and a set of associated explanatory frameworks built to guide the systematic search for answers to these questions. An example of how this can be done is given in Table 1.1, which describes a series of different policy orientations, their core research questions, and related frameworks.[5]

We can tackle the field(s) of public policy by taking these different orientations on their own merits. The questions they pursue are undoubtedly important, and the frameworks generated to answer them orient research toward conclusions that can have important, real-world consequences. But is it possible to go further than this, to somehow connect these different pieces into a larger picture of a coherent field that can take its place as a social science in its own right?

Most policy orientations can be traced to a common root, that of the policy sciences. Lasswell formulated the policy sciences as an independent field of study, but that vision simply collapsed under the weight of its own contradictions. Stitching the various orientations together into a coherent, independent field requires what neither Lasswell nor anyone thus far has managed to supply: general theories of public policy that are not bounded by space or time. Public policy scholarship has, deservedly or not, gained a reputation as doing a poor job of constructing original theories, instead preferring to borrow bits and pieces from others where it proves useful or convenient to do so.

TABLE 1.1 **Fields of Policy Study**

Field of Policy Study	Representative Research Questions	Representative Conceptual Frameworks	Methodological Approach and Examples	Representative Disciplines
Policy and politics	Does politics cause policy, or policy cause politics?	Policy typologies Stages heuristic	Quantitative and qualitative classification (typology and taxonomy) Statistical analysis Case studies	Political science
Policy process	Why does government pay attention to some problems and not others? How are policy options formulated? Why does policy change?	Bounded Rationality Multiple streams (garbage can models) Punctuated equilibrium Advocacy coalitions Diffusion theory Systems theory	Quantitative	Political science Economics

TABLE 1.1 **Fields of Policy Study** *(continued)*

Field of Policy Study	Representative Research Questions	Representative Conceptual Frameworks	Methodological Approach and Examples	Representative Disciplines
Policy analysis	What should we do? What options exist to address a particular problem? What policy option should be chosen?	Welfare economics /utilitarianism	Quantitative Formal/Qualitative Cost-benefit analysis Risk assessment Delphi technique	Political science Economics Public administration Policy-specific subfields (education, health, etc.)
Policy evaluation	What have we done? What impact did a particular program or policy have?	Program theory Research design frameworks	Quantitative/Qualitative Statistics Expert judgment	Political science Economics Public administration Policy evaluation Policy-specific subfields
Policy design	How do people perceive problems and policies? How do policies distribute power and why?	Discourse theory Hermeneutics	Qualitative Text analysis	Political science Philosophy/Theory Sociology

23

TABLE 1.1 **Fields of Policy Study** (*continued*)

Policy design (*continued*)	Whose values are represented by policy? How does policy socially construct particular groups? Is there common ground to different policy stories and perspectives?			Political science Economics Public administration
Policymakers and policymaking institutions	Who makes policy decisions? How do policymakers decide what to do? Why do they make the decisions they do?	Public choice Incrementalism	Formal theory Quantitative analysis	Political science Economics Public administration
Policy Implementation	Why did a policy fail (or succeed)? How was a policy decision translated into action?	Bounded rationality Ad hoc	Quantitative analysis Qualitative analysis	Political science Economics Public administration Policy-specific subfields

In what follows we hope to achieve two primary goals. First we seek to provide the reader with a guided tour of the particular fields of public policy studies as exemplified in Table 1.1. In particular, what we want to illuminate are the key research questions and the conceptual frameworks formulated to address them. In doing this we have the explicit aim of countering the oft-made argument that those who study public policy have done little original work in theory. Second, in doing all of this we intend to equip the reader with the tools necessary to make up their own mind about the present and future of the field (singular) of policy studies. Within particular orientations to studying public policy, we are fairly confident we can make the case for coherence. But is there any possibility that these orientations can be joined together into a comprehensive picture of an academic discipline? In other words, is there such a thing as a field of public policy studies?

Notes

1. The exceptions, though, are notable. Lasswell was the preeminent example of a policy scientist who moved easily between academia and government. In a more contemporary context there are a handful of policy scholars whose work and willingness to advocate solutions to particular problems have had an enormous impact on shaping real world policy. Examples include James Q. Wilson (crime), John Chubb and Terry Moe (education), and Milton Friedman (everything from the best way to staff the U.S. military to creating the basic economic policies of the entire country of Chile).

2. Most chapters in this book hammer on this theme, so it is not being pursued in-depth here. This contrarian claim, though, can be backed by a few examples (all discussed in-depth elsewhere in the book): policy typologies, punctuated equilibrium, and the advocacy coalition framework. Although there are some notable black holes of theory in the policy world (e.g., implementation), there are other areas (e.g., policy process) where there are a number of systematic, comprehensive, and empirically testable frameworks.

3. Except, of course, when that model *is* mainstream economics. Public choice, for example, takes the fundamental assumptions of economics (e.g., utility maximization, individual rationality) and applies them to the political world. Such approaches have been enormously influential in explaining "why government does what it does" (e.g., Buchanan and Tullock 1962; Niskanen 1971).

4. Over the years a number of our graduate students for whom English is not a native language have pushed us particularly hard in clearly distinguishing politics from policy and have mostly been less than satisfied with our answers. Several of these students have stated that in their native languages there is no equivalent word for the concept of policy as it is employed in the political science policy literature.

5. Please note that this is supposed to be a descriptive rather than an exhaustive table.

CHAPTER TWO

Does Politics Cause Policy?
Does Policy Cause Politics?

As detailed in Chapter 1, the field of policy studies is often criticized for its theoretical poverty. Yet even though conventional wisdom regards the policy sciences as contributing few explanatory frameworks that help us systematically understand the political and social world, we believe the evidence suggests otherwise. In fact, the policy sciences have produced at least two frameworks that continue to serve as standard conceptual tools to organize virtually the entire political world: policy typologies and the stages theory.

These two frameworks are generally remembered as theoretical failures, either failing to live up to their original promise because of the universal inability to separate fact and value in the political realm (typologies), or failing to be a causal theory at all (policy stages). These criticisms are, as we shall see, not without merit. Yet both of these frameworks suggest the policy field conceives of its theoretical jurisdiction in very broad terms, and that even when its conceptual frameworks come up short, they leave a legacy of insight and understanding that help organize and make sense of a complicated world.

The stages theory (or what many would more accurately term the stages heuristic) is perhaps the best-known framework of the policy process. Yet by most criteria it does not qualify as a good theory because it is descriptive rather than causal and it does little to explain why the process happens the way it does. Theodore Lowi's original notion of a policy typology was nothing less than a general theory of politics—it raised the possibility that the study of politics would become, in effect, a subdiscipline of the study of public policy. Lowi posited the startling possibility that policy caused politics, rather than the reverse causal pathway still assumed by most students of politics and policy. Typologies ultimately foundered on a set of operational difficulties, difficulties quickly identified but never fully resolved. For these reasons typologies and the stages heuristic, if anything, are more likely to be used as evidence for the theoretical shortcomings of policy studies as opposed to evidence for its worthy contributions. Yet despite their problems, both are still employed to bring systematic coherence to a difficult and disparate field. Even though both are arguably "bad" in the sense that they did not live up to their original promise (typologies) or are not a theory at all (stages heuristic), at a bare minimum they continue to help clarify what is being studied (the process of policymaking, the outcomes of policymaking), why it is important, and how systematic sense can be made of the subject. The general point to be made in this chapter is that if there is such a thing as a distinct field of policy studies, it must define itself by its ability to clarify its concepts and its key questions and to contribute robust answers to those questions. This is what good theory does. And as two of the better-known "failures" in policy theory clearly demonstrate, the field of policy studies is not just attempting to achieve these ends, it is at least partially succeeding.

Good Policy Theory

What are the characteristics of a good theory, and what are the characteristics of a good theory of public policy? Lasswell's notion of the policy sciences, with its applied problem orientation, its multidisciplinary background, and its call for complex conceptual frameworks, sets a high bar for policy theory. Standing on a very diffuse academic foundation, it was not only expected to explain a lot but also to literally solve democracy's biggest problems. It is little wonder theory in public policy when measured against this yardstick is judged as falling short. Such expectations are perhaps the right goal to shoot for, but no conceptual framework in social science is going to live up to them.

McCool (1995c, 13–17) suggested good theory in public policy should exhibit these characteristics: validity (an accurate representation of reality), economy, testability, organization/understanding (it imposes order), heuristic (it serves as a guidepost for further research), causal explanation, predictive, relevance/usefulness, powerful (it offers nontrivial inferences), reliability (it supports replication), objectivity, and honesty (it makes clear the role of values). The exhaustiveness of McCool's list makes it almost as ambitious as the burdens placed on policy theory by the Lasswellian vision. Getting any single theory to reflect all of these traits would present serious challenges in any discipline, let alone one attempting to describe the chaotic world of politics and the policy process. In fact, McCool readily admitted that it is highly unlikely that policy theory would contain all of these characteristics. Policy typologies and the stages heuristic certainly do not accomplish this feat; they both lack some of these key traits (e.g., the stages heuristic is not predictive; policy typologies arguably have reliability problems). Yet both frameworks reflect a majority of this intimidating list of theoretical ideals, which is perhaps why they continue to be used to make sense of the policy and political world.

Policy Stages: A First Attempt at Policy Theory

Given the broad scope of its studies and the vagueness about key concepts, a not inconsiderable challenge for policy theory is trying to figure out what it is trying to explain. Individual behavior? Institutional decision making? Process? In his "pre-view" of the policy sciences, Lasswell (1971, 1) argued the primary objective was to obtain "knowledge *of* and *in* the decision processes of the public and civic order." For Lasswell, this knowledge takes the form of "systematic, empirical studies of how policies are made and put into effect" (1971, 1). Given this initial focus, policy process was an early focal point of theoretical work in the field. But where in the policy process to start? What does the policy process look like? What exactly should we be observing when we are studying public policy? What is the unit of analysis?

TABLE 2.1 **The Evolution of Stages Theory**

Policy Scholar	Proposed Stages Model
An Introduction to the Study of Public Policy Charles O. Jones (1970, 11–12)	*Elements:* Perception Definition Aggregation/organization Representation Formulation Legitimation Application/administration Reaction Evaluation/appraisal Resolution/termination *Categories:* Problem to government Action in government Government to problem Policy to government Problem resolution or change
A Pre-View of the Policy Sciences Harold D. Lasswell (1971, 28)	Intelligence Promotion Prescription Invocation Application Termination Appraisal
Public Policy-Making James E. Anderson (1974, 19)	Problem identification and agenda formation Formulation Adoption Implementation Evaluation
The Foundations of Policy Analysis Garry D. Brewer and Peter deLeon (1983, 18)	Initiation Estimation Selection Implementation Evaluation Termination
Policy Analysis in Political Science Randall B. Ripley (1985, 49)	Agenda setting Formulation and legitimation of goals and programs Program implementation Evaluation of implementation, performance, and impacts Decisions about the future of the policy and program

Table 2.1 traces the lineage of what would become the stages model of the policy process. The similarity across the models should be evident. First a problem must come to the attention of the government. Policymakers then develop solutions to address the problem, ultimately implementing what they perceive as the most appropriate solution, and then evaluate whether or not it served its purpose.

For Lasswell (1971), the policy process was fundamentally about how policymakers make decisions. As such, Lasswell's initial attempt to model the policy process was based more generally on how best to model decision processes. Lasswell identified a set of phases common to any decision process: the recognition of a problem, the gathering of information and proposals to address the problem, implementation of a proposal, followed by possible termination and then appraisal of the proposal. The seven stages listed in Table 2.1 were meant to descriptively capture this process as it applied to policy decisions.

Writing at roughly the same time as Lasswell, Charles Jones (1970) also placed a strong emphasis on examining the process of policymaking. For Jones, the focus should not be solely on the outputs of the political system but instead on the entire policy process, from how a problem is defined to how governmental actors respond to the problem to the effectiveness of a policy. As Jones wrote, this "policy" approach is an attempt to "describe a variety of processes designed to complete the policy cycle" (1970, 4). Although Lasswell identified what could be considered stages of the decision process, it is with Jones that we see the first attempt to model the process of public policy decisions. For Jones, the policy process could aptly be summarized by a distinct set of "elements" listed in Table 2.1.

Jones's focus on the elements of the policy process is very much in line with Lasswell's interest in "knowledge *of*" the policy process. The policy process begins with perception of a problem and ends with some sort of resolution or termination of the policy. Jones, however, moved the evaluation element, what Lasswell (1971) would describe as "appraisal," to immediately prior to the decision to terminate or adjust a policy. Because public problems are never "solved" (C. Jones 1970, 135), evaluations of the enacted policy must be made to best decide how to adjust the current policy to fit with existing demands. Jones went on to more broadly classify these ten elements as fitting within five general categories. These categories are meant to illustrate "what government does to act on public problems" (C. Jones 1970, 11).

The phases laid out by Lasswell and Jones conceptualize public policy as a linear decision-making process of linked stages that very much reflects a rationalist perspective: a problem is identified; alternative responses considered; the "best" solution adopted; the impact of this solution evaluated; and on the basis of evaluation the policy is continued, revised, or terminated. In laying out this linear process Lasswell and Jones were essentially trying to describe the policy process and organize it into coherent and manageable terms. The "phases" or "elements" are merely descriptive terms they used for patterns regularly observed by policy scholars at the time.

The big advantage of the stages approach formulated by Lasswell and Jones, as well as contemporary stages models such as that forwarded by James Anderson (1974), is that they provided an intuitive and practical means of conceptualizing and organizing the study of public policy. They provided a basic frame of reference to understand what the field of policy studies was about.

Various refinements of the stages model have been offered, though all retain the basic formulation of a linear process, albeit one in a continuous loop (e.g., Brewer and deLeon 1983; Ripley 1985). The common patterns are clearly evident in Table 2.1, which all portray public policy as a continuous process, one where problems are never solved, they are only addressed.

The stages model provides a generally agreed upon, and widely used, description of the process of public policymaking. Although different variations used different labels for the phases or stages, the fundamental model was always a rationalistic, problem-oriented, linear process in a continual loop. While the stages models seemed to impose order and make intuitive sense of an incredibly complex process, policy scholars were quick to identify their drawbacks, not the least of which were that they did not seem to be testable.

Stages Model: Descriptive or Predictive?

Critics have cited two main drawbacks of the stages approach. First, it tends to produce piecemeal theories for studying the policy process. Those interested in agenda setting focus on one set of policy research, whereas those interested in policy analysis focus on another, whereas those interested in policy implementation focus on still another aspect of the process. In other words, the stages model divides rather than unites the field of policy studies, reducing the likelihood of producing a unifying theory of public policy. Such a view also tends to create the perception that the stages are disconnected from one another, or at least can be disconnected and studied in isolation, and that the policy process is best viewed as proceeding neatly between stages. This criticism is far from fatal. A unified model of public policy is a very tall order, and it is unlikely that viewing policy from the stages perspective is a major obstacle to developing such a theory. Indeed, in the absence of a unifying theory, the stages model arguably creates an intuitive and useful division of labor for policy scholars, putting focus on the construction of more manageable conceptual frameworks in specific stages such as agenda setting or implementation.

A second frequent criticism is that the stages model assumes a linear model of the policymaking, discounting the notion of feedback loops between different stages or different starting points for the entire process (P. deLeon 1999b, 23). Again, we do not see this as a fatal flaw in the stages model. If the process is continuous, disagreements over starting points and feedback loops are all but unavoidable. The most damaging criticism, especially for a conceptual model arising from the policy sciences, was the claim that the stages model was not particularly scientific.

The basis of any scientific theory is the production of empirically falsifiable hypotheses. What are the hypotheses that come from the stages model? What hypothesis can we test about how a problem reaches the government agenda? What hypothesis can we test about the alternative that will be selected for implementation? What hypothesis can we test about policy evaluation? These questions point to the fundamental flaw with the stages model as a theory of public policy—it is not really a theory at all. It is a descriptive classification of the policy process; it says what happens without saying anything about why it happens. Paul Sabatier (1991a, 145) has written that the stages model "is not really a causal theory at all . . . [with] no coherent assumptions about what forces are driving the process from stage to stage and very few falsifiable hypotheses." In fact, Sabatier (1991b, 147) went on to refer to the stages approach as the "stages heuristic." A scientific study of public policy should allow for hypothesis testing about relationships between variables in the policy process. This is the central flaw for many policy scholars: because the stages model does not really generate any hypotheses to test, it renders the whole framework as little more than a useful example of what a bad theory of policy looks like.

The stages model does not even suggest a useful list of variables for policy scholars. The stages heuristic suffers from the process it seeks to explain. Variables that explain some aspect of the policy process at one stage may be insignificant at another (Greenberg et al. 1977). It is generally accepted that the stages approach provides weak guidance for those interested in empirical tests of the causal relationships underlying public policymaking. But does this warrant complete rejection of the model? Does the stages model contribute nothing to our understanding of the policy process?

The stages heuristic or stages model is useful for its simplicity and direction. It provides policy researchers with a broad and generalizable outline of the policy process as well as a way of organizing policy research. Good policy theory should be generalizable and broad in scope (Sabatier 2007). The stages model fits these criteria. Because of the stages approach, we also know what makes up what Peter deLeon (1999b, 28) referred to as the "parts" of the policy process. In fact, within the field of academic policy research, scholarly interest tends to break down along the stages model. There is a definitive research agenda that focuses on problem definition and how a policy problem reaches the decision-making and government agenda, often referred to as the agenda-setting literature (Cobb and Elder 1983; Nelson 1984; Baumgartner and Jones 1993; Kingdon 1995; Stone 2002). Another research agenda focuses on policy implementation and policy evaluation (Fischer 1995). For this group of scholars, the key question is: what should we do? A third group of researchers is more broadly interested in how policies change over time and what causes significant breaks from existing policies (Carmines and Stimson 1989; Baumgartner and Jones 1993; Jones and Baumgartner 2005). And still another group is interested in the effects of policy design on citizen attitudes and behavior (Schneider and Ingram 1997).

The burgeoning literature in each of these stages has no doubt contributed immensely to our understanding of various aspects of the policy process. In fact, Paul Sabatier, a prominent critic of the utility of the stages model for studying public policy (see Jenkins-Smith and Sabatier 1993), has credited the work of Nelson (1984) and Kingdon (1995) as evidence of theory testing within public policy (Sabatier 1991a, 145). In other words, there are useful theories within each stage of the stages approach (see also Chapter 1, Table 1.1). For Sabatier, the stages model is best viewed not as a model but as a "heuristic" for understanding the policy process. Although the stages approach may lack falsifiability, it continues to provide a (perhaps the) major conceptualization of the scope of public policy studies and provides a handy means of organizing and dividing labor in the field. We would venture to guess that most introductory graduate seminars in public policy include Baumgartner and Jones (1993), Jenkins-Smith and Sabatier (1993), Kingdon (1995), and Stone (2002), as well as some readings in policy evaluation and policy analysis. In short, the stages heuristic has organized, and continues to organize, the discipline for researchers and students.

From a Kuhnian perspective, the stages model remains viable (Kuhn 1970). As Kuhn has argued, "paradigms" are not completely rejected until a new replacement paradigm is presented. A replacement theory of the policy process is still lacking. Thus, completely discarding the stages model ignores the organizational benefits it has provided. The stages approach has morphed over time. The various stages frameworks shown in Table 2.1 have helped to clarify the "how" of Lasswell's emphasis on "how policies are made and put into effect." Although the nominal conception of the stages of the model varies ever so slightly across researchers, there is a great deal of substantive commonality. Moreover, most process scholars agree that the stages model is a useful analytic tool for studying the policy process even if they differ over the labeling of the stages. Given such widespread agreement, any new model of the policy process will most likely retain some aspects of the stages approach.

The Lasswellian approach placed a strong emphasis on developing complex models capable of explaining the policy process, and the stages model represents one of the first comprehensive conceptual frameworks constructed with that goal in mind. Although critics argue that the stages approach provides little in terms of testable hypotheses, it does provide an organizing function for the study of public policy. The stages model has rationally divided labor within the field of public policy. Because of the stages approach, policy scholars know what to look for in the policy process, where it starts, and where it ends (at least temporarily). The "policy sciences" were first and foremost about bringing the scientific process into the study of public policy. Good theories simplify the phenomena they seek to explain. The policy process consists of numerous actors at different levels of government from different disciplinary backgrounds with different training and different levels of knowledge on any given policy. These actors converge throughout the process, making decisions that affect future policy analyses. Yet despite such overwhelming complexity, the stages model provides a way for policy researchers to conceptualize the process of policymaking.

Thinking back to McCool's elements of good theory, the stages model actually does quite well. It is economical, it provides an organizing function, it is a heuristic, it is useful, it is reliable, it is objective, and it is powerful both in the sense of guiding the study of the policy process as well as the effect it has had on the field of public policy. What the researcher must decide is where simplification actually inhibits testability and predictability, and if so, whether to discard the theory or to make adjustments. For many scholars, the stages model has been discarded without any adjustments or a replacement.

Another "Theory" of Public Policy: Policy Typologies

The stages model conceives of public policy as the product of the linear progression of political events: Problems are put on the agenda, there is debate over potential solutions, legislatures adopt alternatives on the basis of practical or partisan favor, bureaucracies implement them, and some impact is felt on the real world. The stages model says nothing about what type of policies are being produced by this process, and what those differences might mean for politics.

Theodore Lowi, a political scientist, was interested in examining what types of policies were being produced by the policy process and what effect those policies had on politics. For Lowi, the question was: What is the output of the policy process, and what does that tell us about politics? Lowi was frustrated by what he perceived to be an inability or disinterest among policy scholars in distinguishing between types of outputs. Prior to Lowi's work, policy outputs were treated uniformly as an outcome of the political system. No attempt was made to determine if the process changed for different types of policies, let alone whether the types of policies determined specific political patterns. A single model of public policymaking was assumed to apply to all types of policy (Lowi 1970). Such overgeneralizations, argued Lowi, led to incomplete inferences about the policy process, and more broadly about the relationship between public policy and politics.

Prior to Lowi's work, the relationship between politics and policy was assumed to be linear and casual; politics determine policies. Lowi (1972, 299), however, argued for the reverse, that "policies determine politics." At a very basic level, public policy is an attempt to influence individual behavior. As Lowi (1972, 299) wrote, "government coerces." However, when classified into general categories, such coercion allows for testable predictions about political behavior. By identifying the type of coercion, it would be possible to predict the type of politics that would follow. Lowi developed a 2 x 2 matrix of government coercion based on its target (individual versus environment) and likelihood of actually being employed (immediate versus remote) (1972, 300). Where the coercion is applicable to the individual, politics will be more decentralized; where coercion is applicable to the environment, politics will be more centralized. Where the likelihood of coercion is immediate, politics will be more conflictual with high levels of bargaining. Where the likelihood of coercion is more remote, politics will be less conflictual, with high levels of logrolling. As Lowi (1970, 320) observed, "each kind of coercion may very well be associated with a quite distinctive political process."

Lowi's basic argument was that if one could identify the type of policy under consideration—in other words, if one could classify a policy into a particular cell in his 2 x 2 table—one could predict the type of politics likely to follow. As others have argued (see Kellow 1988), Lowi's model is theoretically similar to the work of E. E. Schattschneider (1965). For Schattschneider, policy and politics are interrelated. How a policy is defined has the potential to "expand the scope of conflict," bringing more groups of people into the policy process, thus shaping politics. Lowi observed that certain types of policy tend to mobilize political actors in predictable patterns. Policies are assumed to fit neatly within one of four boxes of coercion, each generating distinct predictions about the type of politics. By classifying a particular policy as falling into one of these four categories, it would be possible to predict the resulting politics.

Lowi used his table to create a typology that put all policies into one of four categories: distributive policy, regulative policy, redistributive policy, and constituent policy. Table 2.2 provides an adapted model of Lowi's (1972, 300) policy typology framework. The policies and resulting politics in Table 2.2 are based on Lowi's observations about federal-level policies from the 1930s through the 1950s. Looking across the rows in Table 2.2, one can see that each policy provides a set of expectations about politics. Each policy category, Lowi (1972) argued, amounted to an "arena of power," and he saw policies as the predictable outcome of a regular subsystem of actors. Thus if one knows the policy type, it is possible to predict the nature of political interactions between actors in the subsystem. The expectations that policy actors have about policies determines the type of political relationships between actors (Lowi 1964). Lowi described his "scheme" in the following way:

1. The types of relationships to be found among people are determined by their expectations.
2. In politics, expectations are determined by governmental outputs or policies.
3. Therefore, a political relationship is determined by the type of policy at stake, so that for every policy there is likely to be a distinctive type of political relationship. (Lowi 1964, 688)

TABLE 2.2 **Lowi's Policy Typologies and Resulting Politics**

Policy Type	Likelihood of coercion/ Applicability of coercion	Type of politics	Congress	President
Distributive	Remote/ Individual	Consensual Stable Logrolling	Strong Little floor activity	Weak
Constituent	Remote/ Environment	Consensual Stable Logrolling	N/A	N/A
Regulatory	Immediate/ Individual	Conflictual Unstable Bargaining	Strong High floor activity	Moderate
Redistributive	Immediate/ Environment	Stable Bargaining	Moderate Moderate floor activity	Strong

Note: Table is adapted from Lowi (1972: 300, 304–306)

Distributive policies are characterized by an ability to distribute benefits and costs on an individual basis. As Lowi (1964, 690) wrote, "the indulged and deprived, the loser and the recipient, need never come into direct confrontation." Lowi cited tariffs, patronage policies, and traditional "pork barrel" programs as primary examples of distributive policy. Because coercion is more remote with distributive policies, the politics tend to be relatively consensual. As Lowi noted, the costs of such policies are spread evenly across the population and as such lead to logrolling and agreement between the president and the Congress. The Congress tends to dominate the process, with the president often serving a relatively passive role.

Redistributive policies, unlike distributive policies, target a broader group of people. These policies, such as welfare, Social Security, Medicare, Medicaid, and even income tax, determine the "haves and have-nots" (Lowi 1964, 691). The politics of redistributive policies tend to be more active than distributive policies, resulting in more floor activity than distributive policies, with the president taking a slightly stronger role than Congress. Redistributive politics are also characterized by a high level of bargaining between large groups of people. Although such bargaining is relatively consensual, because it takes place between larger groups of people than with distributive policies, there is a greater potential for conflict.

Regulatory policies are policies aimed at directly influencing the behavior of a specific individual or group of individuals through the use of sanctions or incentives. The purpose of regulatory policies is to increase the costs of violating public laws. Examples include policies regulating market competition, prohibiting unfair labor practices, and ensuring workplace safety (Lowi 1972, 300). Regulatory policies, because the likelihood of coercion is more immediate and applicable to the individual, tend to result in more conflictual politics than either distributive or redistributive policies. These policies also tend to be characterized by a high level of bargaining and floor activity, resulting in a high number of amendments (Lowi 1972, 306). As would be expected, groups tend to argue over who should be the target and incur the costs of government coercion. The result is more "unstable" or combative and divisive politics than is typically observed with distributive or redistributive policies. Commenting on the history of public policy in the United States, Lowi argued that these classifications follow a linear pattern; distributive policies dominated the nineteenth and early twentieth centuries, followed by an increase in regulatory policies as a result of the rise in business and labor, followed by an increase in redistributive policies as a result of the Great Depression and the inability of state governments to cope with national crises.

Lowi's fourth category, constituent policy, is considerably less clear than the other three classifications. It was not considered at all in his original typology formulation (1964) but is included in subsequent work to fill in the empty fourth cell (Lowi 1970, 1972). Lowi provides no empirical evidence regarding the role of Congress and the president in debating constituent policy. As such, we leave these boxes blank in Table 2.2. However, from the examples Lowi (1972, 300) uses (reapportionment, setting up a new agency, and propaganda), and the applicability and likelihood of coercion, we are left to assume that such policies are low salience and result in consensual politics. Little has been done to clarify constituent policies; they seem to cover a miscellaneous category that includes everything not in the original three classifications.

The typology framework was an attempt to redefine how policy and political scientists conceptualize the process of policymaking. Moreover, it was a bold attempt to put the discipline of public policy at the forefront of the study of politics. The typology framework posited that politics can only really be understood from the perspective of public policy. Lowi was frustrated by what he perceived as two general problems with existing research: 1) that the study of public policy to that point treated policy outputs uniformly, with no effort to distinguish between types of policy; and 2) a general acceptance among policy and political scientists that the president dominated the political process. The typology framework suggests otherwise on both fronts. In fact, it is only with redistributive policies that the president tends to have a stronger role than the Congress; Lowi further argued that the role of the president is conditional on whether the president is "strong" or "weak" (1972, 308).

Lowi's typology framework was also a departure from the Lasswellian approach to public policy. In fact, the notion that "policies determine politics" turns the "policy sciences for democracy" argument on its head. Instead of studying public policy to improve the political system, public policy should be studied because it will help to predict the type of politics displayed in the political system. The normative aspect in the Lasswellian approach, however, is not completely absent. Rather, Lowi argued that the ability to predict the type of politics given a particular policy should give policy and political scientists a framework for determining what type of policies will succeed and what type will fail. As Lowi (1972, 308) wrote, this "reaches to the very foundation of democratic politics and the public interest." In other words, policy typologies contribute to the policy sciences by providing an additional method for improving public policy.

Typologies as Non–Mutually Exclusive Categories

If politics is a function of policy type, then classifying policies is crucial for making accurate inferences about politics. For any classification to be useful, the categories must be inclusive and mutually exclusive (McCool 1995b, 174–175). If policies can be objectively classified in such a fashion, then Lowi's notion of policy typologies becomes a testable theory of politics. If it is correct, then specific patterns of political behavior and predictable power relationships should be observed to vary systematically across different policy types. This turned out to be the big weakness of the framework: the key independent variable (policy type) needs to be clearly operationalized to have a useful and predictive model of politics. For Lowi, policy classification was easy. If a policy distributes costs broadly, with controllable benefits, it is most likely distributive. If coercion is directed at specific individuals, it is regulative. If it distributes benefits broadly across social groups, it is redistributive. Most policies, however, do not fit neatly within a single category. This critique has plagued the typology framework since its inception.

Greenberg and others (1977) provided the most systematic and sharpest critique of the typology framework. Because Lowi gave scant attention to the actual classification of each policy type, Greenberg and colleagues argued that his framework was doomed from the start. Take, for example, a bill proposing to increase the sales tax on cigarettes. At face value, this is clearly a regulatory policy. But if the added revenue from the tax goes toward health care or public education, then it becomes a redistributive policy. A higher tax on cigarettes is also meant to reduce the number of smokers in the general population as well as the effects of secondhand smoke. From this perspective, the bill is a public health issue and would most likely result in relatively consensual politics—the type of politics associated with distributive and constituent policies. This is not an unexceptional case; most policies can be reasonably argued to fit into more than one category. Yet from Lowi's framework, we see widely varying predictions regarding the type of politics surrounding such a bill. This creates a fundamental problem for formulating falsifiable hypotheses. What type of politics can we expect from [fill in the blank] bill? is that it depends on whom you ask. In the example provided here, Lowi's model gives us three different outcomes. The point is that without a clear set of criteria for identifying policies, the typology framework is of little use (see also Kjellberg 1977).

If policy actors come to different conclusions about the type of policy under consideration, predicting politics becomes difficult if not impossible. To account for such complexity, some scholars have advocated the use of non-positivist methodology. Implicit in Greenberg et al.'s (1977) argument is a call for a diverse methodological approach to public policy. For this group of authors, Lowi's model is too simplistic; it ignores the complexity of the policy process, namely that multiple actors will tend to view a particular policy through multiple lenses. As a way around this dilemma, Greenberg and others argued that policy scholars should view public policy as a continuous process with multiple outputs, and that predicting politics depends on what output is being studied. Policy should be broken down into smaller units or key decisions, what Greenberg et al. label "points of first significant controversy" and "point of last significant controversy" (1977, 1542). Both provide focal points for policy researchers, the latter of which is useful for classifying policy type.

Steinberger (1980) agreed with Greenberg et al. (1977) about the need for accounting for multiple participants but took it a step further by suggesting that positivist methodology is simply inadequate to deal with the subjectivity of the policy process. Instead, a phenomenological approach is required. Policy actors attach different meanings to policy proposals according to their own beliefs, values, norms, and life experiences. To account for such variation requires a more intersubjective or constructivist approach to the study of public policy. For Steinberger, this requires accounting for the multiple dimensions of policy, namely substantive impact, political impact, scope of impact, exhaustibility, and tangibility. Presumably, such dimensions are regularly assessed by policy analysts. But at the heart of the phenomenological approach is the notion that each person has a different set of values. Thus, while those dimensions may in fact be the dimensions along which people attach meaning to policy, some dimensions may be more valued than others. Complicating Steinberger's argument is the expansion of categories of public policy from three in Lowi's model to eleven. Policies can be categorized as falling into one or more categories with crosscutting dimensions. Although this expands the realm of classification, it does little in terms of providing a parsimonious model of policy classification; indeed, it moves the whole typology project out of the rationalist framework and pushes it into post-positivist territory where subjective perception takes precedence over a single objective reality.[1] In fact, Steinberger admitted that "the range of possibilities is obviously enormous" (193). It also means prediction becomes a post hoc exercise, possible only when we know how specific actors subjectively classify a particular policy proposal.

That policy actors potentially view the same bill differently presents a serious problem for the typology framework. Whereas Greenberg et al. and Steinberger are right to argue that multiple actors will tend to have varying expectations about a single policy proposal, their solutions muddy the waters of policy analysis. If Steinberger's model were adopted, this would complicate the tasks of the traditional, rationalist policy analyst. In addition to assessing the substantive, cost-benefit impact of public policy, policy analysts would now also play the role of policy psychologist. Not only does this present a problem in terms of identifying the key independent variable in Lowi's model, but it also raises doubts about whether objective empirical research on policy classification is even possible.

Debate over the utility of Lowi's model came to a head in the late 1980s. A series of articles published in *Policy Studies Journal* demonstrated the enormity of this debate. Working within Lowi's framework, Spitzer (1987) saw a way out of the problems documented by Greenberg et al. (1977) and others. Rather than adding typologies, Spitzer revised existing typologies. Spitzer, like others, recognized that many policies do not fit neatly within one of Lowi's four categories. To accommodate such cases, Spitzer placed a diagonal line through each policy typology to distinguish between "pure" and "mixed" cases. Pure cases were those that fit clearly within Lowi's original framework, whereas mixed cases were those that generally followed the pattern described by Lowi but also shared characteristics of other types of policy. The result was ten categories of public policy.[2]

Spitzer's article provoked a sharp reply from Kellow (1988). For Kellow, the distinguishing trait of good theory is simplicity. Spitzer's model added unneeded complexity to Lowi's original framework. As Kellow wrote, "the simpler and more powerful the theory the better" (1988, 714). Rather than adding categories, Kellow revised Lowi's model in accordance with work by James Q. Wilson (1973b, Chapter 16). Rather than defining policy types according to the likelihood and applicability of coercion, policy types were defined according to the distribution of costs and benefits. Regulatory policy was divided into public and private interest regulatory policy, and constituent policy was dropped in Kellow's revisions.[3] Simplification was critical to preventing "an infinite parade of subcategories" (Kellow 1988, 722).

The problems with Lowi's original typology are numerous and have been well documented: it is not testable, it is not predictive, it is too simplistic—the categories are not mutually exclusive, it is post hoc, it does not provide causal explanation, and it does not account for the dynamic aspect of the policy process. The difference between Greenberg and colleagues, Steinberger, Spitzer, and others who question Lowi's typology (see Kjellberg 1977; Kellow 1988) tend to revolve around the inclusiveness of Lowi's model. Is the model too simplistic? Should future researchers work around or within the original four typologies? Sharp disagreement over these questions also prompted an important exchange between Kellow and Spitzer. Rather than continuing to press the criterion for classification, however, the debate appears to have settled on the question of epistemology. Spitzer (1989) advocates for a Kuhnian and inductive approach to policy studies. The "tough" cases ignored by Kellow are critical to the theory-building process (532). Spitzer (1989) further criticizes Kellow on the grounds that his theory is not a theory at all but rather a tautological attempt to preserve Lowi's original framework. If, as Kellow observed, policy proposals determine politics, but political actors can manipulate the expectations surrounding policy proposals, then does it not follow that policy proposals determine politics, which determine policy proposals? For Kellow (1989), the tough cases cited by Spitzer and others as creating problems for models of policy classification do not warrant a revision of the theory. In fact, Kellow is skeptical of the inductive and behavioralist approach he attributes to Spitzer. Lowi's model provides a theory, a frame of reference for looking for supporting observations. Cases that do not fit neatly within one of Lowi's four categories simply represent limitations of the model; they do not warrant a paradigm shift.

This leaves policy studies in a bit of a dilemma. Did Lowi give policy studies a new paradigm from which to view the relationship between policy and politics? Or, because his model fails the classic Popperian test of falsifiability, is the typology framework useless? Many have come to the latter conclusion, consigning policy typologies into the same category as the stages model. It is a handy way to impose order on a complex topic, a good heuristic for compactly conveying information in the classroom and on the page, but it's not really an explanatory framework that is going to advance the field. Yet the typology framework does contain some attributes of good policy theory.

Public policy is often criticized for being devoid of generalizable and "ambitious" theory (Hill 1997). It is hard to make that claim for the typology framework, which was nothing if not bold. The proposition that "policies determine politics" essentially renders the study of politics a subfield of public policy. In many ways, the typology framework is a victim of its own ambition. On the one hand, it was an attempt to redefine the relationship between politics and policy. On the other hand, it was an attempt to introduce an important but overlooked independent variable in the study of public policy. Lowi's typology framework also fits with Lasswell's emphasis on developing testable "models" about public policy. The typology framework essentially gives us four different models about the relationship between policy and politics. By Lowi's (1972, 299) own admission, "Finding different manifestations or types of a given phenomena is the beginning of orderly control and prediction." Policy typologies give us a distinct set of "variables" for testing theories about the policy process (Lowi 1972, 299). Given a type of policy, we can make predictions about the type of politics that are likely to ensue. If such predictions do not hold up to rigorous testing, that provides a cue that a paradigm shift is warranted or at least can be expected. A null hypothesis that fails to be disproven still contributes to scientific knowledge.

Ultimately, if the methodological issues surrounding policy classification are solved—and we recognize that is a big "if"—the generalizability of the framework is still possible. Lowi's framework did not fail because its first principles did not fit together logically nor because it was empirically falsified; it has been kept in suspended animation because no one has figured out how to objectively and empirically classify policies into different types. If that problem can be overcome, the framework may yet prove to be a new paradigm for understanding politics. Most are rightly skeptical about objective classification, though there are still periodic attempts to do so, and they have been met with at least some success (Smith 2002). There is still potential for progress in this area.

Even if typologies never overcome this problem, however, the general framework has still made a contribution comparable to the stages model. It provides a workable frame of reference for studying public policy and has influenced generations of policy scholarship, but it contains many problems.

Where Do We Go from Here?

Does the field of public policy have a unifying theoretical framework? The answer is no. Has the field attempted to create such unifying frameworks? The answer is yes. The stages model and policy typologies, for all their inherent flaws, do provide a broad conceptualization of public policy and what public policy scholars should be doing. Most policy scholars view these frameworks more as historical artifacts than theoretical tools to guide research, and with some justification. The last major evolution of the stages model came with Ripley in 1985. Although more journal space has been devoted to criticizing the typology framework, the last major attempt at revision came with the sharp exchange between Spitzer and Kellow in 1989, and Smith's (2002) call to shift to a taxonomic (as opposed to typological) approach to policy classification. The typology framework and stages model both provide a way of organizing the field (one regarding policy process, the other regarding policy outputs), but there are important flaws in each. Such flaws, such as causality, testability, falsifiability, predictability, and others documented in this chapter, are fodder for theory-building within each framework. Attempts at revisions of both theories, however, appear to have stalled. Does this mean both theories are irrelevant?

The answer, like most in the social sciences, is "it depends." Most policy theories, including Lowi's typologies and the stages heuristic, fall short of scientific theory or are inadequate in ways that prevent systematic testing (Sabatier 2007). For the typology framework, the problem lies with the operationalization of the key independent variable. For the stage heuristic, the problem lies in the fact that it presents an untestable and non-falsifiable model. Greenberg et al. (1977, 1543) conclude that policy theory "should be parsimonious to be sure, but not oversimplified." Both the stages heuristic and policy typologies appear to have fallen into the trap of over-simplifying the policy process at the expense of rigorous scientific theory. The stages approach ignores institutions and critical individual actors such as policy specialists and advocacy groups, as well as systemic characteristics such as political feasibility, all of which can affect the policy process in varying ways. All are assumed to be static in the stages model. Policy typologies ignore the complexity of policy content as well as the fact that the causal arrow can flow in both directions. That is, political actors may attempt to shape the content of public policy as a way to shape the ensuing political debate. Both the stages model and policy typologies also fall short of the Lasswellian call for improving the quality of public policy. The stages model is simply a descriptive model of the policy process, and despite Lowi's claim, the typology framework does not give us any sense as to how to improve policy outputs. Good policy research includes substantive policy information that can potentially be used by policy practitioners (Sabatier 1991b). Neither the stages model nor the typology framework does this.

Even though both theories have serious limitations, both theories are also useful in terms of laying the groundwork for what good public policy theories should look like. The paradox of the stages model is that while most scholars argue it lacks testable hypotheses, most scholars also agree on the basic framework: problems must come to the attention of government before they can be addressed, alternatives are debated and the best option is selected and then implemented, with the implemented policy being subject to evaluation and revision. The same holds for the typology framework. Whereas critics of Lowi argue that most policies do not fit neatly within one of his three categories, they do agree that most policies share characteristics of these original categories. Moreover, policies that are "pure" cases do tend to be characterized by the politics predicted in Lowi's original model (Spitzer 1987). The utility of the stages model and typology framework is that they both show what not to do while also contributing to the field of policy studies. The number of books and journal pages devoted to both topics are a testament to their effect on the field.

The real dilemma for policy theory is whether it should be held to the same standards as theory in the natural or hard sciences. Paul Sabatier has written extensively on the need for "better theories" of public policy. For Sabatier (2007), the path to better theories is most likely to be characterized by a mix of inductive and deductive approaches. Policy theories should be broad in scope and attempt to develop causal relationships. Following Lowi, critics regularly chastised the simplicity of the typology framework on the grounds that it led to an incomplete and untestable model of politics. Revisions called for expanding the number of categories and adopting post-positivist methodology. Although such models were perhaps more inclusive, they did little to organize our understanding of policy classification. Lowi (1988, 725) himself wrote that his original typology framework outlined in his 1964 book review should be viewed "not for what it accomplished but for what started." The complexity of the policy process as well as policy content most likely means that any theory of public policy will continually be subject to revision. This is not meant to detract from the quality of such theories, it is simply recognition of the nature of the unit of analysis.

Notes

1. This sort of post-positivist approach has been used to construct some useful alternate typologies of politics and public policy. See, for example, Schneider and Ingram 1997, 109.

2. Ten rather than eight because regulatory policy is further subdivided between economic and social regulation, resulting in four types of regulative policy.

3. Policy with widely distributed costs and benefits was labeled redistributive policy; policy with widely dispersed costs and narrow benefits was labeled distributive; policy with narrow costs and widely dispersed benefits was labeled public interest regulatory; and policy with narrow costs and narrow benefits was labeled private interest regulatory (Kellow 1988, 718).

CHAPTER THREE

Who Makes Decisions? How Do They Make Decisions? Actors and Institutions

At a fundamental level, public policy is the study of decision making. Public policies, after all, represent choices backed by the coercive powers of the state. Who makes these decisions and why they make the decisions they do have always been important research questions for policy scholars.

How are decisions explained by policy scholars? Broadly speaking, policy studies have borrowed heavily from rational choice theory to explain decision making. In the ideal rationalist world, policy choices would be made objectively and efficiently. Policymakers would identify a problem; search though all possible alternatives for addressing the problem, weighing the pros and cons of each; and select the most efficient and effective solution. Most policy scholars, though, recognize such a model of decision making is wildly unrealistic, falling short of the rational ideal for at least two reasons, one political and one practical. On the political dimension, citizens tend to want immediate solutions to policy dilemmas. This compresses the time horizons of policymakers, limiting not just their time but also their ability to marshal the other resources needed (labor, information, etc.) to make fully rational decisions. On the practical dimension, the sheer complexity of most policy issues, and the limited cognitive capacity of humans, makes fully rational decision making virtually impossible. This does not mean that policy decisions are irrational. Many policy scholars agree that policymakers are at least intendedly rational; that is, their decision making is goal-oriented and they make choices with the intent of achieving those goals.

The assumption of at least intended rationality fits well with the Lasswellian notion of the problem orientation of public policy. If the purpose of policy is to solve problems, then the rational choice framework, with its focus on systematically linking means to desired ends, is an attractive model to help explain public policy decision making. As rational choice theory is predicated on the notion of methodological individualism, it sets up the study of decision making in public policy as the study of how individuals make choices. Yet individuals do not make choices, especially choices about public policy, in a vacuum where self-interest is allowed free rein. There are strong expectations that public policy will be made to advance the public interest, not just the individual interests of the decision maker. What might cause policymakers to ignore their own self-interest in favor of producing better public policy? The answer: institutions. Institutional rules shape policy decisions and can solve collective-action dilemmas that emerge from a rational choice framework. If public organizations are producing inefficient or ineffective policy, the solution is to redesign the institution. In the end, it is not the individual policy actor nor the institution that shapes public policy. Both dictate decision making in the public policy process.

Bounded Rationality and Incrementalism

Herbert Simon's seminal work *Administrative Behavior* (1947) has for more than half a century provided a foundation for understanding how policy choices get made. At the core of Simon's theory is the notion that people are not completely rational actors but instead are limited by cognitive and environmental constraints. Policy actors do not operate with complete information nor engage in exhaustive cost-benefit analyses when making policy decisions. Instead, policymakers make compromises, adapting to the situation at hand.

For Simon, complete rationality is unattainable for three reasons:

1. Rationality requires a complete knowledge and anticipation of the consequences that will follow on each choice. In fact, knowledge of consequences is always temporary.
2. Since these consequences lie in the future, imagination must supply the lack of experienced feeling in attaching value to them. But values can be only imperfectly anticipated.
3. Rationality requires a choice among all possible alternative behaviors. In actual behavior, only a very few of all these possible alternatives ever come to mind. (Simon 1997, 93–94).

In short, "It is impossible for the behavior of a single, isolated individual to reach any high degree of rationality" (Simon 1997, 92). Organizational constraints, time constraints, and cognitive limitations all prevent decision makers from making fully rational decisions.

If decision makers are limited by their cognitive abilities, then how do they go about making decisions? For Simon, decision making is best characterized by what is known as "bounded rationality." The basic tenet of bounded rationality is that humans are intendedly rational but are prevented from behaving in a fully rational manner due to cognitive limitations. Humans are simply limited in their ability to engage in an exhaustive search of all possible alternatives when making decisions. Memory, attention span, information processing capabilities, and so forth, all limit a person's ability to achieve complete rationality. Instead, the information search is incomplete and people choose among options that are not completely optimal but are good enough for the situation (Simon 1947). Such behavior, Simon has labeled, is best characterized as "satisficing." According to Simon, satisficing allows policymakers to make decisions that, although not completely rational, are capable of solving the issue at hand. In other words, policymakers make the best decision given the situation. Importantly, this allows policymakers to make "good enough" public policy decisions.

Simon (1985) contrasted the debate between complete and bounded rationality as one between "substantive" and "procedural" rationality. Substantive rationality assumes the tenets of complete rationality as conceived in economics—people have complete information before making a decision, weighing the costs and benefits of all alternatives. Bounded rationality, by contrast, is best characterized as "procedural" rationality, most closely associated with the field of cognitive psychology (Simon 1985, 295; see also B. Jones 2001). People are limited in their mental abilities to process incoming information. This in turn limits their ability to conduct comprehensive informational searches when considering policy alternatives or the goals of a particular policy. Procedural rationality implies that policymakers rely on mental shortcuts when processing incoming policy information. Instead of starting anew with each new policy problem, policymakers relate new problems to existing problems, drawing on existing solutions rather than starting from scratch.

That people are bounded when making decisions, however, does not imply an absence of intention. From an economic perspective, irrationality is defined as a lack of consistent preferences. Simon was explicit about the fact that "bounded rationality is not irrationality" (see Simon 1985, 297). Bounded rationality, unlike what Simon described as irrationality, consists of goal-oriented behavior. People, as Simon (1985, 297) wrote, "usually have reasons for what they do." Decision makers strive for and achieve rationality; it is just a degree of rationality that falls short of "substantive" rationality. So, while policymakers may not fit with what most people would picture as the ideal decision maker, they are still capable of making rational decisions. That is, they are still capable of making good policy decisions.

Rational decision theory implies that people operate with complete information and engage in exhaustive cost-benefit analyses when making policy decisions. Simon challenged this assumption head on. To suggest that policy actors and organizations employ rational decision-making processes is unrealistic. But, despite Simon's initial argument, there remained a lack of systematic empirical evidence documenting how policymakers make policy decisions.

Shortly after Simon's groundbreaking work on bounded rationality (1947, 1955), Charles Lindblom (1959) applied such concepts directly to the study of public policymaking. According to Lindblom, rather than engaging in a rational and comprehensive updating of specific policies, policymakers "muddle through"—making policy decisions based on small changes from existing policies. In other words, policymakers address each new policy problem from the perspective of what had been done in the past. Lindblom argued that both cognitive and situational constraints prevent policymakers from articulating clearly defined goals and conducting a wide and comprehensive search for alternatives. As a result the policymaking process, according to Lindblom, is best characterized by small, incremental adjustments, a model of policymaking that became known as "incrementalism."

Incremental decision making allows policymakers to process incoming information more quickly and deal with the complexity of many policy issues. As with Simon, decision making for Lindblom is governed by cognitive and environmental constraints—policymakers do not consider the full range of alternatives prior to making a decision, instead relying on heuristics that limit the information search. "Incrementalism," as conceptualized by Lindblom, is simply "satisficing" in practice. Like Simon, Lindblom saw a disconnect between the assumptions of substantive rationality, or the rational-comprehensive model of decision making, and the reality of decision making. Policymakers lack the time, financial, and mental resources to explore all policy alternatives. Because it is impossible to know all the viable policy options, as well as their consequences, policymakers tend to seek agreement where it can be found. In most cases, this occurs when policymakers make incremental, as opposed to comprehensive, changes to existing policies.

Lindblom clarified this distinction by distinguishing between the "root" and "branch" methods to policy decision making (1959, 81). The rational-comprehensive approach, because it treats each decision as an isolated event, is characterized by root decision making, whereas incrementalism, because it is based on small changes building off previous decisions, is based on branching. Policy decisions are not based on a new process for each decision; instead, they branch off from previous decisions. For Lindblom, the root method requires a separation of the means and ends. Policymakers first decide what the desired outcome of particular policy is, then proceed by deciding the best means to achieve such an outcome. The branch method, by contrast, combines the means and ends. Policy decisions are a process of "successive limited comparisons," with each decision building off previous decisions (81). Admittedly, Lindblom confessed that the disadvantages of such an approach include overlooking optimal means and ends. However, the branch method is a more realistic depiction of how policymakers actually make policy decisions.

Just like a boundedly rational decision maker can still be rational, so too can policymakers employing the branch method make rational, or "good," policy decisions (Lindblom 1959, 83). Decision making based on successive limited comparisons is the most efficient way to achieve policy agreement. It is unlikely, Lindblom has argued, that policymakers employing the root approach will ever agree on the end goal of old age insurance or agricultural economic policy, nor do policymakers have the time or mental resources to comprehend all possible consequences of such complex policies (1959, 83–84). Policymakers can, however, agree on small changes to existing policies.

Although satisficing was originally developed within the context of organizational decision making—specifically decision making in public bureaucracies—Simon was more interested in applying to it all human decision making. Lindblom's "muddling through" can be viewed as an extension of "satisficing" applied to the field of public policy. The only way for policymakers to agree and move forward with a policy is through successive limited comparisons. The end result, Lindblom argued is a process of "mutual adjustment" (1959, 85). Policymakers, recognizing their individual and institutional limitations, agree on small adjustments as a way to improve policy. Such adjustments may not be optimal, but they keep the policy process moving forward. And for policymakers, this is the most efficient way of pleasing a demanding public.

Lindblom's seminal work was purely a theoretical exercise in the application of satisficing to the study of public policy. Despite Lindblom's well-articulated argument about policy decision making, the empirical evidence to support such a claim was lacking. Moreover, incrementalism seemed to actually move us further away from the notion of the rational decision maker. That is, while it seemed difficult to comprehend how a boundedly rational decision maker could make sound policy decisions, the idea of an incremental decision maker making such decisions seemed even more unrealistic.

Davis, Dempster, and Wildavsky (1966) were the first to systematically test Lindblom's notion of incrementalism as a way of conceptualizing public budgetary processes. Despite the complexity of the federal budget, budgetary decisions are based on a relatively simple formula: agency requests and congressional appropriations tend to be predicted by small deviations from the previous year's request or appropriation. Though Davis, Dempster, and Wildavsky have admitted that their work is largely descriptive, it does provide empirical backing to Simon's and Lindblom's claims that decision making is primarily bounded and incremental. Rather than reviewing each program anew prior to the beginning of a new fiscal year, these authors have found that policymakers make adjustments in budgets based on the previous year's allotment. As Davis, Dempster, and Wildavsky argued, attempting to engage in a rational and comprehensive updating of the federal budget would simply overwhelm policymakers with information and prevent the policy process from ever moving forward. Simply put, the complexity of budgetary decisions forces the policymaker's hand to accept small, incremental changes, resulting in agency requests and congressional appropriations deviating only slightly from the previous year's decision. To sum up, gradual, incremental adjustments in policy best explain how policy actors make budgetary decisions—a process of decision making that is predicted by the tenets of bounded rationality.

At face value, incrementalism appears to be a useful explanatory framework for answering the question: Why do policymakers make the decisions that they do? The answer: because they are boundedly rational. Policymakers do not start from scratch with each new policy problem. Limitations in their ability to consider all possible policy goals or alternatives leads to a heavy and necessary reliance on past decisions, mental heuristics, and institutional rules. Outside of the work of Davis, Dempster, and Wildavsky, however, some scholars have argued that incrementalism offers little in the way of testable predictions. These critics have questioned its predictability and suggested that the tenets of incrementalism are little more than a descriptive model of policymaking. Reviewing the Davis, Dempster, and Wildavsky model of budget incrementalism, Wanat (1974, 1221) wrote that incrementalism "infrequently meets the canons of academic and scientific explanation." As Wanat explained, existing models of budget incrementalism are descriptive rather than explanatory. Using the Davis, Dempster, and Wildavsky model, Wanat demonstrated that political factors, such as the size of the request made by Congress, provide the explanatory backing as to why incremental changes occur. Whereas Davis, Dempster, and Wildavsky's model demonstrates that budgetary decisions tend to follow the pattern originally described by Lindblom, Wanat's theory contends it offers little in the way of predicting the degree of incrementalism.

More recent work by Jones, Baumgartner, and True (1998; see also True, Jones, Baumgartner 1999) has suggested incrementalism may be even less prevalent than originally indicated by Lindblom and Davis, Dempster, and Wildavsky. As we discuss in Chapter 4, these scholars have found that policy decisions are subject to relatively frequent "punctuations," or significant changes in policy. Although not completely discrediting incrementalism, this line of research casts further doubt on the predictive power of the incrementalist framework.

Nevertheless, Simon's research remains fundamental to policy decision theory because most policy scholars realize that policy actors are not completely rational. Few policy scholars question whether policymakers make decisions with incomplete information. Bounded rationality is based on the notion of individuals being limited in their information-processing capabilities. Incrementalism is a product of this framework and explains why policies seem to exhibit relatively little change from year to year. However, the degree of incremental change that takes place and how much change is considered incremental remains a theoretical and empirical question. For example, what explains significant policy change? What explains why a problem that received no money in the previous year's budget suddenly receives significant attention and a substantial amount of money? Nor does incrementalism explain rapid change in a policy. Until such questions are answered, incrementalism and bounded rationality will remain useful and powerful explanatory frameworks. But their predictive abilities will remain in question.

Public Choice and the Tiebout Hypothesis

One of the inherent contradictions in the Lasswellian notion of policy studies is the paradox of an elitist technocrat, a policy scientist, playing a central role in democratic decision making. As we shall see throughout this book, one of the issues that consistently divides the rationalist project from its post-positivist critics is the desire to make public policy more bottom-up and participatory. Neither the study nor the practice of policy-making can be democratic, the argument goes, if it is driven by the policy science elites.

The study of policy decision making, with its roots in classical economics and its heavy reliance on rational choice theory, is typically thought of as squarely in the rationalist tradition. Yet drawn from this perspective is perhaps the most participatory, systematic theory of who should make policy decisions and how they should be made. Public choice is essentially the application of neoclassical economic ideas to the public sector; the basic idea is to transfer the logic and theory of how markets work and apply it to politics. Public choice claims normative and objective status (i.e., it claims to be how the world does work and also how the world should work). From a public choice perspective, government should supply public programs and services in a similar fashion to private sector businesses; in other words, they should respond to demand from their "customers." Customers, i.e., citizens, should be given choices in terms of the public programs and services they can consume (and the associated costs of providing them), and driven by these quasi-market forces, government will supply the demanded services efficiently.

One of the earliest public choice frameworks was proposed by Charles Tiebout (1956). In his short essay on public service delivery, Tiebout described the ideal structure for local governance. The primary objective of any community is to serve its citizens by providing services. Certain services, such as water service, garbage service, police protection, fire service, and so forth, take the form of a public good. According to Tiebout, centralized or consolidated communities are inefficient in delivering such goods and unresponsive to the demands of individual citizens. Such inefficiency, argued Tiebout, stems from the nature of public goods. Because public goods, by definition, are indivisible, the provision of such goods is traditionally left to a centralized governmental structure. Having a monopoly over the provision of such goods, centralized structures have little incentive to respond to citizen preferences. As a result, public goods are inefficiently produced. Tiebout saw multijurisdictional communities as a way around this dilemma.

Local jurisdictions, like large, centralized bureaucracies, are prevented from distributing public goods. But what localities can do is offer service that is comparatively superior to surrounding localities. For example, localities do have control over the quality of water service, garbage service, education, and most important, tax burden they offer to citizens. By varying the level of service, localities are, in effect, offering citizens a choice about in which communities to establish residence. This choice is the hallmark of the Tiebout model. Citizens expressing their preferences for certain localities over others change the monopolistic relationship prevalent in centralized jurisdictions. Municipalities must respond to citizen demands or risk losing their tax base. When citizens are choosing communities based on the quality of service provided, and communities are responding to such choice, the market model takes hold. Thus, for Tiebout, citizen choice is the key to improving organizational efficiency. This choice manifests itself in the form of fragmented local government.

Two key assumptions rest at the heart of the Tiebout model: perfect information and perfect mobility. First, citizens are assumed to be rational decision makers with perfect information about the services provided by surrounding communities. Second, they are assumed to have the financial means to pick up and move at any time to a more satisfactory community. Other factors, such as employment opportunities, are considered irrelevant (Tiebout 1956, 419). That is, if people are presented with an "exit" option that offers superior service, they will choose the community that best represents their interests. Because people choose which community to reside in based on the quality of service provided, communities will be composed of people of similar interests. This has important policy implications. On the one hand, organizations and policymakers in such communities will be more responsive to citizen demands. And responsiveness breeds satisfaction; citizens will be more informed and more satisfied in a community in which they had a choice to reside.

That citizens act on their preferences is fundamental to the Tiebout hypothesis. As Tiebout wrote, "The act of moving or failing to move is crucial. Moving or failing to move replaces the usual market test of willingness to buy a good and reveals the consumer-voter's demand for public goods" (1956, 420). For the Tiebout hypothesis to hold, citizens must be willing to move when they become dissatisfied with the service being provided. Without acting on such choices, competition between jurisdictions becomes nonexistent, and there will be an inefficient production of public goods.

The Tiebout hypothesis is one of the most influential applications of the public choice model to public service delivery, and its intellectual heirs continue to shape policy debates in areas ranging from school vouchers to tradable pollution permits. The Tiebout framework is interesting because it seeks to devolve sovereignty over local-level policymaking to the level of the individual citizen; policymakers either respond to citizen preferences, or the citizens "vote with their feet" and, in effect, put that "brand" of public program or service out of business. Centralized governments are inefficient in the delivery of public goods because they have no incentive to respond to their primary clientele. The solution: offer citizens a choice about where to reside. The policy implications that stem from this are clear. Multijurisdictional communities are more efficient than single-jurisdictional communities. When citizens vote with their feet, they are making a statement about the current state of public policy. To be competitive, policymakers must respond, and in doing so, they improve the quality of services being provided. This citizen-as-policymaker perspective offered by the Tiebout hypothesis was purely a theoretical exercise aimed at solving the dilemma of inefficient provision of a public good. Upon further scrutiny, however, empirical support for the Tiebout hypothesis has been mixed.

Because of its emphasis on giving individual citizens influence over what programs and services are provided by government, public choice frameworks such as the Tiebout hypothesis have been championed as a means to resolve the democratic dilemma of the policy sciences. From this perspective, public choice represents much of the positive of the Lasswellian vision; a systematic theory generated by academic technocrats, moreover one that is rigorously examined across disciplines, and aimed at setting up an institutional mechanism to guide policy solutions to social problems (essentially a public sector equivalent of the "invisible hand" of the market place). Yet it does not set up the technocrats to make the decisions; public choice's relentless focus on the freedom of the individual to make choices gave it a claim to be a truly democratic system of governance (V. Ostrom 1973).

Two major objections stand in the way of public choice achieving the status of the Lasswellian ideal. First, on a theoretical level it equates democracy with free markets, and they are not synonymous. Democracy makes no guarantee that you get what you want—the customer is not always right—it simply guarantees you have a voice in the public space. Public choice basically eliminates public space; everyone is sovereign and his or her civic duties extend no further than narrow self-interest. For such reasons, post-positivists reject public choice as the democratic white knight of the rationalist project. Quite the contrary, they see public choice and its market-based institutional prescriptions as atomizing public policy preferences rather than effectively aggregating citizen preference. Democracy institutionalizes voice, not exit. Second, and perhaps more damning from the rationalist project's point of view, is the fact that it is not at all clear that public choice works as well in practice as it does in theory.

Citizens as Efficient Policymakers?

The Tiebout hypothesis rests on the assumption that citizens will choose municipalities that offer the best service. Scholars have picked up on this assumption, testing whether multijurisdiction (fragmented) or single-jurisdiction (centralized) government is better in terms of increasing citizen satisfaction. Such work tends to center around the basis of choice for individual citizens. If citizens choose jurisdictions based on concerns other than service quality (say, for example, they choose on the basis of racial segregation), the Tiebout hypothesis breaks down empirically, and its normative claims in terms of democratic principles also start to appear suspect. Similarly, if people living in fragmented communities lack perfect information about surrounding jurisdictions, or people living in consolidated communities are equally satisfied as those living in fragmented communities, the Tiebout hypothesis becomes problematic. The Tiebout hypothesis also posits that people have perfect mobility, that citizens are capable of "exiting" a community if services become unsatisfactory. Moreover, for Tiebout, these mobility decisions should not be affected by external considerations. As Tiebout wrote, "restrictions due to employment opportunities are not considered" (1956, 419). In other words, people should not be constrained in their ability to change communities. Like other assumptions in Tiebout's model, these assumptions have been challenged by scholars as unrealistic and deserving of empirical scrutiny.

Lyons, Lowery, and DeHoog (1992) offer one of the most comprehensive and systematic empirical tests of the Tiebout hypothesis. To do so, the authors draw on data obtained in a survey of citizen attitudes in a fragmented community and a centralized community. The data are based on a matched sample in both communities. The Tiebout hypothesis rests on the assumption that citizens treat their decision about in which community to reside similar to decisions in the marketplace; citizens will shop around for the community that delivers the best quality service. As a consequence of such behavior, Tiebout argued, a clear set of testable hypotheses emerges: citizens should be more informed, more satisfied, and more aware of alternative jurisdictions in fragmented communities as compared to single-jurisdiction or centralized communities. The results of the Lyons, Lowery, and DeHoog (1992) study cast considerable doubt on these assumptions.

Reviewing citizen responses to surveys in polycentric (fragmented) and monocentric (centralized) jurisdictions, Lyons, Lowery, and DeHoog found little support for Tiebout's model. Specifically, citizens in polycentric jurisdictions tend to be *less* informed about surrounding jurisdictions and *less* informed about what services are provided by their own local government (1992, 98–99). Moreover, there was no statistical difference in the level of satisfaction of the service provided between citizens in polycentric communities and citizens in monocentric communities (1992, 101). Finally, despite Tiebout's assumption that people "vote with their feet," there was relatively little difference in the use of the exit option between the two communities. In short, citizens in centralized communities tend to be happy about the quality of service being provided and have little desire to exit.

The debate between Tiebout and the findings presented by Lyons, Lowery, and DeHoog is critical to understanding how and why policymakers make the decisions they do. If the evidence presented by Lyons, Lowery, and DeHoog is correct, then citizens and policymakers are making inefficient public policy. From a purely democratic point of view, this is not a problem; democracy, as scholars like Stone (2002) have taken some pains to point out, is not particularly efficient and makes no claim to be so. For public choice, however, the empirical claim that more marketlike arrangements do not increase efficiency in public policy is fairly devastating. Unlike democracy, efficiency *is* the central normative value of economic theory, and efficiency is the central normative justification for public choice. If policymaking remains inefficient under a public choice framework, then public choice does not provide a solution to the problem originally proposed by Tiebout—that all centralized communities are producing inefficient public goods. Are citizens actually staying in communities in which public service delivery is inefficient? Probably, but it does not seem to bother them that much, at least if one looks at levels of service satisfaction in studies like those by Lyons, Lowery, and De-Hoog. So do citizens really not care about inefficient service? This also seems questionable given the level of knowledge citizens in centralized communities have about services being provided relative to citizens in fragmented communities. In an attempt to resolve this dilemma, Paul Teske and his colleagues further examined the Tiebout model.

Teske et al. (1993) began with the assumption that not all citizens are fully informed. Like Herbert Simon, Teske and his colleagues see citizens as making decisions appropriate for the situation. The situation, for most citizens, rarely involves decisions about tax-service packages or the quality of garbage service in a community. As such, the average citizen is unaware, or has no incentive to be aware, of the difference in services between jurisdictions.

Teske et al. challenged Lyons, Lowery, and DeHoog on the notion that for Tiebout's hypothesis to be correct, all citizens must be fully informed. Teske et al. contended that for markets to function efficiently, only a "subset" of actors must make fully informed decisions. This "subset" most likely consists of people who have the most to gain from being fully informed, specifically those who are actually moving between jurisdictions. Teske et al. tested this proposition by surveying "established" residents and movers in a single county in New York about school district expenditures and taxes. They hypothesized that movers, because they have an incentive to obtain information about tax-service packages, are more likely to be informed and therefore are more likely to fit the assumptions of Tiebout's model.

The results of the survey by Teske and his colleagues do provide some empirical support for their hypothesis. Examining citizen perceptions about school district expenditures and taxes, Teske et al. found that a small group of citizen consumers were well-informed about educational policy in their district as well as surrounding districts. Importantly, however, this group of "marginal consumers" did not consist of general movers as originally proposed by the authors. Instead, it was high-income movers who were most well-informed about school district taxes. The utility of this finding, according to Teske et al., is that it resolves the problem presented by Lyons, Lowery, and DeHoog—how can relatively uninformed citizens make for efficient public policy? The findings of Teske et al. suggest local governments can be competitive and efficient simply by responding to a small group of citizen-consumers. High-income, mobile citizens tend to be the most well-informed citizens because they are the ones "shopping" around for a new community and are most likely to have the time and resources to do so. And, as Teske et al. (1993, 709) wrote, it is this group "communities have the strongest incentive to attract."

Teske et al.'s finding provides a lifeboat for the Tiebout hypothesis and presents an important revision to the conclusion of Lyons, Lowery, and DeHoog (1992). However, in doing so it undercuts a key normative claim of public choice and brings back the paradox inherent in the policy sciences of democracy. Rather than all citizens actively participating in the policy process, only a small minority will drive the marketplace for public goods and services. These citizens are not technocrats, but they are an elite minority, and there is no guarantee they are representative of the preferences of others. In other words, this vision of public choice ends up being more elitist that egalitarian; it simply switches the elitist policy technocrat for an almost certainly socioeconomically distinct minority. To post-positivist critics, and perhaps many others, that tradeoff is unlikely to provide a satisfactory squaring of the democratic circle.

There are also some empirical objections to the reformulation of public choice provided by Teske et al. Lowery, Lyons, and DeHoog (1995) challenged the key findings in two ways. First, Teske et al. focused on education policy, a policy Lowery, Lyons, and DeHoog describe as "atypical" and highly salient, particularly for the county from which the sample was derived (1995, 705). A less salient policy, such as water or garbage service, would be more appropriate. Second, Teske et al.'s measure of "informed" citizens was rather simplistic, asking respondents whether the school district's expenditures were average, above average, or below average for the area. As Lowery, Lyons, and DeHoog wrote, given the "absurdly unchallenging level" of being informed, that high-income movers perform better on this question does not necessarily imply a great deal of depth to their knowledge of school expenditures. Thus, we seem to be back to the original dilemma. Citizens are not behaving as proposed by Tiebout, but they are not any less satisfied with the service being provided, nor are they any less informed. So what explains public service delivery in local governments, and how are policy decisions being made?

Applied narrowly, some scholars argue that the Tiebout hypothesis provides a means for constructing a more efficient system of delivering public goods (Chubb and Moe 1988, 1990). Applied more broadly, however, as evidenced by the debate between Lyons, Lowery, and DeHoog and Teske et al., the Tiebout hypothesis receives mixed support. One way to interpret the findings of Lyons, Lowery, and DeHoog is that polycentric communities do not increase the efficiency of the public service delivery. This of course assumes people are making decisions based on the quality of service provided. An alternative explanation is that people actually make decisions based on factors other than the service being provided.

The quality of water service or garbage service being provided may have no effect on people's level of satisfaction or their desire to exit. Acknowledging the relatively low level of knowledge citizens have about local government service provision, Lyons, Lowery, and DeHoog (1992, 103) speculated that "local factors are probably more important in determining satisfaction and responses to dissatisfaction than the kinds of institutional factors addressed by both the Tiebout exiting hypothesis and traditional civic reformers." The question then becomes: what are these local factors, and how do they affect how policy decisions are being made?

Policy scholars have struggled to determine exactly how citizens make mobility decisions. Even though "marginal consumers" may make fully informed decisions, how do nonmarginal consumers make decisions? The Tiebout hypothesis, by the admission of its author, is an "extreme" model (Tiebout 1956, 419). If local factors are important, the range of possible alternatives is potentially endless. To narrow the search, scholars have revisited educational policy, specifically the issue of school choice. School choice provides a nice example because it assumes people make decisions on the basis of a specific policy outcome: academic performance.

Mark Schneider, Paul Teske, and others (M. Schneider et al. 1998) asked the question: what factors drive school choice? The voucher system is based on the assumption that parents are choosing schools on the basis of academic performance. If, however, other factors are driving such choice, this has important policy implications. What Schneider et al. found is that parents tend to pick schools based on their own individual preferences, but those preferences are not always related to academic performance. Marginal parents, who tend to be high-income parents, are more informed about schools' academic outcomes. These parents, argue Schneider et al., are enough to induce competitive pressures on the school to improve academic performance. However, for nonmarginal parents, school choice decisions are more complex. Although parents tend to have erroneous assumptions about school characteristics, they are able to match their preferences about schools. These preferences, however, are based on the demographic characteristics of the school and the reported number of violent incidents at the school. Citizens are making public policy decisions, but the basis of such decisions varies widely. Like Teske et al., Schneider et al. found that high-income citizens with a vested interest in the policy do make "rational" decisions. However, for the vast majority of citizens, policy decisions are being made in such a way that violates the underlying assumptions of the existing policy.

Mark Schneider and Jack Buckley (2002) picked up on this notion of "local factors" or non-outcome factors as dictating school choice and mobility decisions. To understand how parents make school choice decisions, Schneider and Buckley monitored Internet usage on a Web site providing school district information for Washington, D.C., schools. Their purpose was to monitor the search behavior of parents to determine what factors are important when making school choice decisions. What they found was that while parents are initially interested in academic performance factors (test scores and programs offered), the most prominent school attributes parents access in the initial search process are racial diversity and school location. In other words, non-outcome factors are much more prevalent in the search process than would be assumed by the Tiebout hypothesis. Such findings put a serious dent in the policy prescriptions offered by school choice advocates and public choice more generally. Perhaps even more revealing from the Schneider and Buckley article is that the demographic attributes are prevalent in the search process of college educated and non–college educated parents and that such attributes tend to dictate the entire search process. "Local" factors pervade policy choice decisions and create an environment ripe for racial disparity.

The findings of Schneider and Buckley (2002) present policymakers with a serious dilemma. Should they respond to citizen preference, whatever those preferences may be? Or should they make decisions based on what they believe is the best outcome? School choice, or the voucher system, is a direct application of Tiebout's exit model. However, as the findings by Schneider et al. and Schneider and Buckley suggest, parents are not making educational decisions based on academic performance but instead on factors unrelated to education, with potentially undemocratic results. Moreover, if the findings of Paul Teske, Mark Schneider, and others regarding the marginal consumer are correct, then public policy is being crafted based on the preferences of the few, the well-off few to be exact, rather than the majority.

Institutional Rational Choice

Using public choice theory as the basis for understanding how policy decisions are made has important policy implications because it provides prescriptions regarding public service delivery (Frederickson and Smith 2003, 187). Those prescriptions, however, have a mixed empirical record. The exchange between Lyons, Lowery, and DeHoog (1992) and Teske et al. (1993) demonstrates that citizens can make policy but that mobility decisions are much more complex than originally proposed by Tiebout. Some citizens may in fact "vote with their feet," but such decisions are not nearly as widespread or as simple as suggested by Tiebout. Subsequent work by policy scholars has also confirmed the potential disadvantages of designing jurisdictions in accordance with the Tiebout hypothesis. If left to their own accord, citizens will make decisions that have the potential to further racial and economic disparities. Summarizing research in the fifty years since the Tiebout hypothesis, Howell-Moroney (2008) has written that while the Tiebout model preserves efficiency and economy, it ignores equity. Left to their own devices, citizens produce if not wholly irrational policies, then certainly suboptimal policies (i.e., policy that is not particularly efficient, and not particularly effective). Does this mean policymaking authority should be removed from the hands of the individual citizen?

Some scholars have argued that rules or institutions can be employed to improve the rationality of individual decision making, thereby improving the overall quality of policymaking. The rational actor model, for this group of scholars, presents a shortsighted and incomplete view of human decision making. Policymakers, citizens, and other human beings make decisions in the context of institutional rules. These rules, in turn, shape individual preferences. Labeled "institutional rational choice," this approach to policy decision making has a leading proponent in Elinor Ostrom. At the heart of this framework is an interest in "how institutions affect the incentives confronting individuals and their resultant behavior" (Ostrom 2007, 21). Quoting evolutionary psychologists Leda Cosmides and John Tooby, Ostrom (1998, 6) contended that institutions allow for individuals to make "better than rational" decisions. The belief among institutional rational choice scholars is that institutions can be designed to solve collective-action problems. Contrary to decision-making models discussed in the previous sections, the independent variable of interest in this framework is the institution or institutional rule.

Institutionalism and School Choice

A good example of institutional rational choice applied to a practical policy problem is John Chubb and Terry Moe's widely cited work on school choice. Chubb and Moe (1990, 1988) began with the assumption that public schools, because they have a monopoly on the service being provided (public education), have no incentive to respond to their consumers (parents). As a result, the public-school system fosters an unresponsive environment. The Tiebout hypothesis is based on citizens having an "exit" option. For parents in public-school systems, the exit option does not exist. The institution (public school) has no incentive to respond to parents' demands. Instead, as Chubb and Moe argued, public schools respond to other actors, namely, the elected officials who provide financial support for the school. In public schools, school administrators become so focused on satisfying the demands of these elected officials that they rarely care to respond to the demands of teachers and parents, the primary users of the service provided by the school. Chubb and Moe view this dilemma as an institutional design flaw, with the solution being a redesign of the institution such that the institution has an incentive to respond to its primary clientele (i.e., parents and teachers).

Coming from a neo-institutionalist perspective, Chubb and Moe have argued that public choice presents opportunities for major reforms in public education. Their argument is based primarily on the assumption of policymakers behaving as rational, self-interested agents (see Niskanen 1971). Applied to education policy, this means that public schools are top-heavy agencies governed by self-interested administrators. This has serious and negative consequences for public schools. Rather than listening to teachers and parents who utilize the service being provided by the school, administrators are more focused on obtaining resources. As a result, academic performance suffers. The policy prescription put forth by Chubb and Moe is rooted in institutional theory: redesign the incentives for the primary policymakers (i.e., school administrators) within the institution. To do so, Chubb and Moe argued for removing policy delivery mechanisms from democratic control. As Chubb and Moe wrote, "Democratic control normally produces ineffective schools" (1990, 227). In other words, remove the connection between administrators and elected officials and give parents a choice about to which school to send their children. Doing so will force administrators to respond to the parents' and teachers' demands to maintain sufficient funding. Chubb and Moe, in short, have argued that democratic control creates a perverse set of top-down incentives, and that policy effectiveness would increase by replacing this institutional arrangement with a market-based framework where incentives are produced from the bottom up.

The market model of public education put forth by Chubb and Moe (1990) is often cited by school choice advocates. The policy prescriptions from this model were designed to maximize the collective good by providing an exit option with competing alternatives. Public education institutions should be reformed by decentralizing, allowing parents a choice about to which school to send their children. Doing so will force school administrators to pay attention to the primary clientele of the school. Some have argued, however, that the assumptions underlying Chubb and Moe's institutionalist approach are flawed. We have already observed that citizens tend not to make school choice decisions on the basis of academic performance outcomes (see Schneider et al. 1998; Schneider and Buckley 2002). Others, however, question the direction of the relationship outlined by Chubb and Moe between school administrators and school performance. Kevin Smith and Kenneth Meier (1995) have asked the question: is it really that school bureaucracy causes negative performance, or is it that school bureaucracy is a response to negative performance? Smith and Meier found in favor of the latter, that the causal arrow presented by Chubb and Moe is actually reversed—bureaucracies are top-heavy because of the needs of the school. In other words, school bureaucracies are a response to demands by parents and teachers, not elected officials (see also Meier, Polinard, and Wrinkle 2000). As schools are required to meet the demands of a more diverse student body, the number of administrators working on behalf of the school is likely to increase. Previous test scores, not the size of the bureaucracy, tend to be a stronger predictor of school performance. And where school choice policies are in place, there is a greater risk for educational segregation (Smith and Meier 1995, 55–58). That citizens are making choices based on non-outcome factors, and that school bureaucracies are responding to the needs of the school as opposed to elected officials, presents two significant challenges to Chubb and Moe's neo-institutionalist framework.

Chubb and Moe proceeded primarily from a rational choice perspective. Policymakers are viewed as acting in their own self-interest, and in doing so they create inefficient public institutions. From a rational choice perspective, collective-action problems or social dilemmas present a significant problem. Rational choice, as originally understood, is based on the following assumptions: 1) behavior is best explained at the level of the individual; and 2) people are self-interested utility maximizers (see Downs 1957 and Buchanan and Tullock 1962).[1] What does this mean for the study of public policy? By definition, the role of public policymakers is to make decisions that are in the public's best interest. If, however, rational choice theory is correct, then policymakers are incapable of making public decisions. The neo-institutionalist framework put forth by Chubb and Moe does little to resolve this dilemma.

Collective-Action Dilemmas: IAD and the Logic of Appropriateness

Despite the mixed success of the institutionalist approach with regard to education policy, scholars continue to recognize that institutions do matter. Like Herbert Simon, Elinor Ostrom (1998) has viewed human decision making as bounded by cognitive constraints. Ostrom has put forth two additional propositions, however. First, institutions can shape individual preferences. Second, people will use institutional rules to solve collective-action problems. Out of the institutional rational choice perspective, Ostrom and her colleagues have developed an entire research agenda focused on the application of institutionalist theory to solving common-pool resource dilemmas. Labeled "institutional analysis and development" or IAD, these scholars focus on common-pool resources for two reasons: 1) common-pool resource dilemmas tend to lack any sort of formal institutional rules; and 2) if people are able to solve such dilemmas in the absence of an external authority, it would provide insight into how best to solve other collective-action dilemmas.

One of the more intriguing findings from this research agenda comes from Ostrom, Walker, and Gardner (1992). Rational choice and noncooperative game theory suggest that the only way to solve collective-action problems in a one-shot dilemma is through the use of external sanctions. These theoretical predictions are then used to justify the allocation of punishment power to the state. To ensure cooperation, there needs to be the threat of punishment. Ostrom, Walker, and Gardner have challenged this assumption, citing evidence that communication can solve collective-action problems, even in one-shot encounters. Using an experimental design, the authors invited subjects to play a common-pool resource game.

In this game, subjects were endowed some payoff at the beginning of the game and had a choice about whether to contribute to one of two public-good markets. The first market gave a fixed return based on the amount contributed by the individual. The second market gave a return that was based on the amount of tokens invested by other players. In the second market, the game-theoretic prediction was for individual players to free ride off others' contributions because investing in this market was both costly and risky.

In the baseline condition, in which no sanction and no communication were possible, players tended to conform to game-theoretic predictions. However, in additional treatments, when communication and sanction were introduced, contribution levels changed. In one-shot and repeated communication treatments, subjects yielded more efficient outcomes than treatments in which subjects were allowed to sanction others, but without communication. In cases where subjects were allowed to communicate and sanction, subjects were able to negotiate a sanctioning mechanism that achieved near-optimal results. In other words, subjects were able to achieve an efficient policy outcome in the absence of an external enforcer.

From an institutionalist perspective, the findings of Ostrom, Walker, and Gardner make perfect sense. A change in rule should lead to a change in behavior. Allowing communication and self-sanctioning increases the ability of policymakers (subjects) to achieve better and more efficient policy outcomes. Since this initial publication, Ostrom and her colleagues have further demonstrated that communication and other institutional rules can increase the efficiency of policy outcomes (Ostrom, Gardner, and Walker 1994). For policymakers, this implies that institutional rules may hold the key to producing better public policy. If certain rules allow individuals to coordinate their behavior to achieve more efficient outcomes, then institutions should be designed accordingly. If Ostrom, Walker, and Gardner (1992, 1994) are correct, there may be situations in which policymakers are able to remove the need and cost for policy oversight.

Ostrom (2007) argued that the IAD framework is useful for policy analysts in explaining and predicting how people will respond to institutional rules. To do so requires conceptualization of what is known as the "action area." The action area consists of seven sets of variables describing the situation and the actor. The seven variables are other participants, positions currently held, potential outcomes, action-outcome linkages, the control that participants exercise, information available, and the costs and benefits assigned to outcomes (Ostrom 2007, 28). The complexity of this framework is readily apparent. In fact, it seems to move us closer to the rational-comprehensive model of decision making or Simon's substantive rationality. This may in fact encompass how people make policy decisions, but it hardly presents a parsimonious model of decision making. In fact, Ostrom has admitted that "strong inferences" about decision making are most likely possible in "tightly constrained, one-shot action situations under conditions of complete information, where participants are motivated to select particular strategies or chains of action that jointly lead to stable equilibria" (32). We doubt that such a situation is common among policymakers. In fact, we would argue that such a model actually reduces our ability to predict policy decision making. Thus, although the IAD framework provides enormous explanatory power and is confirmed in experimental settings designed to simulate common-pool resource dilemmas, its applicability outside the lab in terms of predicting how policy decisions are made is still in question.

A more simplistic model of decision making is presented by James March's (1994) "logic of appropriateness." The logic of appropriateness states: "Action, policy making included, is seen as driven by rules of appropriate or exemplary behavior, organized into institutions" (March and Olsen 2006, 689). Put simply, people will do what is appropriate given the situation. In any given situation, the logic of appropriateness states that people will ask: What kind of situation is this? What kind of person am I? What does a person like me do in a situation such as this? (March and Olsen 2006, 690). People tend to adapt to the situation at hand and to make the decision that will best satisfy their preferences given the current set of rules and norms, as well as their past experiences and expectations of their position within the organization.

The logic of appropriateness, like bounded rationality, is a departure from models of pure rationality. "Appropriate" goes beyond standard operating procedures to include informal rules and norms within an organization, thus helping to explain extreme decisions such as organizational protests and defiance of authority (March and Olsen 2006, 692). Institutional rules and norms define what is in one's best interest, thus guiding individual behavior. Like Ostrom's IAD framework, the logic of appropriateness relies on institutional rules to solve collective-action dilemmas. What is appropriate seems to be an intuitive understanding among policymakers. We would venture to guess that most policymakers can recall when a colleague acted inappropriately, and probably can recall even more vividly when their own actions violated the "logic of appropriateness." Like the IAD framework, the logic of appropriateness enhances the explanatory power of models of policy decision making, but with greater parsimony.

Despite this intuitive appeal, questions still linger. For example, who or what defines what is "appropriate"? How do changes in what is appropriate occur? If "appropriate" is defined only after someone is working within an organization, how are we able to predict policy decisions? Without answers to these questions, it is difficult to make predictions with any degree of certainty about how people will respond to changes in institutional rules.[2] Even March and Olsen (2006, 695) have admitted that "rules, laws, identities, and institutions provide parameters for action" rather than exact predictions about what decisions will be made. As policymakers take on more roles and identities within an organization, determining what is appropriate in any given situation becomes ever more important to understanding how people make policy decisions.

There seem to be two glaring problems with the institutionalist framework. One is that, when applied to real-world policy problems, empirical and theoretical support tend to be lacking. The causality of Chubb and Moe's neo-institutionalist approach has been questioned extensively. Although the Tiebout hypothesis is based on assumptions about citizen choice, the policy prescriptions clearly fit within the institutionalist framework. In the more than fifty years since its publication, scholars have struggled to find any empirical support for its assumptions (see Howell-Moroney 2008). Second is that, where empirical support does exist as in the area of common-pool resources demonstrated by Ostrom and her colleagues, there is little theoretical backing as to why communication, particularly face-to-face communication, is so important for coordinating behavior. Ostrom (1998) has speculated that such mechanisms allow for "better than rational" decisions, and although her more recent work (see Ostrom 2005) has been devoted to theoretically modeling such mechanisms, it has yet to be fully tested. Theoretical insight is critical to identifying the conditions under which communication in common-pool resource dilemmas and other collective-action problems will fail. The complexity of the IAD framework makes it difficult to make predictions about when institutional rules will work. Ostrom (2007, 22) has written that the effects of rules at any one level of decision making are likely to be affected by rules made at other levels. Yes, institutions matter. Most scholars agree on this point. But when? The interaction between rules and norms and between policymakers of varying levels of authority makes it difficult to assess the exact effect of institutions on individual decision making. Thus, in their current form, institutional rational choice and IAD remain powerful explanatory frameworks, with uncertain predictive qualities.

Conclusion

What do we know about how policy actors make decisions? First and foremost, policy actors are not fully rational. They do not make decisions with complete information, nor do they weigh the pros and cons of all possible alternatives prior to making a decision. As Herbert Simon established more than fifty years ago, policy actors, whether they are top-level officials or the ordinary citizen, are bounded in their degree of rationality. Policymakers rely on cues, heuristics, institutional context, and what is "appropriate" when making decisions. Simon's (1947, 1955) early work on bounded rationality spawned an entire subfield of public policy based on incrementalism (Lindblom 1959, 1979; Davis, Dempster, and Wildavsky 1966; see also Goodin 1999, 72) that provides a glimpse into how policymakers deal with complex policy problems. Second, if left to the decisions of ordinary citizens, public policy would potentially create an inequitable social environment. Citizens do not make choices based on the quality of service provided or what would be the most efficient public policy. Instead, they are more interested in demographic factors. This raises questions about whether boundedly rational citizens are capable of making good policy decisions. So, where does this leave us?

Institutionalist scholars argue that the problem rests not with individual policymakers or citizens; when it comes to making choices, humans are what they are. Instead, the problem lies with the design of public institutions, which could be better constructed to channel individual self-interest toward choices that result in more effective and efficient policy outcomes. If certain policies are delivering inefficient or inequitable outcomes, then there must be a design flaw in existing institutions. Although some important policy prescriptions have emerged from this framework, particularly regarding behavior in a public goods setting or a collective-action dilemma (see Ostrom, Gardner, and Walker 1994 for an application to common-pool resources), others have not been so successful (Chubb and Moe's 1990 neo-institutionalist approach to school choice and Tiebout's 1956 hypothesis on public service delivery).

Common to both the individual and institutionalist framework is a desire to understand and ultimately predict the choices of policy actors. Unfortunately, research on decision making in public policy seems unable to get away from its rational choice/public choice roots. Most policy scholars now seem to accept the bounded rationality view of human decision making, and most seem to accept that institutions matter. What is missing is a theoretical framework that explains the origins of our boundedly rational preferences. Why does face-to-face communication increase cooperation so dramatically? Why are people extremely sensitive to violations of fairness norms in group settings such as common-pool resource dilemmas? From an institutionalist perspective, answers to such questions are desirable because they present an opportunity for the implementation of a new set of rules. The current state of policy research, however, seems less interested in answering these and other questions about preference formation, instead taking bounded rationality as a given. The result has been a series of policy decision-making models with a high degree of explanatory power but little predictive ability. Whereas this descriptive framework is useful, the lack of predictive power forces policymakers into a largely trial-and-error approach to policymaking. Thus, we are left with policy decisions being made by boundedly rational actors who may or may not change depending on the situation and existing institutional rules.

Notes

1. Since the work of Downs and Buchanan and Tullock, many scholars have questioned the feasibility of rational choice assumptions. See Green and Shapiro (1994) for an exhaustive critique of the assumptions of rational choice theory, with a response by Friedman (1996).

2. For a review of what is "appropriate" in social dilemmas of varying characteristics, see Weber, Kopelman, and Messick (2004).

CHAPTER FOUR

Where Does Policy Come From?
The Policy Process

Foundational to the notion of the policy sciences is the problem orientation, the assumption that public policy is a solution-oriented response to major social problems. Although this assumption can be (and has been) challenged, it fits with intuitive notions and generally accepted definitions of what public policy is and what it is supposed to do, i.e., policy is a deliberative action (or nonaction) undertaken by government to achieve some desired end. Accepting the problem orientation, however, raises a series of complex questions. What problems should government pay attention to? Who decides what a problem is and whether it merits government attention and action? When and why do policies change? Is it because the problem is solved, is it because the problem is redefined, or is it something else?

These sorts of questions are at the heart of the study of policy process, which can be thought of as the study of how public policy is made. This includes the means by which problems are identified and brought to the attention of government as well as how solutions are formulated and decided upon. The primary objective of this broad research literature is to try to understand where policy comes from and how and why it changes.

Policymakers are inundated with pressure for action from constituents, issue interest groups, think tanks, the media, and numerous other information sources. And more often than not, such groups tend to be in disagreement over what are the most pressing issues. So what determines whether government will pay attention to an issue and take some purposive action to address it? For example, why did child care suddenly become a problem meriting intensive government attention in the 1960s and 1970s (see Nelson 1984)? Why did special education become such a high-profile policy issue during the same time period (see Cremins 1983; Turnbull 1986). Certainly such issues were prevalent long before legislation was enacted to address such concerns, and certainly lawmakers were aware of such issues. So why did policymakers decide to act when they did? How did these issues move from relative obscurity to the government agenda?

Ultimately what issues government pays attention to is the result of a highly complex and dynamic process known as agenda setting. As Bryan Jones and Frank Baumgartner wrote, agenda setting is "the process by which information is prioritized for action, and attention allocated to some problems rather than others" (2005, ix). It is frequently assumed that this process is logical and rational; in reality, the process is as much political as it is logical, and some theorists have claimed that it is more rationalized than rational (e.g., Kingdon 1995).

Process and Power

Policy process may be frustratingly complex and hard to understand, but this has not stopped scholars—particularly political scientists—from trying to identify and understand systematic causal relationships. The special attraction for political science is not hard to fathom: the study of policy process is ultimately the study of political power. Think of political power as relative influence over policy outcomes, i.e., what decisions and actions are backed by the coercive powers of the state. What are effective ways to wield such influence? Students of policy process readily affirm that an effective means to wield such power is to influence the government's policy agenda, to determine the list of problems and proposed solutions government is actively paying attention to.

The power of agenda setting, the process of bringing certain topics to the attention of decision makers to make policy, has long been recognized by scholars (Cobb and Elder 1983; Majone 2006; Page 2006). Thus a central research question for policy process scholars revolves around how problems gain government attention, and who gets to define those problems and suggest solutions. This has particularly important implications for democratic systems because policy scholars quickly established that whatever the intricacies of the process of policymaking, they frequently did not conform to the notions of a pluralist democracy. The ability to decide what is being decided upon is often referred to as "indirect power." Most scholars agree that such power is more influential in determining the outcomes of the policy process than direct power, or the ability to actually make policy decisions (Bachrach and Baratz 1962). The actors who wield true political power within a given system are those who can influence or control the problems and policy alternatives that are placed on the government agenda. Theories of the policy process are largely devoted to understanding who these actors are and how they wield this influence.

Policy Subsystems and Issue Networks

So who does get to decide what topics are important enough for the government to address? How do they go about making such decisions? Is this process democratic, or is it dominated by elites? The pluralist theoretical tradition in political science suggests that the policy process is mainly a competition among organized groups that account for all interests, each vying to get the government to pay attention to its problems or concerns and to do so by taking particular actions (Truman 1951). Some policy process scholars—and certainly some theories of the policy process—tend to be a good deal more skeptical of this pluralist framework. At the extreme, iron triangle theorists argue that the Congress, the bureaucracy, and special interest groups form an unbreakable triad, offering ideas and policy solutions with narrow benefits at the expense of the public interest. The power of iron triangles to control policy agendas, however, has also come under fire. In the late 1970s and early 1980s, scholars revised the notion of the iron triangle. Rather than the policy process being dominated by a select group of actors, these scholars argued that policy process was more open. Known as subsystems theory, these scholars emphasized the role of public and private organizations, including think tanks, research institutes, interest groups, and ordinary citizens. The main premise of subsystems theory was that the policy process was, or at least had become, decentralized and fragmented, allowing for informal alliances in the policymaking process.

Although Freeman (1965) was the first to discuss the existence of policy subsystems, Hugh Heclo (1977, 1978) was the first to theoretically expand on this notion and what it meant for understanding the source of agenda setting and policy change. Heclo argued that existing studies of the iron triangle were incomplete because they were unable to account for decentralization and change in the policy process. If the iron triangle is the only source of public policy, how do new policy proposals emerge? How can the iron triangle explain rapid change in public policy? Examining the policy landscape system in the 1970s, Heclo did not see a rigid and impenetrable structure as suggested by iron triangle scholars. Rather, Heclo noticed a tremendous increase in intergovernmental lobbies coupled with a rise in the role of state governments in public policymaking. The growth in governmental activity and the complexity of emerging policies had also spawned a massive increase in interest group activity. For Heclo, the political system was highly fragmented and much more dynamic than suggested by iron triangle scholars.

Heclo's research (1978) coined two important terms relevant to agenda-setting scholars: "issue networks" and "technopols." Instead of the tight-knit policy groups within government acting as the sole administrators of public policy, there had been a significant increase in informal alliances among interest groups, public and private organizations, and ordinary citizens. These groups tended to coalesce around certain issues to form autonomous policy subunits that exerted considerable influence on the policymaking process. Because of their mutual interest in a particular policy arena, Heclo labeled such groups "issue networks."

For Heclo, these issue networks "overlay" rather than replace existing alliances (1978, 103–104, 105). Issue networks are different from groups based on what he describes as "shared-attention, shared-action, or shared-belief" groups (103–104). Instead, issue networks tend to consist of individuals with highly active citizens with specialized policy knowledge who are drawn to the group for noneconomic benefits. Heclo (1978, 116) observed the rise of issue networks as having three important advantages for the policy process: 1) issue networks tend to reflect the general sentiment of citizens who are less constrained by party identification and who tend to engage in issue-based politics; 2) they provide more policymaking options to members of Congress and the executive branch; and 3) political actors in the legislative and executive branch are less constrained in their policymaking decisions than would be expected in an iron triangle. Put simply, issue networks tend to be highly fluid groups, expanding or detracting depending on the level of attention surrounding a particular issue, and provide governing bodies with more alternatives in the policymaking process.[1]

Using issue networks to conceptualize and understand the policy process suggests a pluralist response to the iron triangle model. Yet whereas issue networks suggest open points of influence within government, the increasing complexity of public policy has further disconnected citizens from the policymaking process. Within issue networks, those with specialized, technical knowledge of the policy at hand tend to wield the most power. Heclo refers to such individuals as "technopols" and maintains that the process of policymaking occurs at the level of policy specialists. Because technopols are located well below high-level political appointees, they operate under the radar and are often disconnected from ordinary citizens. Elected officials rarely have the time and resources to obtain complete information about a particular issue. Instead, they rely on technopols.

The emergence of issue networks run by technopols has splintered the connection between policymakers and citizens. According to Heclo, the dependence on specialized experts has created a push-pull effect in the political system. While responsibility for public policy is being pushed away from the federal government and iron triangle politics, the overreliance on technopols pulls the policymaking process further away from ordinary citizens. This highlights one of the drawbacks of Heclo's subsystems theory for democratic politics. Even though the policy process may be susceptible to influence from a multiplicity of groups, technopols maintain a strong grip on policymaking. Issue networks and technopols thus present a dilemma for Heclo. On the one hand, Heclo argued that the rise of issue networks created a situation in which "no one, as far as one can tell, is in control of the policy process" (1978, 102). On the other hand, policy experts within these issue networks have a distinct informational advantage over other participants.

For Heclo, the origins of public policy lie with the main actors in an increasingly complex policy process, namely, those with highly specialized policy expertise—technopols. As issues become more complex, the connection between ordinary citizens and elected officials and those with the most policymaking authority is likely to decrease. Following Heclo, agenda-setting scholars embraced subsystems theory, but not without important revisions. Keith Hamm (1983) was the first to systematically apply Heclo's research to the study of federal policymaking. Like Heclo, Hamm perceived the policy process as highly decentralized, consisting of numerous and complex subgovernments. Hamm's research, however, also highlighted the tight-knit nature of policy subsystems. Focusing on the relationships between congressional committees, interest groups, and federal agencies, Hamm's research indicates that these groups work closely together in the formation of public policy, often to the benefit of their own self-interest. Interest groups and committee staff play vital informational roles for members of Congress. Federal agencies also provide valuable information, but their role is dependent upon the degree to which they are able to provide constituency benefits for members of Congress. Although Hamm's analysis fits within the subsystems framework, it is also suggestive of multiple but closed policy subsystems. Hamm's research is similar to Freeman's (1965) in that both contend that whereas the policy process has become more decentralized, it is still controlled by specialized subunits. Committee staff, as portrayed by Hamm, are akin to Heclo's technopols, possessing specialized policy knowledge upon which members of Congress depend for making significant policy decisions. Thus, Hamm's research does little to quell the democratic concerns raised by Heclo; the emergence of policy subsystems has done nothing to narrow the gap between ordinary citizens and actual policymakers.

In short, the issue networks and policy subsystems frameworks have largely displaced the notion of a fairly narrow and inaccessible group of actors who exercise primary influence over what problems are or are not addressed. Yet these frameworks do not necessarily support a pluralist model of the policy process. In these frameworks, elites—the technopols, to use Heclo's term—still exercise a disproportionate share of indirect power.

Advocacy Coalitions: Theory or Framework?

The work of Hugh Heclo provided a solid theoretical basis to subsystems theory. Later work by Hamm, however, revealed that these policy subsystems were in fact more similar to the iron triangle than originally suggested by Heclo. This left subsystems theorists at an impasse. Was agenda setting controlled by elites? Or were policy subsystems permeable and accessible? If the latter, how were they permeable and who could gain access? Following Heclo, Paul Sabatier and his colleagues maintained that the policy process was indeed a dynamic and ongoing process, with multiple participants from diverse backgrounds. As we discuss below, Sabatier's framework provided solid theoretical footing to the notion that the best way to understand the policy process and policy change is by studying relationships within and between policy subsystems.

Similar to Heclo, Sabatier (1988) argued that the iron triangle of politics is highly permeable and often unpredictable. Multiple participants are able to wield power throughout the policy process. This stands in direct contrast to traditional iron triangle scholars as well as Easton's (1965) stages model, which describes the policy process as a predictable and repeated pattern among a select group of actors. For Sabatier, the answer to the question, "where do policy proposals come from?" is similar to Heclo's answer and much broader than suggested by iron triangle scholars. To address such a complex and changeable process, Sabatier (1988), and later Sabatier and Jenkins-Smith (1999), developed what became known as the "advocacy coalition framework." Although Sabatier and Jenkins-Smith (1999, 118) contended that there are five "premises" to this framework, implicit in each assumption is the notion that the policy process is dynamic and permeable.

Described as "advocacy coalitions," Sabatier (1988) argued that policy process and policy change are best characterized as a slew of policy subsystems interacting throughout the policy process. Advocacy coalitions, like issue networks, represent groups with shared beliefs that coordinate activity following the emergence of a particular policy on the governmental agenda. These coalitions tend to consist of legislators, interest groups, public agencies, policy researchers, journalists, and indeed many other subnational actors who wield tremendous influence in the policy process (Sabatier and Jenkins-Smith 1999, 119). Although these coalitions may disagree on the details of a particular policy, or "secondary beliefs," there is widespread agreement on the fundamental or "policy core" beliefs of the group. As Sabatier and Jenkins-Smith (1999, 126) pointed out, the advocacy coalition framework has been used to explain various types of regulatory and distributive policies. Advocacy coalitions, however, differ from Heclo's issue networks in that the former are usually organized around core policy beliefs while the latter tend to be organized around technical expertise and ideology (Sabatier 1988).

Critical to explaining change in the policy process, advocacy coalitions engage in what Sabatier (1988) described as "policy-oriented learning." Subsystems or advocacy coalitions are not static or monolithic creatures. Rather, such groups continually update their beliefs, adapting to changes in the political and socioeconomic environment. Indeed, other scholars have noted that policy actors engage in "policy learning," revising their beliefs about policy design and policy goals in response to new information (May 1992, 336). Like issue networks, the size and strength of advocacy coalitions are affected by the reframing of an issue and the ebbs and flows in attention on a particular issue. For Sabatier, an emphasis on core beliefs means that coalitions tend to be long-term alliances. Policy actors are foremost motivated toward advancing the beliefs of their policy domain or subsystem. As such, they are less prone to free riding than other types of coalitions (Sabatier and Jenkins-Smith 1999). Core belief systems are at the center of Sabatier's call for a longitudinal approach to the study of public policy. Like Heclo, Sabatier viewed policymaking as a dynamic and ongoing process. Sabatier's depiction of policy-oriented learning was itself a continual process with constant feedback.

Sabatier's advocacy coalition framework (ACF) is important for multiple reasons. First, it provides a theoretical basis for explaining both stability and rapid change in the policy process (Sabatier and Jenkins-Smith 1999). As public agencies, interest groups, or issue networks develop relationships, their ability to coordinate activity on a particular issue increases. Such reinforcement allows for the development of long-term and stable policy alliances. Rapid change, according to Sabatier, is most likely when dissatisfaction with existing policies creates an atmosphere ripe for the emergence of new coalitions. Second, the advocacy coalition framework moves scholars away from the notion of the policy process as a linear progression of predictable events as originally suggested by Easton (1965). And, relatedly, it moves scholars away from a conception of policymaking as a rational process based purely on economic benefits. The ACF does not dictate that core policy belief systems operate on purely instrumental terms.

Subsystems theory is based on the view that policy proposals emerge from multiple access points in the political system. Fragmentation of the political process has resulted in a decrease in the influence of party politics and a subsequent rise in issue-oriented groups. Early findings from Heclo and Hamm, however, revealed that although the process has become more decentralized, it is not necessarily more open. These early analyses indicated that policy proposals emerge only from those with highly specialized and technical knowledge about a particular policy. In other words, a small group of elites still controls the policy process. Policy subsystems exist, but they operate as highly specialized policy subunits. The work of Paul Sabatier and his colleagues has expanded the number of participants and the complexity of these participants even further. The question remains: Have subsystems theorists simply recast the iron triangle with additional sides for specialized subunits? Or, as other scholars have suggested, instead of one iron triangle, is the policy process best characterized as multiple iron triangles competing against one another? As McCool (1995d, 382) wrote, "all three corners of the triangle now have multiple participants."

Punctuated Equilibrium: Predictive or Descriptive?

We now have some sense of where policy proposals come from: they originate in issue-centric subsystems characterized by one or more advocacy coalitions. But how and why do policies change, if they change at all?

For decades the mainstream answer to this question was centered on the concept of incrementalism. According to Charles Lindblom (1959), time constraints and/or political limitations prevent policymakers from articulating clearly defined goals and conducting a wide and comprehensive search for alternatives, weighing the costs and benefits of each. Instead, policymakers rely on previous policy decisions, resulting in a policy process that is characterized by small, incremental adjustments. In effect, incrementalism is the notion that policymakers start from an existing baseline and make adjustments to that baseline based on pressures from the current task environment (Lindblom 1959, 1979; Wildavsky 1964; see also Davis, Dempster, and Wildavsky 1966 for an application of incrementalism to federal budgeting).[2] For many years, the incrementalist framework was viewed as the primary model for explaining stability in the policy process.

Incrementalism is simply bounded rationality in practice. Incrementalism views policy actors who would rely heavily on past experience as a guide to making choices as boundedly rational. Incrementalism, however, has an obvious flaw: policymaking is not always incremental. The framework of boundedly rational actors in policy subsystems producing incremental change simply breaks down when public policy undergoes radical change.

Baumgartner and Jones (1993) have argued that the theory of incrementalism, though important for explaining periods of stability in the policy process, is unable to account for periods of rapid change. Following Heclo and Sabatier, they have accepted that the policy process is complex and dynamic, but that the pace of change is not always constant or linear. To test their suspicions, Baumgartner and Jones conducted a longitudinal analysis of the tone of media coverage as well as congressional activity on a number of policy issues. From their analysis, the authors concluded that an important aspect of the policy process often overlooked by incremental scholars is the "long-run fragility" of policy subsystems (1993, 3). Drawing off the work of biologist Stephen Jay Gould, Baumgartner and Jones suggested that while there are periods of stability in the process—periods compatible with an incremental view of the policy process—there are also periods of rapid and significant change. Borrowing a term from Gould and his colleague Niles Eldredge, Baumgartner and Jones labeled these periods of rapid change "punctuated equilibria." Significant change in the political system (i.e., policy punctuation) results in a new point of equilibrium from which to evaluate public policy. In effect, these punctuations cause the political system to "shift from one point of stability to another" (Baumgartner and Jones 1993, 17). For Baumgartner and Jones, periods of change are characterized by the theory of punctuated equilibrium, whereas periods of relative stability are characterized by the theory of incrementalism.

The big question, of course, is what punctuates equilibria? What forces disrupt the process of incremental policy change and precipitate a radical shift in policymaking? Baumgartner and Jones argue that underlying these shifts are the breakdown of traditional policy subsystems. Baumgartner and Jones (1993, 4) described a particular sort of subsystem they termed a "policy monopoly," defined as a set of structural arrangements that keep policymaking in the hands of a relatively small group of interested policy actors. What Baumgartner and Jones recognize is that, for a variety of reasons, these policy monopolies periodically come under extreme stress. At these points, other actors penetrate these subsystems, creating instability in the policy process and the opportunity for significant shifts in policymaking.

The driving force for the theory of punctuated equilibrium, and by default the driving force for stability and instability in the policy process, is issue definition. As long as issue definition does not change, it is unlikely the underlying policy subsystem will change. However, changes in the tone of an issue can lead to changes in the level of attention the issue receives, fostering a change in image and a change in the institutional venue upon which the issue is considered. In short, changes in issue definition can alter the structural arrangements of a policy subsystem, breaking the policy monopoly and paving the way for radical shifts in policymaking. An example provided by Baumgartner and Jones is that of nuclear power. In the 1950s the image of nuclear power was positive—a clean and cheap source of energy—and the policy monopoly built around the regulation and expansion of the nuclear power industry benefited from this image. The incident at Three Mile Island produced a radical shift in this image; suddenly nuclear power was the focus of intense questioning and was viewed as dangerous, a threat to the safety of millions. The intensity of attention and the change in issue definition brought different government decision-making bodies into the policy monopoly (what Baumgartner and Jones termed "venues"), which shattered the policy monopoly. The result was a significant change in policy from regular endorsement of nuclear power to a sudden withdrawal of funding for such power.

Important to the theory of punctuated equilibrium is the notion of positive and negative feedback. Lindblom, drawing off Downs (1957), argued that increased attention in the policy process often fails to result in any institutional adjustments. As suggested by Downs and Lindblom, public interest in an issue declines following a wave of enthusiasm as the cost of change becomes apparent, resulting in a process of negative feedback. The theory of punctuated equilibrium, however, posits that as theories emerge on the formal agenda, they leave behind an "institutional legacy" (Baumgartner and Jones 1993, 37), resulting in a *positive* feedback system. Positive feedback is the process by which a change in policy image based on criticism results in a new point of stability. According to Baumgartner and Jones, positive feedback is "anti-Downs" because increased attention does not necessarily result in a favoring of the status quo (1993, 64). Although heightened media attention can lead to public uncertainty, this does not constitute a ruling in favor of the opposition. Baumgartner and Jones characterized this process of relative stability, followed by rapid change, followed by a new point of stability as an "S-shaped diffusion curve." This represents an important distinction from Lindblom's work on incrementalism. A change in image can produce a change in venue and a change in the institutional structures addressing the issue. Policy entrepreneurs, issue networks, or advocacy coalitions are well aware of this fact and tend to engage in what Baumgartner and Jones described as "venue shopping." Policy actors will continue to redefine an issue until it reaches a favorable venue, thus ensuring a favorable governmental response.[3] When this occurs, the policy process is subject to rapid change.

As would be expected, the media is an influential actor in shaping public opinion about an issue. How the media defines an issue ultimately shapes who will be involved in the public debate. Drawing on Schattschneider (1965), Baumgartner and Jones argued that the "losers" in the policy debate have an incentive to manipulate the image of an issue to increase political receptivity and the likelihood of finding a favorable venue. Redefining an issue has the potential to motivate previously uninterested groups of society into taking action, destabilizing a once-stable policy process. Baumgartner and Jones have referred to such cases as the "mobilization of the apathetic" (1993, 21). Policymakers thus have an incentive to preserve the status quo, to preserve existing policy monopolies by limiting or discouraging debate.

Baumgartner and Jones have cited attempts by those within the nuclear power industry to control the image of nuclear power by highlighting only the cost-savings and energy-efficient aspects of nuclear power. With the disaster at Three Mile Island as well as dissension among top nuclear scientists regarding safety concerns, the public image began to change, resulting in more groups emerging against nuclear power. The rapid rejection of nuclear power as simply a cheap and clean source of energy resulted in a significant shift in policy such that the new policy equilibrium was one in which nuclear power was viewed with skepticism. The nuclear power industry, once a dominant policy subsystem, immediately collapsed due to a change in how the issue of nuclear power was defined. Similarly, in tracing the political progress of child abuse policies, Barbara Nelson (1984, 17) argued that governmental activity and public concern significantly increased as the issue of child care was redefined as social illness rather than an individual dilemma.[4] Policy monopolies, then, are simply policy subsystems that contend to offer the best solution with a single, positive policy image. This means they can either be created or destroyed depending upon how an issue is defined (Baumgartner and Jones 1993, 161). Stability in the policy process is thus deceptive because it can be disrupted very quickly through issue redefinition and mobilization of those previously uninvolved in the policymaking process.

How an issue is defined ultimately determines the institutional response and whether the policy process is characterized by stability or instability. A change in the image associated with a particular issue will tend to lead to a change in venue in which the issue is advanced. Stability in the policy process is contingent upon two factors: 1) existing structure of institutions; and 2) definition of issues processed by the institutions. As Baumgartner and Jones argued, the latter is the first to change and represents the source of rapid shifts in the policy process. Institutions provide stability in the policy process, and political entrepreneurs seek to maintain that stability if they are part of a policy monopoly perceived favorably by existing institutional structures. Baumgartner and Jones describe such stalemate in the policy process as "structure-induced equilibrium." Because images are inherently tied to venues, those on the opposing side of policy monopolies seek to manipulate the image of a certain policy in order to reach an alternative institutional venue. Institutional structures are contingent upon the attention and intensity of citizen preferences. The mobilization of the apathetic represents a destabilizing force in the policy process. Thus, the answer to the question, why do policies change? is that as issues are redefined, preferences change, which leads to political instability. Political and policy actors that were either disinterested or unmotivated are brought into the policy process through policy definition and/or redefinition.

Like incrementalism, Baumgartner and Jones's theory of punctuated equilibrium policy change rests on the notion that political and policy actors are boundedly rational. People do not engage in fully rational decision-making processes; rather, cognitive limitations and the task environment lead to a heavy reliance on heuristics (Simon 1947, 1985). Bounded rationality, for many scholars, provides an explanation for why individuals often behave in ways contrary to the predictions of the rational actor model. For example, preference reversals (Kahneman and Tversky 1978), over-cooperation (Dawes and Thaler 1988), and susceptibility to framing effects (Druckman 2004), according to Simon (1985), are the result of limits in cognitive abilities. Later work by Bryan Jones (2001, 2003) and Jones and Frank Baumgartner (2005) clearly fits within Simon's notion of bounded rationality, as does Sabatier's (1988) work on core belief systems within advocacy coalitions.[5] The work of Baumgartner and Jones simply extends this theory to account for periods of rapid change. Like bounded rationality, punctuated equilibrium posits that individuals react to the external task environment rather than offering a theory for why individuals react in the way that they do. By departing from complete rationality in favor of bounded rationality, punctuated equilibrium is able to explain both periods of equilibrium and periods of disequilibrium (True, Jones, and Baumgartner 1999, 101).

Critics, however, suggest that by attempting to explain everything in the policy process, the theory of punctuated equilibrium provides little in terms of predicting when change will occur. Although punctuated equilibrium provides a descriptive account for why rapid changes in policy occur, it fails to offer a theory for when such changes will occur or can be expected. In other words, the theory of punctuated equilibrium is not a theory in terms of providing point predictions about when significant fluctuations in the policy process will occur. Punctuated equilibrium does, however, offer a useful explanatory framework for policy change. We agree that the theory of punctuated equilibrium as articulated by Baumgartner and Jones is incomplete; more work is needed as to why certain issues are more receptive than others and what factors contribute to punctuations. Bounded rationality is based on the notion of individuals being limited in their information-processing capabilities. Punctuated equilibrium theory simply extends this argument to conclude that it is possible to redefine an issue so as to capture the attention of those previously left out of the policy process. However, the theory of punctuated equilibrium, like bounded rationality, fails to offer a theory as to why cognitive capacities are limited in the way they are. This reduces the ability of policy scholars to offer a predictive framework for when policy punctuations will occur. In fact, acknowledging the problems with their theory, Baumgartner and Jones (with True) wrote that "a complete model will not be locally predictable, since we cannot predict the timing or outcomes of the punctuations" (True, Jones, and Baumgartner 1999, 111).

Do the above limitations limit punctuated equilibrium to a useful explanatory framework, but with little predictive power? True, Jones, and Baumgartner (1999, 109–110) argued that policy punctuations occur more frequently than would be expected if the policy process were random or conformed strictly to rational choice theory. Instead, policy change tends to reflect a leptokurtic distribution (a large number of data points near the center and in the tails of the distribution) as opposed to a normal distribution that would be expected if the process were completely random. That such punctuations occur more frequently than originally believed is important for explaining policy change, but what are the key causal factors?

Jones, Sulkin, and Larsen (2003) expanded on this notion of a leptokurtic distribution of policy change. These authors found that bargaining and information-gathering costs contribute to the size of the policy punctuation. Highly complex organizations with a large number of participants tend to have more of what Jones, Sulkin, and Larsen (2003, 155) described as "institutional friction." More friction tends to equal a higher probability of punctuation and a higher likelihood that policy change is leptokurtic rather than normal. Following in the footsteps of Jones, Sulkin, and Larsen (2003), Scott Robinson and his colleagues (2007) also found evidence linking institutional structures to the likelihood of policy punctuation. Analyzing budgetary data from school districts, Robinson et al. found that highly centralized school districts are more susceptible to "nonincremental changes" (2007, 147). Centralized districts tend to increase the probability of large policy changes whereas increases in organizational size decrease such probability. If the purpose of studying policy change is to uncover what factors predict policy change, then the contributions of Jones, Sulkin, and Larsen and Robinson et al. are significant. Both provide policy scholars with concrete independent variables to add to equations predicting policy change.

Despite some limitations, the work of Baumgartner and Jones has significantly improved our understanding of the policy process in many ways. First, and perhaps most important, the theory of punctuated equilibrium, unlike incrementalism, recognizes that significant change in the policy process can and often does occur. In fact, one of the main objectives of Baumgartner and Jones's work is to explain why policy monopolies, such as the nuclear power industry, fail. Punctuated equilibrium is also evidence that the policy process is not rational. Rather than progressing through a series of stages (Ripley 1985), the arguments presented by Baumgartner and Jones suggest the policy process is susceptible to rapid change due to highly irrational processes.

Second, punctuated equilibrium recognizes that changes in institutional design occur following the emergence of an issue on the government agenda, moving policy scholars away from the Downs (1972) model of negative policy feedback. This has important implications for policy entrepreneurs. The key to disrupting policy equilibrium is finding the appropriate policy image that mobilizes citizens previously disengaged from the political process. No one group controls the policy process, and no one issue fits neatly into a particular venue. Immigration policy, for example, is both a national security issue as well as an economic development issue. Policy entrepreneurs, utilizing the media and other political actors, can continually redefine their policy image until it receives a receptive audience, setting the stage for rapid policy change.

Third, Baumgartner and Jones's original research has spawned numerous attempts to improve our ability to predict policy change. Most notably, the work of Jones, Sulkin, and Larsen (2003) and Robinson et al. (2007) improves our understanding of the policy process and provides viable theoretical and methodological alternatives to incrementalism.

Garbage Cans and Windows: Another Theory of Policy Change?

Heclo and Hamm's research has suggested that the policy process is indeed fragmented. Policies can originate from numerous sources, allowing for multiple sources of change in the policy process. Baumgartner and Jones's analyses take this a step further, demonstrating that the policy process is dynamic and subject to rapid change. However, whereas Baumgartner and Jones have provided an explanatory framework for suggesting the policy process is subject to stability as well as change, they have readily admitted that the punctuated equilibrium framework put forth is not predictive. Thus, we are still left with the question: Why do policies change? Why are some policies more successful than others in terms of garnering public support? And, similarly, why does the government pay attention to some policies but not others?

Like Baumgartner and Jones, John Kingdon (1995) has argued that the best way to understand the policy process is by examining policy images. In fact, Baumgartner and Jones's analyses are based in part off Kingdon's original research on agenda setting. How a policy is defined and how it is perceived by the public and policymakers ultimately determines whether the policy will receive positive or negative feedback. Kingdon has also agreed that Lindblom's incrementalist approach is incomplete. And, like Heclo and Sabatier, Kingdon has asserted that actors both inside and outside of government are important to understanding the policy process and policy change. Kingdon, however, took a different approach to agenda setting. Beyond providing evidence of rapid policy change, Kingdon identified what components are necessary for such change to take place.

Kingdon's research on policy change is instructive for the simple and parsimonious model it presents. It begins with the question (1995, 1), "What makes people in and around government attend, at any given time, to some subjects and not to others?" For Kingdon, the level of analysis is the government agenda and the items government pays attention to, and the unit of analysis is "predecisions," decisions made by relevant actors that affect whether an issue reaches the government agenda. Rather than focus on policy stability, Kingdon is interested in explaining the process by which issues reach the government agenda and allow for significant policy change to take place. To do this, he examined health and transportation policy in the late 1970s, focusing on cases of policy initiation and cases in which policy initiation seemed likely but never occurred.

Analyzing the agenda-setting process and alternative selection, Kingdon incorporated the "garbage can model" of Cohen, March, and Olsen (1972). This model is centered on the concept of "organized anarchies" (Kingdon 1995, 84), or organizations that share three general characteristics: problematic preferences, fluid participation, and unclear technology. People routinely move in and out of organizations or organizational subunits and thus rarely understand the organization's purpose or their role within the organization. Various participants work autonomously to provide independent solutions to similar problems. In the process, ideas are jumbled together, with solutions actually searching for problems, rather than the reverse, as would be suggested by the stages model of public policy or the rational-comprehensive model (Kingdon 1995, 85). According to the garbage can model, policy entrepreneurs learn by trial and error regarding alternative selection. The end result is that both problems and solutions are "dumped" into the policymaking garbage can. What does this mean for Kingdon's model and the agenda-setting process? In essence, the policy process is not linear nor does it always move in incremental stages. Rather, it is best described as relative chaos among competing policy communities. Kingdon revised the garbage can model to include three separate "streams": problems, policies, and politics. Each stream, as we discuss below, contributes to our understanding of why government pays attention to some problems more than others.

The first stream is the problem stream. For policy change to take place, policy actors must first recognize that there is an existing problem. The most obvious way for a condition to become a problem is through a "focusing event." Focusing events are highly public events that call attention to a particular issue. For example, the disaster at Three Mile Island was a focusing event for nuclear power, ultimately shifting the focus away from energy efficiency to health and safety concerns. "Indicators" such as regularly conducted surveys or published reports can also raise awareness of an existing condition, but focusing events tend to be more effective. The media also plays an important role in shaping the saliency of a particular issue. Again, as other agenda-setting scholars have suggested, policy definition and policy image are crucial to moving a condition onto the government agenda (see Stone 2002).

Policy is the second of Kingdon's streams. It is here where policy alternatives are generated to address emerging problems. Participants in the policy stream are represented by both "visible" and "hidden cluster" actors (Kingdon 1995, 199). The visible cluster represents prominent policy actors such as the president and members of Congress. The hidden cluster tends to be composed of policy specialists, operating deep within federal or state agencies that set the available alternatives upon which policy decisions are made. Like Heclo, Kingdon described the policy entrepreneur as highly influential in the policy process, capable of determining policy outcomes by manipulating and narrowing the number of policy alternatives. This differs from the role of visible participants, who are less effective in the policy stream but more important in the problem stream and in getting items on the government agenda (Kingdon 1995, 30). Kingdon (1995, 116) described the policy stream as consisting of a "policy primordial soup" in which multiple ideas are just "floating" around, waiting to be scooped up by prominent government actors. The primordial soup is akin to the garbage can put forth by Cohen, March, and Olsen (1972). Both problems and solutions get dumped into the same policy can, resulting in an unpredictable process of policy change.

The process of selecting policy alternatives is not random, however. Within the policy stream, Kingdon has argued that there are two important aspects to understanding how alternatives move from the primordial soup to being a viable policy option: 1) through "softening up"; and 2) through "coupling" (1995, 200–201). Policy specialists in the hidden cluster, interest groups, and even academics and researchers can help to soften up the agenda to ensure favorable political receptivity. As Kingdon noted, the softening up process is critical in terms of determining whether a policy actually reaches the government agenda. The coupling process is the ability to link alternatives with problems. For elected officials, policy alternatives must be justified in terms of costs and benefits, with particular attention to core constituencies, and must also be workable solutions to the problem. Although many good ideas may be floating around among policy specialists, without a specific problem, they are unlikely to reach the government agenda.

The third and final stream of Kingdon's model is the political stream. It is useful to think of Baumgartner and Jones's notion of venue shopping as well as May's (1992) "political learning" when discussing the political stream. For Kingdon, elections and the national mood determine whether a problem will find a receptive venue. A significant shift in the national political ideology and/or a realigning election can cause a significant shift in the type of policies that reach the attention of elected officials. Existing conditions that were previously not considered problems can suddenly move onto the government agenda. The political stream is characterized by bargaining among elected officials, constituents, and organized political forces. Even though hidden participants are important within their own agency, Kingdon (1995, 30) argued that such experts tend to be less influential outside their agency, and thus less effective in the political stream. Instead, more visible participants within the executive branch are critical to raising national awareness of a policy and to moving a condition to a problem to be addressed by the government.

When the three streams converge, Kingdon stated, the convergence creates a "policy window" for rapid policy change. Importantly, however, the problem and political streams open the window. For significant change to take place, the savvy policy entrepreneur operating in the policy stream must be capable of recognizing the opportunity the window presents. The role of the policy entrepreneur is to "couple" the three streams before the window closes, which, according to Kingdon, can occur quickly and without notice: "Once a window opens, it does not stay open long" (Kingdon 1995, 169). Thus, on the one hand, policy entrepreneurs and policy communities are limited by the political stream. Without a receptive political venue and/or receptive national mood, coupling of the policy and political streams is unlikely. On the other hand, the problem and political streams depend on existing policy communities. Cases of "partial coupling," in which one or two streams are joined without the remaining stream(s), rarely lead to policy change (Kingdon 1995, 200–201).

The importance of predecisions, or what others refer to as nondecisions, in the policymaking process can be traced back to the work of Bachrach and Baratz (1962). As we noted at the beginning of the chapter, decisions about what is being decided upon represent a critical and important source of power in the policymaking process. Similar to Bachrach and Baratz, Schattschneider (1965, 68) argued that the ability to "expand the scope of conflict" has a direct impact on the final policy outcome. Whereas Kingdon described the process of agenda setting and alternative selection as the result of three separate and independent streams, the first two streams of Kingdon's theoretical framework are directly linked to the issue of nondecisions. Problem definition and the alternative development (problem stream and policy stream) are critical in determining the nature of the final policy outcome. These nondecisions determine whether a policy window will be useful in achieving policy change. This lead Kingdon to conclude that policy entrepreneurs are actually more important than individuals considered responsible for the original creation of the policy.

As we discuss in Chapter 8, policies that serve social or public problems have been identified as more likely to find an appropriate venue in the policy community than policies based on an image of individual or private misfortune (Baumgartner and Jones 1993; Kingdon 1995; Schneider and Ingram 1997). As a result, whether an issue reaches the decision-making agenda ultimately depends on how an issue is defined. Barbara Nelson's (1984) work on child abuse mentioned earlier is illustrative of Kingdon's policy windows. In the case of child abuse, the focusing event was part issue redefinition, part media attention, and part a product of a changing national mood. Child abuse slowly shifted from a parental issue to a social problem (problem stream). As the national mood shifted, prominent political actors, including U.S. Senator Walter Mondale, spoke publicly and adamantly about the need to take action on the issue (Nelson 1984, 134). Such events, in turn, created a receptive political venue (political stream). For policy change to take place, however, policy entrepreneurs must recognize the existence of an open policy window (policy stream). On the issue of child abuse, the policy community consisted of federal agencies such as the U.S. Children's Bureau and also particularly the media and policy researchers who were able to maintain national focus on the potential social problems stemming from child abuse. The three streams coalesced and created an environment ripe for significant policy change.

Not only do nondecisions have the potential to determine who is involved in the policy process, nondecisions significantly affect the nature of political debate throughout the policymaking process. However, whereas nondecisions remain critical to explaining the policy process as well as policy outcomes, they remain difficult to systematically study. What is a nondecision? Are different types of nondecisions more important than others? Extending the "garbage can model," Kingdon (1995) simply asserted that the policy process is complex and that nondecisions are influential in determining policy outcomes. However, describing the policy process as complex does not move us closer to a comprehensive theory of policy change. The same limitation facing Baumgartner and Jones (1993) can also be applied to Kingdon. Do certain indicators increase the probability of conditions turning into problems? Why do some policy images lead to more public receptivity than others? Nonetheless, like Baumgartner and Jones's seminal work, Kingdon laid the groundwork for systematically studying the policy process and provided us with a powerful explanatory framework for policy incrementalism and rapid policy change. In fact, we would suggest that the three streams approach gives policy scholars the tools to make point predictions about when significant policy change will occur.

Conclusion

The study of policy process has important implications for the study of interest representation. If elites or policy experts are able to wield control of the policy process, often through indirect and unobservable decisions, then the potential exists for the abrogation of citizen interests. If public policy is simply the study of what government does, why it does it, and what implications this has (Dye 1976), then the study of public policy process, particularly agenda setting and policy subsystems, clearly fits within the confines of Lasswell's (1936) definition of politics. Moreover,

as we have discussed in this chapter, scholars have provided useful explanatory frameworks for studying policy change. Although there is disagreement over the predictability of the policy process, there exist several
well-developed theories that help explain this process. For many agenda-
setting scholars, the policy process is best viewed through the lens of policy definition and policy image. The study of policy subsystems is also
clearly linked to the study of politics and the distribution of governmental resources. Given that policy subsystems represent responses to the issues that emerge on the policy agenda, the study of both agenda setting
and policy subsystems is fundamental to the study of political power.

The core research questions of policy process scholarship are: Where do
policy proposals come from? Why do policies change? Why does the government pay attention to some policies but not to others? Where does the
process of policymaking actually take place? The research literature on
subsystems and agenda setting has provided systematic responses to all of
these questions, though it is fair to say that none of these provides definitive answers.

From Heclo and Sabatier we know that policy proposals tend to emerge
from large informal alliances comprised of highly diverse policy actors.
What we do not know, however, is what type of alliances are the most
successful in terms of pushing an issue onto the government agenda.
Within advocacy coalitions or issue networks, which type of actors tend
to be the most influential? Heclo theorized that technopols wield the
most policymaking power, but this is not tested empirically. Sabatier
did provide a more rigorous framework but failed to identify which
type of participants are the most critical for ensuring policy change. Finally, what is success for a policy subsystem? Is it simply raising awareness
of an issue, or is it actually causing significant policy change? Heclo's
work frequently mentions policy change, but how much change is required for an issue network to be successful? Sabatier and Jenkins-Smith
(1999, 147) distinguished between "major" and "minor" policy change
but readily admitted that the type of change depends on the subsystem.[6]
To empirically assess the role of advocacy coalitions and issue networks in
the policy process, these questions need to be answered (see also Sabatier
1991b).

From the existing literature, we also know that how policies reach the
government agenda is a bit of mystery. As we have discussed in this chapter, Baumgartner and Jones's (1993) punctuated equilibrium is less a

theoretical framework for predicting policy change and more of a descriptive analysis of the policy landscape. Without a theory regarding why the particular frame of an issue is more receptive than another frame, the theory of punctuated equilibrium fails to offer a predictive account for when "losers" will be successful in reframing the debate, and thereby successful in terms of causing a major disruption in the policy process. By depicting policymakers as decision makers guided by bounded rationality, Baumgartner and Jones were less interested in predicting why policymakers make the decisions they do than in explaining how policymakers respond to the task environment. The question also remains as to what constitutes a policy punctuation. How much change constitutes a significant enough departure from the previous policy to qualify as a punctuation?

Kingdon's (1995) research on policy windows is a step in the right direction of providing a more rigorous theoretical framework. In terms of answering the question of why policies change, Kingdon has indicated that certain political and policy factors are necessary for change to take place. But, as we alluded to earlier in the chapter, there are also limitations to Kingdon's work. For the three streams framework to apply to the study of policy change, policy actors must first recognize that a problem exists. Kingdon argued that focusing events are the first of the three streams necessary for triggering a policy window. But what constitutes a focusing event? Can we really predict a focusing event, or even if a focusing event occurs, whether it will ignite significant policy change? These questions are left unaddressed by Kingdon's analyses (see also Zahariadis 1999). The fact that the political stream in Kingdon's model depends on the "national mood" casts further doubt about the ability to predict significant policy change.

Although subsystems theory and the agenda-setting literature fall short in terms of predictive power, there are some important contributions. First and foremost, subsystems scholars shifted the focus away from iron triangle politics to a more open and complex policymaking process (see Bardach 2006). The policy process is not rational, but it is also not random. Thanks to Heclo and Sabatier, a policy scholar interested in identifying key policy actors knows to look beyond the traditional actors identified by the iron triangle model of politics. We agree with Sabatier and Jenkins-Smith (1999, 154) that revisions to the ACF provide an important framework, not theory, for evaluating policy change. The agenda-setting literature has also improved our understanding of the policy process. From Baumgartner and Jones, as well as Kingdon, a policy entrepreneur seeking to find receptive policy venues will know that policy image and policy definition are important. What all of these scholars have in common is an agreement that the policy process is just that, a process. Policy outcomes are not the final say in the policymaking process. Rather, multiple actors within and outside of government are constantly seeking to influence the government agenda, resulting in a highly dynamic and highly complex process. Punctuated equilibrium and "policy windows" frameworks also move us away from an overreliance on incrementalism and a recognition that rapid policy change is possible and in need of examination.

Even though the agenda-setting and subsystems literatures have their fair share of critics, the important thing is that both sets provide a great deal of explanatory power and are moving forward. Agenda-setting studies are based on how policymakers and the public respond to policy images and issue definitions. Emerging work in experimental economics, social psychology, and even neuroeconomics on how the human mind processes incoming information will no doubt contribute to this agenda. And, as the work of Leach and Sabatier (2005) illustrates, policy scholars are beginning to incorporate these literatures into their research on the policy process. The ability to predict policy change is also improving. Scholars are continuing to increase our understanding of what factors contribute to policy punctuations (see Jones, Sulkin, and Larsen 2003; Robinson et al. 2007), thereby increasing the predictive power of when punctuation will occur. We believe this is a promising occurrence for the agenda-setting and subsystems literatures as well as for those seeking to better understand policy change.

Notes

1. See Gormley (1986) for an examination of how issue networks operate concerning regulatory policy.

2. We discuss the tenets of incrementalism and its pros and cons more fully in Chapter 3.

3. "Venue shopping" is akin to what May (1992) described as "political learning," whereby policy elites "learn" how to adapt their proposals to garner the most political support.

4. Other issues have also reached the government agenda following redefinition from an individual problem to a social dilemma. For example, federal attention to the issue of special education began to shift as evidence was presented indicating the deleterious effects of ignoring special education on disabled *and* nondisabled individuals. Noting the primary reasons for "dramatic changes in public attitude" concerning special education in the 1960s, Cremins (1983) cited "social consciousness and upheaval" as a major determinant of the enactment of favorable policy (83).

5. Sabatier (1988) contended that individual belief systems are cognitively limited, that people are capable of processing only a limited amount of information and tend to engage in bias information processing, in other words, processing favorable information while discarding disconfirming or controversial information.

6. Sabatier and Jenkins-Smith (1999, 153) also identify a number of limitations to the advocacy coalition framework, including lack of knowledge regarding the conditions for coalition formation and the need for more longitudinal studies on how subsystems and belief systems change over time.

CHAPTER FIVE

What Should We Do?
The Field of Policy Analysis

Government has a finite ability to address the infinite claims placed upon it. It is asked to address a virtually unlimited set of issues and problems within an all too limited set of political, financial, institutional, personnel, legal, temporal, and informational constraints. Say a particular issue or problem—educational performance, a budget deficit, or whatever—has made its way onto the institutional agenda. The government now has to decide what action (if any) to take to address that problem. Pay teachers more? Increase test standards? Cut spending? Raise taxes? Something else? Whenever policymakers seek to address a pressing issue or problem, the starting point boils down to a single question: What should we do? (Rose 1993, 19). The fundamental task of policy analysis is to seek an answer to this question.

There is considerable disagreement over how to approach the question at the heart of policy analysis. On the one hand are those who believe the question charges the analyst with an obligation to provide a reasonably objective, single response; an answer that, in effect, says a particular policy alternative is the best choice. On the other hand are those who view the idea of expert policy analysts being society's problem-solvers as naive, or even worse, as dangerous. They argue the question raises a normative problem, not a series of technical or instrumental problems. When a government faces a question of "what should we do?" it is confronting what is most likely to be a clash of values. Liberals want one thing, conservatives another, particular policy responses to a problem create winners and losers, and the various stakeholders in this process clash noisily over whose preferences will gain the favor of government. This is the reality of politics, and the job of the analyst is better conceived as a task of interpretation and facilitation: understanding the different perspectives that create the conflict of values and judging them on their own terms. "What should we do?" is a question best answered by reflective deliberation and discourse among these various perspectives, not by a causal theory or a regression coefficient.

There are, of course, numerous degrees of each of these positions, and the orientation of policy analysis is more accurately described as a continuum rather than as two competing camps. It is useful, however, to roughly divide the field into two such generic approaches to understand how the field of policy analysis goes about answering its central research question. So, although a number of frameworks have been formulated to structure the search for answers to the question of "what should we do?" for our purposes we will collapse these into what we will term the rationalist approach and the post-positivist approach. The rationalist approach views policy analysis as a linear problem-solving process, "as a tool for choosing among alternatives in an effort to solve problems" (Shulock 1997, 227). Proponents of this orientation to policy analysis favor deploying the theoretical and methodological tool kit of social science to generate a reasonably objective and neutral ranking of policy alternatives. Post-positivists argue that it is impossible for policy analysis to inoculate itself against the normative nature of answering the key question. The conceptual framework of science and the sophisticated methodological firepower wielded by the rationalists are propped up by their own value systems (Fischer 2003). Post-positivists seek to put other values and perspectives on an equal footing with science in the process of deciding what should be done.

As traditionally and currently practiced, policy analysis is dominated by the rationalist approach. In general, this means policy analysis has a strong bias toward quantitative methods and conceptual frameworks taken from the positivist traditions in social science (economic theory, especially, is used to structure many analyses). Post-positivists, drawing on decidedly less positivist theoretical foundations like discourse and critical theory, have leveled some important criticisms of the rationalist approach. Post-positivist policy analysis, however, has struggled to establish a practical set of methodological alternatives to those employed by the rationalists and conceptually has yet to convince the mainstream of the field that it is not leading a charge into the swamp of relativism. The rationalist approach at least produces an answer to the fundamental question of the field. According to its critics, post-positivism produces as many answers as there are opinions and perspectives, all of them given equal value and validity. That, the rationalists argue, is no answer at all, just an amplification of the confusion in politics.

In this chapter we are going to examine these two approaches to policy analysis and assess their ability to provide useful explanatory frameworks for answering the question, "what should we do?"

The Rationalist Approach

Joseph Priestly was a notable eighteenth-century scientist, philosopher, and theologian. His many accomplishments include discovering oxygen gas, authoring scholarly manuscripts on electricity, and helping to found the Christian denomination of Unitarianism. He also, indirectly, prompted an early expression of the rationalist approach to policy analysis. In the early 1790s, Priestly was struggling with a decision over whether to leave the ministry and take up a more lucrative offer from the Earl of Shelburne, a well-known British statesman of the time. Priestly was struggling with the individual version of the public policy analyst's question, his being a dilemma of "What should I do?" One of his friends, Benjamin Franklin, wrote Priestly a letter saying he had devised a system of "prudential or moral algebra" to solve exactly this sort of dilemma. When unsure what course of action constituted the best response to a question, Franklin said he did the following:

1. Divided a sheet of paper in half and listed the pros of a decision or course of action on one side and the cons on the other.
2. Assigned weights to the pros and cons, i.e., assigned them numbers reflecting their importance or desirability.

3. Struck out equalities. If one pro carried equal weight as one con, he would strike them both out. If one pro carried the weight of three cons, he would strike those out. Eventually, the pro or con side would reveal itself to have more weight.
4. Used the information from these calculations to make the decision. [1]

Franklin's method of "moral algebra" succinctly captures the basic notion of the rationalist approach to policy analysis (indeed, it has been cited as an early form of cost-benefit analysis; see Boardman et al. 2001, 1). When faced with a question of what to do, the best approach is to employ a means of systematically ranking the various alternatives and choosing the one that ranks highest. More formally, policy analysis is traditionally defined as "an applied social science discipline which uses multiple methods of inquiry and argument to produce and transform policy-relevant information that may be utilized in political settings to resolve policy problems" (Dunn 1981, 35).[2]

As such, the rationalist approach to policy analysis clearly takes its cue from Lasswell's notion of the policy sciences. It takes an instrumental view of public policy: policies are viewed as means to address problems or achieve goals, and the central objective of policy analysis is to identify the most desirable means to achieve these ends. Identifying those means is a largely technocratic undertaking that draws on multiple disciplines, is heavily quantitative, and is keenly interested in assessing causal relationships. The rationalist approach follows this generic process for generating knowledge useful for answering questions about what should be done:

1. Define the problem. For a policy analyst, a "problem" typically implies some state of the world that is and will remain unsatisfactory or undesirable without government intervention (Mohr 1995, 14).
2. Identify alternative courses of action. This means generate a series of policy options that will have a desired impact on the problem. Linking alternatives to problems implies a causal link—if government does X, Y will happen. Rationalists draw heavily on social science theories to understand such causal links.

3. Estimate outcomes. This involves creating a set of criteria on which to judge different policy alternatives, then generating estimates of how each policy alternative is likely to perform on those criteria. For example, a policy analyst may wish to estimate the impact of various policy alternatives on the basis of costs, impact on a particular outcome (say a reading program on test scores), and distribution (who bears the costs and who reaps the benefits).
4. Compare alternatives. This means ranking the different alternatives according to their performance on the various criteria from step 3.
5. Choose the most preferred alternative. The alternative that scores the highest, or is judged most likely to achieve a desired objective or fulfill a desired value, is the alternative forwarded as the best option to translate into government action, i.e., to become a public policy.[3]

The rationalist approach, in other words, is an updated version of Franklin's moral algebra. The theoretical and methodological horsepower employed in modern rationalist approaches has increased considerably since Franklin's time, but the basic concept remains the same. Resolving questions of what to do is best approached as a systematic, problem-solving exercise.

In its modern Lasswell-like form, the original idea behind the field of policy analysis was to put teams of experts—who would employ social science theory and methods to put this problem solving process into action—into the highest reaches of government (Dror 1968). The hope (since proven naive) was that policy analysts would deal in facts more than values; they would produce relatively objective assessments of what would and what would not work for a given problem.[4] Policymakers would take the role of clients, meaning they would come to the analysts with the problems, specify the desired outcomes, and set values that would serve to rank different policy alternatives. The analyst's job was to develop and supply the technical know-how in order to employ the best social science theory and methods to identify the alternatives that addressed client needs.

Many aspects of this vision have become firmly entrenched as mainstream policy analysis. For example, graduate courses in policy analysis by and large train students to view policy analysis as a linear problem-solving paradigm whose main objective is to advise a client on the best policy alternative for a given problem (Shulock 1997, 228; Weimer and Vining 2005, 1). This is often accomplished using sophisticated quantitative methods; just about everything in the statisticians', econometricians', and game theorists' tool kit has been adapted to serve the needs of policy analysis (for a comprehensive introduction to the range of quantitative policy analysis methods, see Gupta 2001). The increasing sophistication of methods, however, has not yet addressed a fundamental conceptual problem the rationalist project has struggled with since its modern inception.

If the underlying purpose of the rationalist project is to come up with some ranking of policy alternatives, it needs a measure with which to rank them. On what grounds does rational policy analysis judge a particular policy alternative "best"? In Franklin's system of moral algebra this was a comparatively easy question to answer. As the problems the system was designed to solve were individual, the subjective judgments of the individual were enough to attach weights to the pros and cons of different choices. The rationalist does not have it so easy; the subjective values of the analyst are not seen as a valid yardstick to judge the worth of public policies that represent collective interests. But if rationalists are not going to incorporate the individualistic values employed in Franklin's moral algebra to operationalize their problem-solving process, what do/should they use? Answering this question has proven to be a central challenge for the rationalist project.

Following the generic problem-solving process listed above requires at some point knowing what outcomes or impacts are going to be used to rank policy alternatives. Presumably, this means knowing the objectives or goals of the policy. If the problem is, say, educational performance, then policy alternatives can be ranked by their estimated impact on educational performance indicators. Unfortunately, in practice, the problems public policies are called upon to solve rarely have a universally agreed upon, precisely defined, easily measurable, single goal. Educational performance, for example, is a pretty vague goal. How do we measure this? Test scores? Graduation rates? What happens if our analysis shows that increasing test scores requires tougher academic standards, which lead to lower graduation rates? Assuming away such issues, what if the policy deemed as best by our analysis of expected impact on educational performance is very expensive? What if it leads to more dropouts, i.e., it is a policy that increases the socioeconomic prospects of some at the expense of decreasing those same opportunities for others?

The issues raised in this brief example are raised in frustratingly complex ways in virtually any attempt to apply the rationalist framework to questions of what should be done. Again, the fundamental problem is normative: what do we use to judge what's best? Identifying and rank ordering policy alternatives inescapably means identifying and ranking values (C. Anderson 1979, 711). Public policy, most agree, should promote social welfare; it should represent decisions and actions that further the public interest. That, however, simply redefines the problem. How does one measure social welfare or the public interest? Anyone with even a passing comprehension of politics recognizes that what best serves the greater good is often in the eye of the beholder.

Rationalists have formulated a number of ways to deal with this key normative issue, ranging from the dismissive (ignore the problem altogether) to the inclusive (i.e., keep the methods and theory, but use a range of values to judge the comparative worth of policy alternatives; see Smith 2003). Perhaps the most common approach to dealing with this question, however, is to judge policy alternatives on the basis of a particular value: efficiency. The rationalist approach takes a good deal of criticism for relying so heavily on efficiency to solve its key normative challenge. In particular, the use of efficiency—as opposed to more democratic values such as equity—serves as the core of a number of post-positivist criticisms. Yet using efficiency as the basis for judging policy alternatives, i.e., as the normative basis for operationalizing the rationalist approach, is not done without justification. In doing so, rationalist analysis draws heavily from welfare economics, a framework that has a well-laid argument for using efficiency as the basis for deciding what is best.

The Welfare Economics Paradigm

Welfare economics is the study of the normative properties of markets. In general terms, welfare economics is devoted to trying to assess what economic policy or regulation is "best" (Zeckhauser and Schaefer 1968; Just, Hueth, and Schmitz 2004). This objective has a clear parallel with the goal of rationalist policy analysis, which is different only in that it seeks to assess what public policy—economic or not—is best.

This similarity in objectives makes adapting the welfare economics framework to the general study of public policy highly attractive. The key question of policy analysis essentially poses a question of social choice. What should we do? The government has limited resources, so how can it best allocate those resources in a way that maximizes the public interest? The conceptual tools of welfare economics are readily adaptable to such questions of social choice. In effect, the welfare economics paradigm offers a systematic framework to answer the critical normative question of what alternative is best.

Welfare economics rests on a foundation of methodological individualism: Individuals are viewed as rational actors, as the best judges of their wants and needs who seek to satisfy those wants and needs in a way that maximizes their individual utility (Campen 1986, 28). Social welfare is seen simply as the aggregation of individual welfare. Policies that maximize the aggregate level of individual welfare are thus viewed as maximizing social welfare. Social welfare is in turn operationalized through the concept of efficiency.

The term "efficiency" comes with considerable baggage and prima facie is frequently viewed as an antidemocratic value (see Stone 2002). At least in a purely theoretical sense, however, efficiency from the view of welfare economics is simply a characteristic of a distribution of resources. Specifically, the most efficient distribution is one that maximizes social welfare. Efficiency from this perspective is defined by the Pareto criterion, which describes an allocation of resources such that "no alternative allocation can make at least one person better off without making anyone worse off" (Boardman et al. 2001, 26). It is easy to convey this concept visually.

Figure 5.1 shows a simple two-person society where individual A has y resources, and individual B has x resources. Where the two lines labeled "x" and "y" intersect is the status quo. Any policy that shifts the distribution of wealth from this status quo point up and to the right would produce a Pareto superior outcome; at a minimum it increases the wealth of one individual while costing the other nothing. Any policy that shifts the distribution down and to the left is Pareto inferior; at least one individual is losing wealth under this distribution. Any policy that results in a move up and/or to the right of the status quo point, in other words, is efficient, and any that shifts down and to the left is inefficient. The Pareto principle strikes many as an intuitively appealing way to conceive of social welfare.

FIGURE 5.1 **The Pareto Principle**

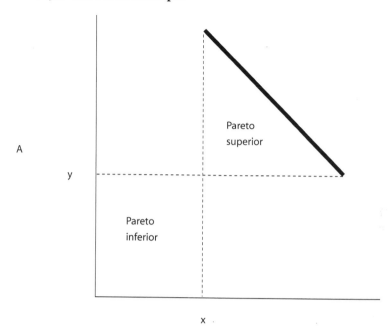

It defines the best or most desirable policy as the one that generates the highest level of benefits while doing no harm to others.

In theory, perfectly functioning markets will allocate resources in such a way as to produce Pareto superior outcomes (Nas 1996, 19). Perfectly functioning markets, of course, are conceptual creatures of theory rather than part of our real-world experience. Still, for many private goods, markets do a remarkably good job of allocating resources efficiently in a more or less Pareto-like way (walk into any supermarket in the United States and what is taken for granted—an astonishing choice of foodstuffs at reasonable prices—is a rough-and-ready example). The problem with using the Pareto principle to operationalize the concept of efficiency, of course, is that even reasonably free markets are not much good at distributing public (as opposed to private) goods. Also, much of public policy is explicitly redistributional in nature, with some people bearing the costs while others enjoy the benefits. There is no reasonable approximation of a free and functioning market for providing national defense or universal social security for the elderly or free parking spaces. Social security, for example, transfers wealth from young workers to provide pensions for elderly nonworkers. Building a new public parking garage may provide benefits to downtown commuters, but to build that garage may mean using taxes taken from people who may not even own a car, homes and businesses may have to be torn down to clear the construction site, and the end result may be a concrete box of an eyesore that changes the character of downtown. These examples, like most public policies, do not fall into the clean categories of Pareto superior or Pareto inferior quadrants of the graph represented in Figure 5.1. They fall into the unlabeled upper-left and lower-right quadrants, where there are some winners and some losers. A shift into those quadrants pretty much describes what happens whenever the government purposively backs an action or inaction with its coercive powers.

To make the Pareto principle tractable in the real world, welfare economics uses what is known as the Kaldor-Hicks compensation principle (developed independently by two British economists in the 1930s; see Hicks 1939; Kaldor 1939). The Kaldor-Hicks principle is simple in notion, if controversial in practice, and serves to make the concept of efficiency a practical means to judge the relative social worth of public policies. Basically Kaldor-Hicks says this: if those who gain from a policy could, in theory, make a set of side payments to those who lose from the policy such that the losers become indifferent, that policy is *potentially* a Pareto superior outcome. This translates in practical terms as, "if the benefits outweigh the costs, the policy is efficient."

The reasoning here is still intuitive; if a decision or an action results in more benefits than costs, or more pros than cons, it is preferable to any decision or action that has the opposite outcomes. The basic notion is not unique to welfare economics—Franklin's moral algebra is, more or less, just the individual version of the same concept. Nor does it necessarily require the inputs and outcomes of a policy to be translated into monetary terms (though this is a requirement for certain analytic methods such as cost-benefit analysis). What is useful from the policy analyst's perspective is that it offers a well-defined and operationalizable concept of social welfare, i.e., a means to measure the comparative worth of different policy alternatives. This concept of social welfare is essentially utilitarian in nature; it judges the policy that generates the most overall benefits as "best." Utilitarianism as expressed through the Kaldor-Hicks efficiency criterion is certainly not the only means to conceive of social welfare, but it is a systematically and normatively defensible way to practically judge the relative worth of public policies (Weimer and Vining 2005, 133–138).

A simple example can serve to show how this concept of social welfare can be used to quantitatively estimate the impact of a public policy or program on social welfare. Imagine a municipality is considering building a new public garage to address a critical shortage of downtown parking spaces. To estimate the impact of the garage on social welfare, the welfare economics approach would seek to construct a demand curve for parking spaces. Such a graph is depicted in Figure 5.2. The graph plots the demand for parking spaces, in terms of average daily parking use, against parking fees. The demand curve (labeled "D") that slopes down and to the right shows that as parking fees decrease, use of public parking facilities increase. A one-dollar fee results in an average of 1,000 motorists using the public parking garage. A five-dollar fee drops demand to zero—this is the point where the demand curve crosses the y axis.

This simple demand curve contains several pieces of important information relative to the pros and cons of the project, as well as its impact on social welfare. The rectangle defined by the points $1, a, 1000, and 0 represents the average daily revenue generated by the garage. The triangle

FIGURE 5.2 **Hypothetical Demand Curve for Parking Spaces** defined by the points a, D, and 1000 represents what economists call a "deadweight loss." This represents unmet demand for parking spaces, parking spaces that motorists want but are not willing to pay a dollar for. Of most interest to the policy analyst, however, is the triangle defined by the points $1, a, and $5. This area represents what economists term consumer surplus; it represents the difference between what consumers are willing to pay for a good or service and what they actually pay for a good or service. Consumer surplus can be thought of as measure of the project's impact on social welfare—it represents in monetary terms the net benefits society receives from the parking garage.[5] This amount is calculated by simply computing the area of the triangle, easily done using the Pythagorean theorem: height multiplied by width divided by 2. In this example, then, the net social benefit of the parking garage is $4 × 1,000/2 = $2,000. Using this approach, the net benefit of the garage can be calculated even if parking is free. If no parking fees are charged, the consumer surplus is simply the area of the triangle 0, D, $5. This conceptual approach, in other words, has no problem estimating the social value of public services and goods as long as the relevant demand curve can be reasonably estimated. The same general conceptual approach can be employed to compare different projects; the project that best maximizes social welfare is the project that produces the most benefits as measured by social surplus.

In short, the welfare economics paradigm offers a rigorous conceptual framework to deal with problems of social choice. It has a clear notion of what is best; the policy that maximizes social welfare. Social welfare is operationalized using the concept of efficiency and can be quantified and directly measured using the standard conceptual and analytic tool kit of economics as seen in Figure 5.2. Actually doing policy analysis within this framework presents considerable technical difficulties (not the least of which is the problem of estimating reasonably accurate demand curves for public goods and services). Conceptually, however, it provides a systematic means to operationalize the rationalist problem-solving approach.

Rationalist Successes and Failures

Drawing on theoretical frameworks such as welfare economics makes rationalist approaches tractable, allowing the basic conceptual framework to be translated into real-world practice. Building off such foundations, rationalist analysis can generate enormous quantities of information that are of potential use to policy decision making. The policy analyses rank policy alternatives not just in terms of efficiency but also in terms of anticipated impacts, in expected payoffs, and by systematically cataloging the trade-offs inherent in different policy choices. Indeed, that's exactly what rationalist analysis has been doing for four or five decades: generating mountains of information from whose peaks it is presumably easier to see solutions to policy problems. As the field has matured, it has become ever more sophisticated in its methods: cost analysis, econometric forecasting, decision theory, and many other tools taken from the social science tool kit have been adapted and refined to make the process of linear problem-solving ever more rigorous and accurate.[6]

Nonetheless, there remain serious questions about the development, direction, and payoffs of the rationalist enterprise. Whereas even its critics acknowledge the primacy of the rationalist approach in driving the field of policy analysis, that field has not really fulfilled its original vision. It has evolved in ways and down paths not forecast by its forebears seeking to implement the Lasswellian vision of the policy sciences.[7] Most obviously, policy analysis is not confined to the high levels of public agencies but rather takes place at all levels of government and in many places outside of government (academia, think tanks, interest groups). Multiple policy analysts often address the same problem and often come to very different conclusions about what constitutes the best solution. This means that policy analysts often give policymakers very different answers to the question, "what should we do?" The contradictions partially occur because of the explicit client orientation that has long been a central feature of rationalist policy analysis (see Meltsner 1976). An agency head, a legislature, a single-interest issue group, a government watchdog organization, and an academic may all be interested in a particular problem and may seek policy analyses following the generic rationalist approach. Because they start from different perspectives and are addressing different audiences with different desired outcomes, the results of such policy analyses may end up with very different recommendations.

It is not just that policy analysts have different clients and thus focus on different elements and alternatives to particular policy problems. More generally it is clear that a gap exists between knowledge generated by policy analysts and the policymakers who are targeted as the primary consumers of such knowledge. Policy analysts in the rationalist tradition have sought to be data- rather than values-driven. Yet political decision making, which is to say policy decision making, is often values-driven. Any analysis, regardless of its theory, methods, or results attains a normative dimension as soon as it enters the political arena—it will support somebody's preferences while opposing others. No analysis can avoid this inevitable political fate, even if an analyst is a genuinely value-free logical positivist. An analysis that is purely data-driven cannot avoid being championed or opposed on the basis of its comfort to a particular ideology or value system.

The bottom line is that political decision makers, the very people policy analysis is supposed to inform, are often explicitly value-driven and not interested in policy analyses that do not support their preferred values. Rationalist policy analysis is instrumental; it seeks a technical solution to a well-defined problem. In the political arena, solutions are championed not just because of their technical efficacy but also on how well their conclusions support preconceived political agendas. Thus connecting the knowledge generated by rationalist analyses to the values that drive the political world, at least in a fashion that does not relegate policy analysis to just another manufacturer of partisan ammunition, has proven to be maddeningly difficult to achieve. Much to the frustration of policy analysis professionals, policymakers have a tendency to cherry-pick their research to suit preexisting preferences or, even worse, to ignore it altogether (Smith 2005).

This has led to considerable hand-wringing among policy analysts. Though policy analysis in the rationalist mode exploded in the last quarter of the twentieth century, a wide range of studies that examined the impact of these studies came to two sobering conclusions: 1) rationalist policy analysis often produced very bad advice, or at least advice that did not result in government actions achieving desired objectives; 2) even when policy analysis produced, by virtually any criteria, good advice, it was often ignored by policymakers.

This seems a disappointingly long way from the rationalist project's promising origins. World War II, for example, clearly demonstrated the usefulness of applying social science methods and thinking to solving policy problems. Operations research, for example, was a basic form of rationalist policy analysis originally developed to solve problems such as stemming losses in Atlantic convoys and in bombing raids on continental

Europe. By applying statistical techniques, analysts could, for example, help determine what bomber formations minimized losses from collisions and enemy fighters.[8] As policy analysis developed from these successful technocratic beginnings into an independent field of Lasswellian-inspired policy sciences in the 1950s, 1960s, and 1970s, it was asked to provide important contributions to major policy problems such as the Vietnam War, the war on poverty, and the energy crisis. Yet the contributions of rationalist policy analysis to these key post–World War II issues were, to put it charitably, mixed.

Rationalist approaches in the Vietnam War, for example, emphasized quantitative indicators of impact and effect: body counts, supplies consumed, and so forth. These "objective" indicators frequently presented a distorted picture of the war and its progress and created incentives to fudge facts rather than verify them (e.g., commanders on the ground being tempted to inflate body counts to demonstrate success). The rationalist approaches of the federal government's so-called whiz kids did relatively little to formulate successful policy alternatives (see deLeon 2006, 42–47). The bottom line was that rationalist analysis could not, or at any rate did not, solve the problems presented by the Vietnam War, the war on poverty, or the energy crisis.

It was, perhaps, expecting too much of an infant discipline to answer the questions raised by such complex policy issues, and even critics of the rationalistic approach acknowledge it can produce useful information. What good this information does, however, is debatable. A number of studies have examined the impact of policy analysis on shaping policy responses to social, political, and economic problems. Such studies show policy analysis rarely functions as the central problem-solving tool it was designed to be; indeed, most studies conclude policy analysis has relatively little impact on policy outputs or outcomes (e.g., C. Jones 1976; Mooney 1991; Rich 2001). This has led to questions in some quarters about whether the rationalist project is doomed to a quiet extinction. For example, Kirp (1992) concludes that policymakers favor anecdote over systematic analysis and that the dynamics of politics mean passion trumps reason. The general conclusion is that politics willfully ignores careful and reasoned policy analysis because its factual goring of valued political oxen is resented. The result is irrational public policies, or at least policies with lower probabilities of actually achieving a desired end. This will lead to the "end of policy analysis," at least in its rationalist variant (Kirp 1992).

Although rationalist policy analysis currently shows no signs of fading away, the problem of practically and meaningfully connecting its positivist and quantitatively generated knowledge with the real, messy, and value-driven world of politics is real enough. And that gap between knowledge and politics is where post-positivist alternatives to the rationalist project thrive.

The Post-Positivist Approach

The rationalist approach, especially as practiced within the welfare economics paradigm, thus represents a distinct theory of public policy. Public policy is seen as a solution to a problem, its central goal is efficiency, and the practice of policy analysis is theoretically and methodologically oriented to identifying the most efficient solution to a given problem. As such, policy analysis lies within the realm of experts, technocrats who supply information to clients but are not directly involved in the political arena. Post-positivists do not necessarily disagree with this as one approach to policy analysis; what they disagree with is any claim that the rationalist project is *the* approach to policy analysis.

Using its scientific basis to claim a privileged place in the hierarchy of policy knowledge, post-positivists argue, leads the rationalist project down a decidedly antidemocratic path. The main criticisms of the antidemocratic nature of the rationalist approach have been succinctly summarized by Dryzek (1989, 101). Rationalism conceives of politics in purely technocratic terms, seeing policy as a means for a political elite to manipulate causal systems to achieve a desired end. It treats ends simplistically, viewing them as being fixed in nature; it explicitly ignores political debate and conflict, preferring to impose its own preferred values such as efficiency. Rationalism falsely assumes that a general consensus supports these favored values; it promotes a form of policymaking where technocrats exercise central influence and leaves little role for citizens. It ends up reinforcing bureaucratic and hierarchical power systems and in doing so has a distinct bias toward the status quo. In short, "the most widely practiced kind of policy analysis aspires to rationality, but this proves to be at the expense of democracy" (Dryzek 1989, 104).

While post-positivists object to the rationalist approach across a range of theoretical and methodological issues, the core of the post-positivist critique is value-based. It argues that the rationalist approach is predicated on the assumption that better—more comprehensive, more accurate—information will lead to better policies (Collingridge and Reeves 1986). Most analysts in the rationalist tradition are not likely to disagree with this claim. The problem from the post-positivist perspective is that policy belongs to the political realm and as such is not particularly likely to respond to empirical claims regardless of their technical sophistication or theoretical rigor. This is exactly the situation, the inability to successfully bridge the gap between knowledge and politics, that has driven scholars in the rationalist tradition to despair over the inability of policy analysis to shape policymaking (Kirp 1992). Policy, like politics in general, is an interpretive exercise that is driven by values rather than data. The nature of a particular problem, its existence, extent, and the best policy alternative to address it rests not on neutral and objective observation but on the social values used to interpret the world (Fischer 2003, 13). Post-positivists view public policy in expressive rather than instrumentalist terms (Yanow 2000, 22). Rather than judging public policy as an objective means to achieve a clearly defined end, post-positivists view policy as a means to communicate, implement, and enforce explicitly political values. The entire realm of public policy is suffused with values, and policy analysis has to account for these values if government actions are going to uphold the norms of liberal democracy and be granted legitimacy by citizens.

Post-positivists argue that the rationalist approach not only cannot escape the fundamentally normative nature of policy, they charge the rationalist approach is itself value-based and promotes its favored values in a fairly ruthless manner. In doing so the entire rationalist project is not just reluctantly dragged into the political realm but is revealed to be an enthusiastic combatant in the arena where values clash. Underlying the supposedly neutral and objective social science foundation of the rationalist orientation is a set of "underlying and usually unspoken political and social assumptions," and it is these values that drive the methods, the theory, and ultimately the results of rationalist research (deLeon 1988, 70).

As an example, consider the oft-repeated claim that money makes no difference to the performance of schools. This claim has considerable support from a large body of empirical research carried out in the rationalist tradition (for reviews, see Hanushek 1997). The vast majority of these studies are carried out in the education production framework. This is an analytical framework appropriated from the study of profit-making firms that typically uses regression models to provide point estimates of how the inputs of schooling (student characteristics, school resources, teaching experience, etc.) relate to the outputs of schooling (test scores, graduation rates, etc.). Such studies have been used repeatedly to support claims that "money does not matter," or more technically that there is no significant positive correlation between monetary inputs (usually measured as per student expenditures) and test scores or other education outputs. These studies are often technically very sophisticated and are presented as objective representations of the causal relationships that exist in the real world. As the data clearly indicate that money does not matter, the response to "what should we do about school performance?" should focus on alternatives such as institutional reform rather than on more resources (e.g., Chubb and Moe 1990; Moe 2001).

Rather than objective policy analysis, post-positivists (and even some self-proclaimed rationalists; see Smith 2003, 50–57) argue that the conclusion that institutional reform and not more resources is the best solution to the problem of school performance is driven as much by values as by data. Values are seen as directing such conclusions at virtually every stage of the rationalist analytic process. These begin with the values inherent in the scientific method. In testing causal claims, the standard scientific approach is to assume the research hypothesis (in this case, that money is positively related to school outputs) is false and requires overwhelming evidence to reject that assumption. In hypothesis testing there is a distinct bias against making Type I errors (concluding something has an effect when in fact it does not). The consequences of a Type II error (concluding something has no effect when in fact it does have an effect) are considered less serious (e.g., Gravetter and Wallnau 2004, 243). This bias shapes how research results are interpreted. Consider Hanushek's (1997) review of 377 studies examining the link between resources and school or student performance, concluding that an extensive research record backs the claim that "money does not matter." Yet most of the studies cited in Hanushek's review actually show positive relationships between resources and outputs. A plurality show positive and statistically significant relationships. The conclusion that money does not matter rests not on overwhelming evidence of an absence of a relationship, but on statistically insignificant results in roughly a third of the studies (Verstegen and King 1998; Unnever, Kerckhoff, and Robinson 2000). That the latter finding is given so much credence, a post-positivist would argue, is because of the values used to interpret the results of research, not an independent and objective "truth."

Post-positivists would also note that the education production framework structuring most of this research tips the scales toward certain policy conclusions. The education production framework conceptualizes schools as "production units" that are expected to translate inputs into outputs in much the same way that businesses use labor and capital to produce goods and services. This framework requires a quantifiable output measure analogous to profit or goods and services produced. This need in turn pushes researchers toward building analyses of quantifiable outputs, e.g., test scores or graduation rates (the vast majority of the education production functions literature uses some form of standardized test score as a dependent variable). Yet public education does not exist solely, or even primarily, to improve performance on the SAT. Public education in the United States is legally authorized through state constitutions, and virtually all state constitutions explicitly justify public education in value-based terms, specifically as a means to promote and transmit democratic values (Rebell 1998). There is very little research on how schools achieve this goal, or what role resources play, within the education production functions literature (see Smith 2003). That so much rationalist-based education policy analysis ends up calling for the imposition of market values—school vouchers and the like—is not surprising from the post-positivist perspective. Market values, after all, are what frame the research, not democratic values.

The bottom line is that the analytical frameworks and the methodological practices of the rationalist approach are seen as carrying and promoting a particular set of values. The post-positivist critique does not seek to eliminate these values (indeed, it would argue that such an effort would be doomed to failure) as much as it seeks to make them explicit. Failure to take account of these values leads to the common perception that the rationalist approach is more neutral and objective than any alternative. This perception, post-positivists argue, is not only incorrect, but dangerous. Ceding policy analysis to technocrats leads to policy alternatives that promote consistently antidemocratic values. Democracy, after all, is supposed to be egalitarian, not efficient; its policies are supposed to uphold democratic values rather than market values.

One of the preeminent forms of rationalist policy analysis is cost-benefit analysis (CBA), a technique whose ultimate objective is to rank policy alternatives on a straightforward measure of allocative efficiency (typically a benefit-cost ratio, or net social benefits expressed in monetary terms). Efficiency in this case is, of course, defined by the Kaldor-Hicks compensation principle. Post-positivists lodge a raft of objections to cost-benefit analysis, ranging from the heroic assumptions often necessary to make the technique mathematically tractable to the perceived affront to democratic values inherent in its intellectual framework. For example, because CBA requires all costs and benefits to be monetized, it requires putting dollar values on things that strike many as beyond the ability of markets—even theoretical benchmark markets—to price. Clean air, human life, and freedom from sickness or disease, for example, have all been monetized by CBA studies (Boardman et al. 2001, 1–3). Such valuations are frequently challenged as either inaccurate, misleading, or meaningless (Wolff and Haubrich 2006).

Kaldor-Hicks, unsurprisingly, comes in for particular criticism as anchoring policy analysis in a market framework that pays little attention to the distributional issues often at the heart of public policy. Remember that Kaldor-Hicks describes a *potential* Pareto, an outcome where the winners could conceivably compensate the losers to the point where they become indifferent to the policy. This is controversial because the side payments are purely theoretical; there is no requirement about compensation to the losers. This raises immediate distributional concerns. Post-positivists are quite right to point out that political conflict is often about just such distributional concerns; that the winners gain more benefits than the costs incurred by the losers will not make that political conflict any less intense. Just because a policy is efficient under Kaldor-Hicks does not make a political decision any less political; it certainly does not stop the potential losers from expending their political capital to prevent the policy from being adopted.

The crux of the post-positivist critique is that the rationalist approach seeks to divorce policy analysis from politics, to set up policy analysis as a neutral and objective generator of knowledge that stands independent of politics. Post-positivists argue that the rationalist approach fails miserably on all counts. Its methods and theories promote a particular set of values (typically those of science and the market) while elevating technocrats and experts into privileged positions of policy influence. The end result is a form of policy analysis that promotes fundamentally undemocratic, or even antidemocratic, values. Efficiency trumps equity and a technocratic elite has more weight in decision making than the citizen (see, for example, Dryzek and Torgerson 1993; deLeon 1997).

Post-Positivist Methods

If policy analysis is not undertaken in the rationalist framework, however, what's the alternative? Post-positivist policy analysis (like rationalist policy analysis) employs a wide range of conceptual frameworks and methods. Generally speaking, however, the post-positivist approach is distinguished by viewing public policy through the lens of deliberative democracy.

Roughly speaking, deliberative democracy is the (normative) notion that public decision making should be made through a process of informed reflection and dialogue between citizens, politicians, and stakeholders. As James Fishkin put it, deliberative democracy is about "how we might bring some of the favorable characteristics of small-group, face-to-face democracy to the large-scale nation-state" (1991, 1). More broadly, deliberative democracy draws on ideas taken from such theorists as John Rawls, Jurgen Habermas, and Amy Gutmann about how polities should deal with issues of social choice.[9] From this perspective, informed deliberation and consensus provide the best answer to the question of "what should we do?"

The big question, of course, is how to go about doing this. Post-positivist frameworks and theories require a radical epistemological shift from the rationalist approach. It means shifting from a focus on "discovering a set of universal laws about objective, sense-based fact to the human capacity for making and communicating meaning" (Yanow 2000, 5). Post-positivist policy analysis is premised on the assumption that the political world is socially constructed. How this world is interpreted is dependent upon one's perspective, and there is no neutral, independent reality that exists outside of this perspective. Accordingly, post-positivist policy analysis rejects the linear, putatively objective, problem-solving approach in favor of discourse and interpretive analysis. The job of a policy analyst is to understand the different perspectives, why they lead to conflict, and how they might accommodate each other in the form of purposive government action or inaction. Post-positivist policy analysis seeks to translate the different stories or narratives of the political world into a coherent argument; it seeks to translate the stories of "what is" from different perspectives into a case for "what ought" (see Fischer 2003).

The post-positivist approach, then, views the policy analyst not as a lab-coated neutral analyzer of facts but instead as an interpreter, a mediator, and a facilitator. A post-positivist analyst is someone who not only understands different perspectives, and why they exist and why they conflict, but someone who understands different modes of communication and seeks to bring disparate views together. One way to go about doing this is through participatory policy analysis (PPA). PPA is a method that seeks to put the ideals of deliberative democracy into action and to create a new role for policy analysis. PPA has a number of different variants, though: "All reject positivism; view phenomenology or a variation of it, as a better way to interpret the nature of knowledge; and accept an interpretive or hermeneutic paradigm of inquiry" (Durning 1993, 300). In other words, PPA is predicated on the assumption that the knowledge of the expert has no privileged position in deciding what to do, and that the best response to a given social-choice situation depends on your point of view. PPA seeks to build consensus among these differing perspectives from informed deliberation.

The general idea behind PPA is to bring together ordinary citizens from different walks of life and with different perspectives, educate them on an issue or problem, and have them deliberate about "what should we do?" These participatory panels would meet for an extended period of time and deal with a single issue. Knowledge from expert policy analysts (analysts in the rationalist tradition) would be made available to the panel and this information, combined with their own perspectives and experiences, would provide a basis for informed deliberation. PPA is not designed to be just a negotiation among stakeholder groups but also to provide "a fair and impartial representation of all citizens' values and preferences, be they organized or not" (Renn et al. 1993, 206). There are a number of studies suggesting such panels can provide an important contribution to policymaking. Kathlene and Martin (1991), for example, found that a panel of roughly 150 citizens provided key input into the public transportation planning in Boulder, Colorado. The Danish Board of Technology has put something very much like PPA into practice in the form of the "consensus conference." The idea of the consensus conference is to weave together expert knowledge with the often clashing social, political, and economic perspectives that surround controversial policy issues, such as the use of nuclear power. A conference typically involves about twenty-five citizens who spend several months on a single issue or topic, guided by a facilitator who is an expert in communication and co-operation techniques. The end result is a report (often presented in a high-profile media setting) to the Danish government, and these reports have had a not insignificant role in shaping policy decisions (Kluver 1995; Fischer 2003, 210–213). Similar experiments with citizen panels have been conducted across the globe through deliberative polling. Deliberative polling bears a strong resemblance to PPA in that it brings together a representative sample of citizens, provides them with expert information and a facilitator, and asks them to deliberate on important political issues. It differs mainly in that the panels meet for relatively brief periods and that there is no direct policy role for the panel (e.g., there is no official report presented to a legislature).[10]

PPA, however, remains a sparsely employed technique for helping to decide questions of "what should we do?" More common are various forms of interpretive analysis (application of hermeneutics, phenomenology, discourse theory, and the like), though even these do not represent mainstream policy analysis (for examples see Yanow 2000; Schneider and Ingram 1997). Most policy analysts are trained in rationalist rather than post-positivist conceptual frameworks and research methodologies, so unsurprisingly rationalist frameworks are more commonly applied in policy analysis (Etzioni 2006, 840–841).

There are a number of reasons for this; key among them is a counter-critique of post-positivism by the rationalist school. Rationalists acknowledge post-positivists have some legitimate criticisms but argue that they have misconceived the rationalist project and offer no viable systematic alternative to policy analysis. For example, in response to the claim that the rationalist approach is value-based, rationalists reply they have never argued otherwise. Hard-core proponents of the welfare economics paradigm freely admit that efficiency is but one value that might be important to policy decision making, not necessarily *the* value that *all* policy decision making should be based on (Weimer and Vining 2005, 478). Their claim is simply that efficiency is, generally speaking, a value of central importance and relevance to political decision making. The government has limited resources, and assessing how to allocate those resources in a way that produces the greatest net social benefit as judged by the concept of (Kaldor-Hicks) efficiency is important information. The welfare economics paradigm is essentially utilitarian—it judges the policy that generates the most benefits as best. Utilitarianism is certainly not the only means to conceive of social welfare, but it is at least as defensible as a means for judging the relative worth of public policies as anything suggested by post-positivists (Weimer and Vining 2005, 133–138). Rationalist methods can, and do, take into account values other than efficiency. Matrix analysis, for example, can incorporate values such as "justice" or "democracy" into a comparative ranking of policy alternatives (e.g., Munger 2000).

Nor does the rationalist approach necessarily ignore the distributional concerns that have formed an important part of the post-positivist critique. Distributionally weighted cost-benefit analysis, for example, decomposes costs and benefits by group or constituency. This provides an estimate of who is winning or losing under a particular policy scenario, and by exactly how much (Boardman et al. 2001, 456–488). This information not only recognizes that there may winners and losers, and that distributional concerns may lead to political conflict, it also offers precise estimates of these underlying imbalances and in doing so offers a platform to recognize and mitigate these conflicts before they happen. In short, rationalist proponents argue their approach produces useful information that is perfectly capable of incorporating some of the value-based concerns. What separates it from the post-positivist approach is that it clearly defines its concepts (including its normative ones) and provides a clear and systematic means for ranking policy alternatives. Post-positivism, with its perspective-equals-truth approach, runs the risk of "sinking into the swamp of relativism." Indeed, post-positivists have devoted considerable effort to countering this charge (see Fischer 2003), though rarely to the satisfaction of rationalist skeptics.

Rationalists also suspect part of the post-positivist critique confuses ends and means. For example, Deborah Stone's (2002, 65) critique of the rationalist approach argues that efficiency is always a politically defined concept. She defines efficiency as the output gained for a given input and uses the example of a library to demonstrate how efficiency is dependent entirely on how one defines inputs and outputs. Outputs are particularly slippery for public agencies such as libraries. Should the output be defined as total circulation, ease of use, the availability of books, total books, or something else? Rationalists might argue that Stone is defining efficiency a particular way, as *technical* rather than *allocative* efficiency. The fundamental argument Stone is getting at is not really the definition of efficiency but the goal of libraries. The rationalist approach makes no claim that it has a better means to define the goal of a library, or any other public agency or program. What it can do is assess how that goal, once defined, can be achieved most efficiently. It can do this allocatively (assess what policy alternative produces the largest net social benefit) or technically (compare alternatives on the basis of their expected output for a given input). The latter, rationalists would claim, is a better basis for systematically informing policy decisions than relying wholly on subjective perspectives that may or may not be reconciled through dialogue.

A post-positivist would be quick to point out that the last sentence reflects the underlying antidemocratic nature of the rationalist enterprise: The rationalist approach seeks to reduce, or optimally eliminate, politics from policymaking. For the rationalist project, politics is viewed "as an unfortunate obstacle to clear-headed, rational analysis and good policy (which are the same thing)" (Stone 2002, xi). For the post-positivist, politics is not an obstacle to good public policy, it is the path to good public policy. Thus the policy analyst must first and foremost understand politics, and understand it up close. For the rationalist this is a dangerous path to go down—policy analysis becomes simply another path to advocacy, a means to promote a set of preferred values. The post-positivist might well reply; "well, yes!"

Conclusion

When considering a problem or matter of concern, the central objective of public authorities is to decide what action to take (or not to take). Public policy thus invariably begins as a question of social choice, and this universal scenario provides the field of policy analysis with its fundamental question: "what should we do?"

Within policy analysis there is a good deal of disagreement about how to structure the search for answers to this fundamental question. Whereas the discussion above has to some extent oversimplified this disagreement by splitting the entire field into rationalist and post-positivist camps, that division does serve to highlight the fundamental theoretical debate in the field. Basically what we have is two conceptual frameworks that in many ways seem to be mutually exclusive, forcing an analyst's loyalties toward one camp or the other. The rationalists cannot—and do not want to—fully release their grip on positivism. These positivist foundations prop up the causal frameworks that rationalists use to explain the world and make systematic sense of policy choices. The post-positivist cannot see those positivist foundations as anything more than one of any number of value systems, and one that has no legitimate claim to hierarchy over any other. The rationalist looks at post-positivism and sees messy relativism, where knowledge cannot accumulate and the information needed for good policymaking is reduced to equal status with the ideologically fueled opinions of the ignorant and uninformed. The post-positivist sees just such information produced repeatedly by rationalists only to be ignored by politicians and claims to know why.

It is quite possible, however, that this debate is producing more heat than light. Rationalists have become increasingly cognizant of the need to account for the fractured and value-laden nature of the political arena (e.g., Radin 1997, 2000). And the rationalist frustrations over the inability of policy analysis to shape policy directions may actually be misplaced. There are good reasons to believe that rationalist policy analysis is having an important impact in shaping public policy, ironically in a fashion that can be appreciated by post-positivists. Shulock (1997) asked, if policy analysis is really so ignored, why is there so much of it being produced? Her answer was that policy analysis is not being ignored and plays a critical role in the policymaking process, just not the role anticipated or intended by the rationalist project. Mainstream (i.e., rationalist) policy analysis was actually being used in a fashion that fit more with post-positivist perspective. Specifically, policy analysis was used to provide substance to policy debates. Though rationalists typically despair that the products of their efforts become just more partisan ammunition, Shulock argued that this is the wrong way to look at things. It is better to engage in disputes with information and ideology rather than with ignorance and ideology. Both sides lean on rationalist analysis to gain an edge in policy debates. That rationalist analysis is shaping the value conflict rather than providing technical solutions to problems is not necessarily a bad thing. Indeed, it can be viewed as a central contribution to the political process. Post-positivist analysis has had a hard time achieving the latter in any sustained fashion because imposing systematic order on a complicated world can be more difficult using its concepts and methods, at least compared to using rationalist concepts and methods.

What should we do? The field of policy analysis currently is incapable of answering that question technically and instrumentally to universal satisfaction. Thus, in one sense, it may be said that the rationalist project has either failed, or at least has not yet achieved consistent success. Nor can the field of policy analysis consistently produce a response that accounts for all perspectives yet still provides a clear enough answer to guide action, so it may also be said that the post-positivist project has done no better than the rationalist approach. Yet, as research such as Shulock's demonstrates, policy analysis clearly has a role in shaping how policy decisions are made. Ironically, it may be that the rationalist approach to policy analysis, however unintentionally, is better at achieving the aims of the post-positivist project.

Notes

1. Franklin's original letter to Priestly is available from a number of Internet sites. A quickly and easily accessible source is: http://www.procon.org/franklinletter.htm.

2. Like public policy, policy analysis is formally defined in a variety of different ways. A representative sampling of these definitions can be found in Weimer and Vining (2005, 24, note 1).

3. The majority of policy analysis textbooks present some version of this generic process. See Bardach (2005) and Levin and McEwan (2001) for representative examples.

4. In embracing the fact-value dichotomy, policy analysis followed the mainstream orientation of public administration, which through roughly the 1960s conceptually separated administration from politics. The fact-value dichotomy theoretically collapsed following the work of a number of public administration scholars, notably Dwight Waldo (1946), who convincingly demonstrated that decision making in public agencies was unavoidably political. In other words, facts could not be separated from values in public-sector decision making. This shattered the theoretical unity at the core of public administration, and the field has struggled to incorporate values into its conceptual frameworks ever since (see Frederickson and Smith 2003). The rise of post-positivist challenges to the rationalist approach shows policy analysis as a field shares a similar intellectual challenge.

5. Technically, the measure used to assess relative efficiency is social surplus, or the combination of consumer and producer surplus (the latter being estimated in a similar fashion to consumer surplus, but using supply rather than demand curves). In practice, however, consumer surplus is typically used as the benchmark for assessing the relative worth of public policy alternatives (see Gupta 2001, 361–363; Weimer and Vining 2005, 57–70).

6. Numerous textbooks have been exclusively devoted to the ever-growing sophistication of the quantitative methods of policy analysis (e.g., Quade 1989; Gupta 2001; Weimer and Vining 2005).

7. For good overviews of the evolution of policy analysis during the last half of the twentieth century, see Radin (1997, 2000).

8. The Royal Air Force provides an interesting history of bomber activities that includes such analytic contributions at http://www.raf.mod.uk/bombercommand /thousands.html.

9. A good introductory overview of the ideas and issues contained in deliberative democracy can be found in Fishkin and Laslett (2003).

10. Deliberative polling is primarily the brainchild of James Fishkin, who sought to use public opinion research to inform policy debate. A good overview of deliberative polling can be found online at the Center for Deliberative Democracy Web site: http://cdd.stanford.edu/polls/docs/summary/.

CHAPTER SIX

What Have We Done?
Impact Analysis and Program Evaluation

Sooner or later, the government is expected to answer the question "what should we do?" by actually doing something, enacting a public policy or program to address the problem or issue at hand. For example, in response to concerns about educational performance, curricular reforms may be adopted, more stringent teacher qualifications approved, or high-stakes systems of standardized testing required. Whether on the basis of efficiency as judged by a cost-benefit analysis or the joint agreement of various stakeholder groups as judged by a participatory policy analysis, one of these policies, or some combination, may be adopted as the preferred answer to "what should we do?"

Taking purposive action on the basis of a systematic policy analysis, however, is no guarantee that a policy will effectively address the targeted problem. Once implemented, a policy's consequences may lead stakeholders, policymakers, and policy analysts to reevaluate how the "what should we do?" question was answered. Even the best ex ante policy analysis is an exercise in crystal-ball gazing. It may be a systematic and informative form of crystal-ball gazing, but it is crystal-ball gazing nonetheless. Unforeseen events, unaccounted for consequences, and misunderstood causal relationships can result in a very different reality from the one projected in a policy analysis. The most careful cost-benefit projections, for example, may be undone by any number of factors that lower anticipated benefits or increase projected costs. The policy judged to provide maximum net social benefit in an ex ante analysis may prove to be a voracious consumer of public resources that produces few of the anticipated benefits.

Because of the uncertainty that policy analysis has to deal with, it is important to make judgments of the worth or benefit of a policy ex post as well as ex ante. Impact analysis (also known as quantitative program evaluation) is the field of policy studies devoted to systematically assessing what impact or effect a public policy has actually had on the real world, and as such is the ex post counterpart of ex ante policy analysis. The latter is the prospective (and, frequently, the prescriptive) assessment of how the coercive powers of the state can/should be used to address a problem or issue of concern. Impact analysis is the retrospective assessment of policies that have been adopted and implemented. If the fundamental question of policy analysis is "what should we do?" then the fundamental question motivating impact analysis is "what have we done?" More formally, impact analysis is defined as "determining the extent to which one set of directed human activities (X) affected the state of some objects or phenomena $(Y_1 \ldots Y_k)$ and . . . determining why the effects were as small or large as they turned out to be" (Mohr 1995, 1). Using Mohr's definition, X represents a program or policy and Y is the observed or intended outcome of the policy.

Generally speaking, it is the ex post nature of impact analysis that conceptually distinguishes it from policy analysis as discussed in the previous chapter, not methodology. Cost-benefit analyses, for example, can be conducted ex post. As described in the chapter on policy analysis, CBA is a tool to systematically answer the question of what *should* be done. Conducted in the impact analysis framework, a CBA is an assessment of what *has* been done. Ex post, a CBA assesses whether X (a program or policy) has resulted in a particular outcome Y (in this case efficient allocation of resources). A CBA is arguably of less practical use in the latter case; it can assess whether a policy results in a net social benefit, but this information does not allow policymakers to revisit their decisions if the policy turns out to be inefficient. Ex post cost analyses, however, provide an important evaluative function and can inform decisions on whether to make changes in a program or policy. Providing this sort of practical, applied, and often narrowly targeted information is often what impact analyses are intended to do. These are the sorts of broader questions that motivate impact analysis: What is the policy actually doing? What outcomes is it effecting? Is it worth the money it costs? Should it be continued, expanded, cut back, changed, or abandoned? (Weiss 1998, 6).

Like policy analysis, impact analysis has struggled with the question of how to go about answering the questions that define it as a field of study. Impact analysis is squarely in the rationalist tradition, and the same post-positivist criticisms that are launched against policy analysis are also made against impact analysis. Yet while the clash between the rationalist project and its post-positivist critics rings at least as loud in impact analysis as it does in policy analysis, at some level impact analysis has a more straightforward theoretical challenge than policy analysis. Policy analysis cannot proceed without coming to some accommodation with the normative justifications for government action. Whether it is efficiency, effectiveness, distributional concerns, or some other yardstick, policy analysis has to impose a normative yardstick to differentiate between alternate policy options. An impact analysis also has to deal with a range of normative difficulties, but dealing with the consequences rather than the justifications of public policy puts a slightly different spin on these normative issues. The fact that a policy exists suggests that somebody at some point must have believed that it would achieve some goal that justified deploying the resources and coercive powers of the state. The central theoretical challenge of impact analysis, then, is not justifying the normative values used to rank policy alternatives. It is more about identifying those objectives and the actions taken to achieve those objectives and then understanding the causal beliefs that link the two. In other words, an impact analysis does not justify the normative values motivating a public policy, it just has to empirically test the causal claim between the means (the policy) and the end (the policy objective). This represents a fairly clear contrast with the central problem of theory in policy analysis, which is providing some normative justification for deploying the resources and coercive powers of the state in the first place.

In practice, of course, these issues become considerably messier. Impact analysis has nearly as hard a time escaping the gravitational pull of normative concerns that bedevil policy analysis. For one thing, public policies and programs are not always adopted with clear objectives, and different stakeholders may attach very different goals to the same policy or program. There may be wildly different beliefs about the causal mechanisms that connect means and ends, and these can (and often are) charged with political meaning. Judging policies as successes or failures on the basis of an empirical test first requires what goals to measure and how to measure them; that choice alone may determine whether an impact analysis concludes that a particular policy is working or not. In education policy, for example, deciding whether to measure educational performance using standardized tests, graduation rates, or some other metric can provide contradictory notions on whether particular educational policies are or are not achieving their desired objectives (Smith and Granberg-Rademacker 2003).

In this chapter we are going to address the key issues and conceptual frameworks involved in trying to evaluate the actual impact of public policy and try to come to some understanding of how policy scholars go about answering the question "what have we done?"

Impact Analysis and Program Evaluation

Impact analysis is actually one part of a much broader field of policy studies called program (or policy) evaluation. Program evaluation, like many concepts in the field of policy studies, has been formally defined in different ways. Such definitions include the "effort to understand the effects of human behavior, and in particular, to evaluate the effects of particular programs . . . on those aspects of behavior indicated as the objectives of this intervention" (Haveman 1987); the "assessment of the overall effectiveness of a national program in meeting its objectives, or an assessment of the relative effectiveness of two or more programs in meeting common objectives" (Wholey et al. 1970, 15); and the "systematic assessment of the operation and/or the outcomes of a program or policy, compared to a set of explicit or implicit standards, as a means of contributing to the improvement of the program or policy" (Weiss 1998, 4). What the various definitions of program evaluation tend to have in common, and what conceptually separates program evaluation from other types of policy studies, is its focus on the consequences of actually initiating a public policy or program, and/or the judgment of these consequences based on some (normative) yardstick (Scriven 1967; Lester and Stewart 2000, 126).

Taken as an entire field, program evaluation is perhaps the most Lasswellian of all areas of policy studies. At its core program evaluation is an explicitly normative enterprise; the motivation is the desire to compare *what is* with *what should be.* Program evaluation is thus ultimately about determining the worth of a program or policy on the basis of some criteria; it is the systematic attempt to assess whether a program or policy is "good" or "worthy" (Scriven 1967; good discussions of purposes of evaluation and the normative and subjective issues that motivate it as a field of study can be found in Talmage 1982; Mark, Henry, and Julnes 1999; Patton 2000; and Fitzpatrick, Sanders, and Worthen 2004, 4–8). Yet in making such assessments, program evaluators employ the full range of (especially quantitative) methods of social science.

Unfortunately, as the most Lasswellian of policy studies it is also the most amorphous—even more so than policy analysis. The demand for evaluation is ubiquitous, within both the public and private sectors, and evaluations can range from academic studies to reports by management consultants, to formal program reviews by the Government Accountability Office, to informal assessments by program managers. It is reasonable to portray the general field of program evaluation as more applied than academically oriented, a point that a number of well-known introductions to the field make explicit. Weiss (1998, 15), for example, has argued that program evaluation differs from more academic approaches to studying policy because of its fundamentally pragmatic raison d'être. According to Weiss, evaluation is more aimed at informing and improving policy rather than generating knowledge per se, and the knowledge generated by program evaluations is often seen as policy and program specific, rather than cumulatively building into a body of generalizable knowledge that applies across different policies and programs. This narrow theoretical focus may explain why program evaluations are often less oriented toward academic publication and more oriented toward applied audiences.[1]

In one sense, program evaluation is probably as old as organized human activity. Figuring out what worked (or did not) and why was as important to the Romans as it is to modern-day public authorities. Formal evaluations, especially in the education field, have a history of at least 150 years, dating back to Horace Mann's annual report on education in

Massachusetts in the 1840s (Fitzpatrick, Sanders, and Worthen 2004, 31). The modern discipline of evaluation, though, traces its roots to many of the same origins as policy analysis: It grew out of a recognition that social science could be useful in guiding public policy; got a significant boost in the 1960s because of demand to assess the impact of big new federal social welfare programs; and developed into a profession with dedicated graduate programs and publications in the 1970s, 1980s, and 1990s. Like the whole field of policy studies, even as graduate curriculums expanded and journals proliferated to disseminate evaluation theory and practice, program evaluation struggled to define itself as a field. Evaluation has been described as a "transdiscipline" that is employed across fields in a comparable sense to logic or statistics (Fitzpatrick, Sanders, and Worthen 2004, 42).

Although there is some conceptual core to the notion of program evaluation, it is also clearly something of an elastic concept that can mean different things to different people. Subsumed under the umbrella of "program evaluation" are a number of distinct ex post conceptual approaches that extend beyond impact analysis. Unfortunately, there is no universally agreed upon definition of the scope and particular subfields of policy evaluation, though a number of typologies seek to clarify these conceptual differences and provide some order to the field (e.g., Trisko and League 1978; Scriven 1991; Mohr 1995; Bingham and Felbinger 2002, 4–8; Smith and Licari 2007, 161–164; Dunn 1981). The most common of these efforts are a pair of twinned categorizations: formative and summative evaluations, and process and outcome evaluations.

Formative and summative evaluations. Formative and summative evaluations are distinguished by timing and by the intent of the individual conducting the study. Formative studies are undertaken in the early stages and are intended to inform the development of a program or policy. Formative evaluations, then, are timed to be *in medias res*, as opposed to ex ante or ex post. A formative evaluation is undertaken when critical decisions have been made and a program or policy has at least some embryonic implementation but is not so developed that policymakers cannot make adjustments to the policy, taking advantage of empirical study to better match means to the desired ends.

Summative evaluations are done at a different part of a program or policy life cycle; the basic role of a summative evaluation is to decide whether to expand, contract, terminate, or continue a program. Summative evaluations, then, are done when a program or policy is relatively mature and are intended to assess the overall worth in the context of whatever values the program or policy is being judged by. While timing clearly differentiates summative and formative evaluations, intent is the more important discriminator. Formative evaluations essentially ask: "should we change anything that we are doing?" Summative evaluations ask: "should we keep doing what we're doing, do something different, or stop doing it altogether?" Scriven (1991, 19) put the difference between formative and summative evaluations this way: "When the cook tastes the soup, that's formative evaluation; when the guest tastes it, that's summative evaluation."

Process and outcome evaluations. Another useful way to categorize evaluation studies is to split them into process and outcome evaluations. Process evaluations focus on what a policy is actually doing, whereas outcome evaluations focus on what a policy has actually achieved.

Process evaluations assess policy actions' program activities with an eye toward these sorts of questions: Are program staff adequately trained to do the job? Is the program/policy operating according to the rules/laws /obligations that govern it? Are contractual obligations being met? Is the policy serving the target population it is supposed to be serving? (Weiss 1998, 75; Bingham and Felbinger 2002, 4). The basic function of a process evaluation is to see whether the actions of those charged with putting a policy into practice (typically a public agency) match the plans and goals that justified the policy in the first place. Process evaluations, then, are oriented toward issues such as compliance (assessing whether a policy or program meets the laws and regulations that authorize and govern its operation) and auditing (assessing whether a target population is receiving the resources or services mandated by the policy or program). A good deal of what is being termed here as process evaluations overlaps with the study of policy implementation; implementation is discussed in depth in Chapter 7.

In contrast to a process evaluation, an outcome evaluation seeks to measure and assess what a policy has actually achieved. Impact analysis is a specific form of outcome evaluation, i.e., a quantitative outcome evaluation. These are the sorts of questions that motivate an impact analysis: Is the policy having any impact on the problem it was designed to address? If it is having an impact, how much of an impact? If it is not having an impact, why not?

To understand the process/outcome distinction, consider the following example. An increase in drunk driving has become a high-profile issue for a municipality. An ex ante policy analysis concludes that the most efficient way to lower drunk driving rates is to implement a program of checkpoints on key roads and heavily advertise that the police are cracking down on drunk driving. Accordingly, the police department implements random checkpoints on these roads and begins a public relations campaign warning drivers that law enforcement is making a point to catch drunk drivers and that the consequences of being caught driving while under the influence impose significant costs on those convicted. A process evaluation of this policy would focus on issues such as whether the checkpoints comply with the civil rights of the drivers, whether they are placed in the best spots to catch drunk drivers, and whether there are enough of them to significantly increase the probabilities of catching drunk drivers. An impact analysis, on the other hand, will focus on whether the number of drunk drivers has decreased as a result of the checkpoint policy, and if so, by how much (Smith and Licari 2007, 162).

Dividing the policy evaluation field into formative/summative and process/outcome categories helps impose some order on a sprawling area of policy studies. However, there is also clear overlap among these categories, and this can lead to confusion. Some scholars seem to view summative/formative studies more as process evaluations (e.g., Scriven 1991), whereas others view formative and summative evaluations as particular types of outcome evaluations (e.g., Mohr 1995, 32). Weiss (1998, 32–33) has suggested that though it is possible to conceptually distinguish between the two pairs of terms based on timing, evaluator intent, and phase of the policy, the most useful way to think about policy evaluation is in process and outcome terms. The original purpose of policy evaluation, after all, was to assess outcomes, to figure out the consequences of public policy. Process studies fit naturally into this effort because they can help explain why the consequences of policy are what they are.

There are three basic approaches to process and outcome program evaluations that can be distinguished by distinct questions. The first is the descriptive evaluation approach, which seeks to describe goals, processes, and outcomes rather than form judgments about them. At the core of the descriptive approach are questions about whether something *is*: Is the goal (or goals) clearly articulated? Is the goal (or goals) clearly communicated? Is there a plan for assessing progress or success? Is there clear accountability? The second approach is normative. At the core of normative program evaluations are questions about the worth of what is being done: Is the goal realistic? Does the policy advance socially desirable goals? Finally, there is the impact approach, which focuses on the outcomes of a policy: To what extent did the policy achieve its goals? How can variation in this outcome be confidently assigned to the policy? Exactly how much of the variation is attributable to the outcome or policy?

Generally speaking, descriptive and normative approaches tend to use qualitative methods and fall into the formative/process categories of program evaluation (though with plenty of exceptions). Impact approaches are concentrated in the outcome category and, at least according to Mohr (1995, 32), are considered summative if they only assess whether a policy had a particular outcome and formative if they also explain why. Impact analysis is the rationalist project's core ex post approach to forming evaluative judgments of public policy and as such will be the focus of most of what follows.

Impact Analysis

An impact analysis is always built around three core elements: the problem, the activity, and the outcome of interest. The problem is some predicted outcome or condition that is considered unsatisfactory and that is expected to remain unsatisfactory without the intervention of a public policy or program. The activity is the human-directed events that constitute the policy, i.e., the state-directed actions undertaken to address the problem. The outcome of interest is the variable that is actually measured to evaluate the impact of the program on the problem (Deniston 1972; Mohr 1995, 3).

Impact analysis, then, goes about systematically answering the question of "what have we done?" by identifying and measuring some outcome of interest and empirically testing its relationship to the activity of the program or policy. This sounds simple enough in theory but can become complex very quickly in practice. For one thing, an impact analysis depends heavily on how an analyst chooses a dependent variable, i.e., an outcome of interest. The outcome of interest has to serve two critical functions. First, it has to operationalize an aspect of the problem. Second, it has to be a variable that can be causally linked to the program or policy.

This choice becomes complicated because the problems public policies are designed to address are often complex and multidimensional, and because programs and policies often have multiple, vague, or even contradictory outcomes. This is because public policies often have unclear goals, or multiple goals that are not prioritized or may even be contradictory (Hogwood and Gunn 1984, 234). This lack of clarity in goals injects an element of choice and subjectivity into the selection of an outcome of interest. The choices on the dependent variable can be echoed with the key independent variable(s). To take away any valid inferences, a researcher has to isolate the effects of the policy under study, not just from all the potential nonpolicy causes of the outcome of interest but from other policies or programs that may be aimed at the same problem.

As Mohr (1995, 25) has pointed out, a central problem here is that outcomes and problems are not necessarily the same thing. It is surprisingly easy to measure outcomes that do not really represent the targeted problem, or to choose an outcome that captures a relatively tangential impact of the program or policy. Test scores, for example, are widely employed as a general yardstick of educational performance and as such are frequently employed as the outcome of interest in impact analyses of education policies. Yet it is not clear that these tests even measure what they were designed to measure, let alone capture some vague and general concept like "educational performance" (Lemann 1995; Rothstein 1997).

Choosing an outcome of interest is further complicated by the fact that one policy may produce more than one outcome, and a single outcome may be influenced by more than one public policy. Mohr (1995, 39) even made a conceptual distinction between multiple outcomes and single outcomes with multiple elements. As an example of the latter, he used the utilization rate of hospitals, an outcome of significant interest in health care policy that consists of three separate parts: the number of patient admissions, length of stay, and resources used in hospital. These are not separate outcomes, rather interdependent elements of a single outcome.

What this means is that analysts typically have a range of options on how to operationalize an outcome of interest, and this choice can predetermine the conclusions of the study. Smith and Granberg-Rademacker (2003), for example, used six different measures of educational performance to test a range of hypotheses about education policies. The specific activities measured included instructional expenditures, the size of a school's bureaucracy, the percent of minority teachers, and the level of competition for educational services. They found that the link between these activities and educational outcomes was critically dependent not just on the choice of outcome of interest but also on the mix of policy activities included. These differences were not just in statistical significance but in substantive direction: the sign of the coefficients in their regression models switched directions across different model specifications. In other words, they concluded that the answer to "what have we done?" across a range of educational policies was a cautious "it depends," mostly on how a researcher operationalizes the outcome of interest and specifies the causal model used to explain it.

These sorts of challenges, unsurprisingly, open impact analysis to the same sorts of post-positivist criticisms leveled at policy analysis. The sophisticated quantitative techniques that characterize impact analysis present a scientific veneer, but lurking underneath are a set of normative biases that help predetermine conclusions (see Fischer 2003). This has led to some cynicism about the objective worth of not just impact analysis, but program evaluation generally. James Q. Wilson (1973b) proposed two immutable laws of policy evaluation. Wilson's First Law is that all policy interventions produce the intended effect . . . if the research is done by those who support the policy. Wilson's Second Law is that no policy intervention works . . . if the research is carried out by third parties who are skeptical of the policy. What drives the first law, Wilson argues, are data supplied by the agency managing the policy or program, a time period selected to maximize the policy's intended effect, and a lack of attention to alternate causes of the outcome of interest. What drives the second law are independently gathered data, a time period (typically short) that minimizes the impact of the policy, and a strong focus on variables that could also be causally linked to the outcome of interest. Wilson (tongue only partly in cheek) suggested that any program evaluation not explained by one of these laws is explained by the other.

The central problem here is not really the data chosen or the technical expertise used to analyze it, but political perspective and context. The primary job of an analyst operating from the rationalist framework (ex ante or ex post) is to provide policymakers with "honest numbers," defined as "policy data produced by competent researchers and analysts who use sound technical methods without the application of political spin to fit partisan needs" (Williams 1998, ix). Walter Williams, a primary advocate of this rationalist approach to analysis and evaluation, sees its main challenge not in the rationalist methods or training of analysts but in political spin and the incentives of partisan need. Policymakers do not always want honest numbers because they are politically distasteful. In this sort of political context, the temptation for policy analysts is to substitute neutral competence (analysis based solely on expertise) for responsive competence (expertise deployed to serve partisan preferences). Analysts in the rationalist tradition can still produce honest numbers; the real question is whether there is a market for their product. Williams claims that bad public policy is often supported by vast reams of supposedly rationalist research that in reality is tailored to sell an underlying political objective (Jones and Williams 2007). This, of course, undercuts the very notion of the rationalist project and makes "honest numbers" anything but.

Does this mean impact analysis unavoidably becomes just another form of partisanship, with the conclusions being driven by the preferences of the analyst producer and/or the policymaking consumer? Although some with post-positivist sympathies certainly argue along these lines, impact analysis makes a stronger claim to objectivity, i.e., to be capable of producing relatively neutral and data-driven answers to the core question of "what have we done?" Scholars such as Williams argue that analysts can (and do) produce honest numbers, data analysis that is not unduly spun or squeezed by partisan perspective. Producing those honest numbers, though, is critically dependent upon the logic and theory underpinning impact analysis.

The Logic and Theory of Impact Analysis

The objective of an impact analysis is clear: to determine whether a policy had an impact on an outcome of interest, and if so, by how much. Impact analysis is thus explicitly causal analysis, the goal is to make an assessment of whether X (a program or policy) caused Y (an outcome of interest), and if so, by how much. Impact analysis thus depends critically on how it addresses the logic of causality. How do we know when X has caused Y?

The concept of causality used in impact analysis is articulated most clearly by such people like Campbell and Stanley (1966) and Mohr (1995), and more broadly by King, Keohane, and Verba (1994). These works share a common logic for establishing a causal claim that is broadly shared throughout the social sciences. Generally speaking, there are three elements needed to support the claim that X causes Y: temporal precedence (if X causes Y, X must precede Y), co-variation (if X causes Y, then Y will change when X changes), and co-occurrence (if there is no X, there is no Y). The first two of these elements are, at least in the abstract, comparatively easy to empirically establish in ex post evaluations of public policy. We expect X (the program or policy) to precede observed changes in Y because the policy exists to bring about those changes and because no such changes are expected until X exists. Establishing co-variation in X and Y is trivial in quantitative terms as long as adequate measures of the policy activity (X) and the outcome of interest (Y) are available. Correlation coefficients, difference of means tests, and the like are often enough to test a statistical relationship between policy and an outcome of interest, and the full range of quantitative tools available to social science can be brought in as needed.

The critical challenge in making a causal claim, then, comes down to generating an estimate of the counterfactual, i.e., estimating what happens to Y in the absence of X. Assuming such an estimate can be generated, the impact of a policy boils down to the difference between the observed level of Y (the resultant), with an estimate of Y when there is no X (the counterfactual). To use Mohr's (1995) notation, I = R − C (impact equals resultant minus counterfactual). An impact analysis systematically answers the question "what have we done?" by identifying the key causal claim between policy activity and the outcome of interest, estimating a counterfactual, and comparing the counterfactual with the resultant. These needs create the two central theoretical challenges of impact analysis: 1) the need to identify the key causal link between policy activity and outcome of interest. A variety of conceptual frameworks can be employed to achieve this goal, though the generic approach is to employ program theory (discussed in detail below); 2) the need to generate a valid estimate of the counterfactual. This is typically handled through careful research design, and for impact analysis this relies heavily on reasoning borrowed directly from the scientific method.

Before examining program theory and research design, though, it is important to note that there are other approaches to policy evaluation that do not rely on the counterfactual to establish causality. These approaches tend to be qualitative (indeed, the absence of a counterfactual is used to conceptually define qualitative approaches to program evaluation; see Mohr 1995, 1999). These alternate approaches can usefully be described as "diagnostic" because they approach causality in much the same way that a medical diagnosis is done. Causality, in this approach, is inferred from symptoms, or from the physical traces of policy activity (these traces are sometimes referred to as "signatures" in policy literature; see Scriven 1967; George and McKeown 1985 for discussions of this approach to causality).

The diagnostic approach to causality is probably more intuitive than the counterfactual approach. Mohr (1999) used the examples of a person dying after a heart attack and a lamppost falling over after being struck by a car. Cause of death in a heart attack is established by noting symptoms consistent with this problem prior to death or through an autopsy that shows damage to the heart. When a car hits a lamppost, we can readily establish a physical cause of the lamppost falling over: the car smashed into it high. Compare both of these examples of establishing causality with the counterfactual approach. The counterfactual approach would require estimating whether the individual would have lived or died without having a heart attack, and estimating whether the lamppost would have fallen over without a car smashing into it. Stated like this, the counterfactual approach seems not only unduly complicated but counterintuitive.

But consider a public policy, say, a drug treatment program designed to target long-term drug users and keep them clean. One way to figure out what this program has done is to take a diagnostic approach, interview the people administering the treatment to get their assessments of the program's effectiveness, do the same with drug users enrolled in the program, and find out how many people enrolled in the program return to using drugs compared to those who stay drug free for a certain period of time. From these data an analyst can fashion an empirically supported answer to the question of what the program has done.

Let's say, however, that the people who administer the policy (the program staffers) view it as very successful, the program's clients (drug users), view it as moderately successful, and 50 percent of the people who enroll fall back into heavy patterns of drug use. What does this mean? Can we claim that the program is responsible for helping half of its clients kick their drug habits? What if the only people who seek out the program's treatment are individuals who genuinely want to be drug free and are committed to doing whatever it takes to achieve this goal? Should the program be judged as a success because it helps half of its clients, or a failure because it does not address the needs of the other half? It is hard to extract from this sort of mixed picture a clear notion of program impact; subjective perspective clearly plays a role in making this determination. From a post-positivist perspective, this is perfectly acceptable. Actually, it is probably more accurate to say that from a post-positivist perspective, there is no real alternative. If truth or reality is constructed from individual viewpoints, there is no independent, objective reality that has a privileged claim to the truth. The counterfactual approach argues otherwise in staking the claim that R − C is perspective free, or at least holds the promise of being more perspective free than any other alternative.

The counterfactual approach to determining the impact of our hypothetical drug program would identify the outcome of interest (say, the rate at which drug users seeking to kick the habit stay drug free for a certain period of time) and seek to compare the observed outcome of interest with the counterfactual. A valid counterfactual might be an estimate of the level of drug use for the same sort of population treated by the program in the absence of that program. In this approach, the judgment of what the program has or has not done boils down to R − C, an impact that can be quantified and readily attributed to the target policy. The big assumption here, of course, is that both the outcome of interest identified and the estimate of the counterfactual are meaningful (i.e., reflective of the underlying problem and the activity designed to address it) and valid. Such claims to validity are often debatable.

This makes the role of theory and research design absolutely critical in supporting the inferences taken from impact analysis. Impact analysis requires a conceptual framework that identifies the correct outcome of interest and explains its causal relationship with the policy activity, and it needs a logical design for generating empirical estimates of this outcome of interest in the absence of that activity. The theoretical frameworks that supply causal explanations for impact analysis come from a number of different places. Some are generalizable frameworks, or theories that make some claim to a universal explanation of human behavior. Public choice and institutional rational choice, for example, are predicated on a universal set of assumptions about human behavior (that humans are rational utility maximizers). This universal notion of why humans do what they do can be employed to help explain how and why institutional reforms would be expected to change certain behaviors. If these behaviors can be encapsulated in an outcome of interest variable, then a causal link between policy activity and outcome is established that can be empirically tested. For example, consider a regulatory policy that fines industries for emitting certain pollutants. The causal expectation here is that fines will create a rational incentive to reduce pollution. Isolating the unique impact of this regulatory policy on the variation in pollution levels provides empirical evidence of what the policy has (or has not) done.

Again, this sounds simple and straightforward in the abstract, but it can be highly complex in practice. For one thing, theory has to be able to identify the problem and the outcome of interest, which, as we've already seen, is not such an easy thing to do, especially within the boundaries of a single policy or program. Rather than generalizable frameworks such as rational choice, impact analysis is often guided by program theory.

Program Theory

Program theory constitutes "the set of beliefs that underlie action" (Weiss 1998, 55). Such beliefs do not have to be generalizable; they may be specific to the single program or policy under consideration. These causal beliefs do not even have to be correct. Program theory assumes that simply the existence of a policy represents a theory in the sense of a causal claim linking inputs to outputs. If policy is purposive, by definition it seeks to achieve some goal or objective. Logically, then, a policy represents some expectation that the activities it mandates will cause those objectives to be met. Impact analysis does not require a single program theory; there may be several theories that can be empirically tested.

A fairly standard approach to program theory is to construct an outcome line. In its simplest form, an outcome line is an exercise in backward induction. It begins with the ultimate desired outcome and from this starting point works backward, building a causal chain out of links consisting of activities and outcomes. The notion of an outcome line is readily grasped through an example. Consider a policy that seeks to increase teacher salaries as a means to increase student achievement. How will increasing teacher salaries increase student achievement? What justifies any public policy that seeks to achieve higher levels of student achievement? There are a number of potential answers to such questions, but from a society-wide perspective, higher levels of student achievement are associated with positive social outcomes, such as higher economic productivity and competitiveness, greater civic engagement, and a reduction in social ills ranging from criminal activity to teenage pregnancy. Let us assume that the ultimate desired outcome is greater economic productivity. How do higher teacher salaries result in this ultimate outcome? An outcome links the policy to the desired outcomes in this sort of fashion:

Higher teacher salaries (activity) → more qualified individuals attracted to teaching as a career (outcome) → schools hire more qualified teachers (activity) → more qualified teachers in the classroom (outcome) → more qualified teachers provide superior learning experience (activity) → student achievement increases (outcome) → students use human capital to advance their economic prospects (activity) → economic productivity increases

Though an extremely simplified example, this gets across the basic idea of program theory and an outcome line.[2] The outcome line makes explicit the causal beliefs that link the policy to its desired objectives. The immediate advantages of an outcome line are that it can help identify the outcome of interest and can alert a researcher to the activities and outcomes that may lie between the policy and this outcome of interest. According to Mohr (1995, 19), a well-constructed outcome line provides a ready method to identify the outcome of interest. One starts from the right and works leftward through the outcomes. The outcome of interest is the outcome where: 1) all outcomes to its right are considered immaterial (we do not care what those outcomes are, or even if they occurred); and/or 2) we are willing to assume that all outcomes to the right will happen if this outcome is achieved. In Mohr's (1995) terminology, the outcome of interest is the leftmost "inherently valued" outcome. In our example, working from left to right, student achievement is a likely candidate to be this leftmost inherently valued outcome and is thus identified as our outcome of interest.

Our outcome line, though, makes clear that the causal link between the policy and the outcome of interest is not direct; there are a number of linked activities and outcomes that have to fall into place. Mohr (1995, 32) calls outcomes that are prerequisites for the outcome of interest to be achieved policy "subobjectives." Subobjectives can be important, especially if the policy is found to have little or no impact on the outcome of interest. This is because they can provide crucial information on why this impact did not occur. If increasing teacher salaries did not attract more qualified people to the teaching profession, the causal beliefs linking policy to outcome of interest break down very early in the outcome line. This raises a question of how an analysis should treat subobjectives: should they be measured and included in an empirical analysis? Mohr's answer was, that it depends. If the central objective is simply to empirically assess whether the policy had an impact on the outcome of interest, then subobjectives can be ignored (this is what Mohr would term an impact summative analysis). If the objective is to also explain why (or why not) the policy caused changes in the outcome of interest, subobjectives should probably be accounted for (this is what Mohr would call a formative impact analysis).

There may be, of course, more than one set of causal beliefs linking a policy to outcomes (increasing teacher salaries may boost the morale of those already in the classroom and spur them to greater efforts that result in higher levels of student achievement). These can be included in an outcome line—there may be parallel and intertwining causal beliefs that connect a policy to an outcome in a variety of different ways, all of which can be plotted on an extended outcome line (see Weiss 1998, 63, for a good example).

Program theory constructed in this fashion has much to recommend it. It specifies the causal reasoning that justifies a policy and helps identify the outcome of interest. However, program theory is also the target of some justified criticisms. Program theory is often very narrow, a causal explanation that is limited to a single policy at a single time in a single place. This makes it an unlikely basis for building cumulative knowledge; a general theory of why policy does or does not work is unlikely to be fashioned out of outcome lines like the one given above. Program theory is also criticized for presenting an oversimplified model of reality. Student achievement is a complex phenomenon, and no outcome line is going to capture exactly how a single variable is going to shape that phenomenon simply because policymakers can manipulate that variable. Finally, program theory is vulnerable to a full range of post-positivist criticisms about what outcomes and activities are selected to be included in the causal chain. Program theory, remember, is often an unabashedly normative notion of how the world works; it is a framework that makes explicit causal beliefs. These beliefs, and thus the program theory, can arise from a number of different sources, including the biases of the analyst. Some critics raise doubt about any individual's ability to consistently identify the true causal mechanisms at work; it is simply too much of a complex and multivariate world. Others argue that program theory is too reductionist; it seeks to understand "what have we done?" by breaking the world down into simple causal chains. It may be that the answer to "what have we done?" can only come from a more holistic view, that outcomes are more than a sum of unrealistically simple and isolated parts (see Shadish, Cook, and Leviton 1991; Cook and Shadish 1994).

Impact analysis, though, does not rely on program theory or an outcome line to make a formal assessment of causality. It uses these conceptual tools to identify the outcome of interest and the causal beliefs linking it to the policy activity. It seeks to assess causality, i.e., whether X brought about changes in Y, by generating a valid estimate of the counterfactual. If X (higher teacher salaries) causes Y (greater student achievement), then Y should look different if there is no X. Once the outcome of interest and the causal beliefs are identified, the key issue in making a formal assessment of whether X has an impact on Y, and if so by how much, is the estimate of the counterfactual. That is more an area of research design than program theory.

Research Design in Impact Analysis

In impact analysis, research design can be defined as the system or means used to estimate a counterfactual. Any impact analysis research design faces the same crucial challenge: how to create equivalency, i.e., how to create a counterfactual that is equivalent in all aspects to the resultant except for the presence of the public policy or program. There are three basic designs to achieve this end—experimental, quasi-experimental, and correlational—and seminal works linking these different approaches to the counterfactual concept of causality employed in impact analysis include Campbell and Stanley (1966); Cook and Campbell (1979); Mohr (1995); and Shadish, Cook, and Campbell (2002). All three frameworks seek to estimate an equivalent estimate of the counterfactual; the key difference among the research designs is how the equivalent comparison group is created.

The true experimental design is widely considered the flagship approach to impact analysis (Rossi and Freeman 1993, 307). In experimental designs the target population is randomly assigned into treatment groups (those who actually receive program benefits) and control groups (those who receive no program benefits). Any observed difference on the outcome of interest is assumed to be a product of random chance (which can be assessed statistically) or caused by the policy. The experimental group's measure on the outcome of interest is thus used as R, and the control group's measure as C, and the impact of the policy as R − C. Though experimental designs come in numerous variants, all share the same basic logic, i.e., the power of randomization creates real equivalency between control and experimental groups, allowing for valid comparisons of R and C (see Mohr 1995 for a thorough discussion of variants of the experimental design).

Of course, the power of experimental designs is predicated on the assumption an analyst (or some other central authority) actually has the power to randomize subjects and thus manipulate the key independent variable (i.e., who does or does not get the policy benefits). When these assumptions hold, experimental designs can represent a social science analogy to the laboratory benchmarks of the hard sciences and justifiably can be considered "flagship" or "gold standard" means of estimating a counterfactual. In the policy realm, however, it is relatively rare for an analyst to have this sort of control. There are good practical, legal, and ethical reasons for this. Randomly withholding, say, educational benefits from a group of disadvantaged youth in order to assess the impact of a reading program will strike many of those assigned to a control group (and certainly their parents) as unfair and may be considered unethical by the governing policy authority or an institutional review board. Even when such control is granted, running such experiments can be resource intensive—a pilot jobs program that involves randomly selecting participants from a designated sample, for example, may take months to implement and may require considerable funding.

Though challenging to execute, experimental designs are not impossible, and true randomized field trials have yielded important insights into the impacts of a wide variety of public policies (for a review, see Burtless 1995). In the field, however, it is often hard to sustain the assumptions of randomization that provide validity to the experimental design's claims to causal explanation. In education, for example, there have been a number of randomized field trials aimed at assessing the impact of school vouchers on outcomes of interest like academic achievement. These are made possible because the demand for vouchers in some programs exceed supply and were thus awarded by lottery—in effect, random assignment.

At first blush, this seems like a perfect opportunity to leverage the power of experimental design to get a true estimate of the impact of vouchers. Given the significant controversy of what vouchers do (or do not) contribute to education outcomes, such an impact analysis could make an important contribution to a high-profile policy debate. The experimental nature of these sorts of field trials, however, tends to break down quickly. To begin with, the experimental and control groups are not necessarily representative of the target population—all public school students—but just those actively seeking a voucher, and there are good reasons to suspect the latter group is systematically different from the former. Attrition also tends to be a problem; as much as 50 percent of those who received vouchers dropped out of the program within a semester or so (i.e., they returned to their assigned public school). If there is any systematic commonalities to those who drop out—again, there are reasons to believe this is the case—randomization is lost and with it the power of experimental designs (General Accounting Office 2001, 2002; Ladd 2002; Metcalf, Beghetto, and Legan 2002).

One of the great advantages of quasi-experimental designs is that they avoid many of the practical limitations of putting experimental designs into practice. At their core, quasi-experimental designs follow the same structure as experimental designs except for randomization.[3] Rather than randomization, equivalency is created by systematically selecting a comparison group (in quasi-experiments, the counterfactual group is called a comparison rather than a control). Obviously, the key issue in quasi-experimental designs, then, is how the comparison group is selected. There are numerous options. Comparison groups can be selected on the basis of their similarity to the experimental group on a set of reference variables. For example, the impact of a community policing program might be assessed by comparing crime rates in cities of roughly similar size and demographics, some of which have a community policing program and some that do not. Similarly, a group of individuals may be systematically assigned to experimental (or treatment) and comparison groups so that both are balanced in terms of socioeconomics, age, gender, or whatever variables are believed important to creating equivalency.

Probably one of the most common quasi-experimental approaches in impact analysis are versions of interrupted time series analysis, which at heart is a simple before-and-after comparison.[4] The basic idea is to take repeated measures across time on the outcome of interest for the unit of analysis, with the introduction of the program or policy occurring somewhere in the middle of those repeated measures. The counterfactual here is intuitively equivalent because it represents not just a similar group to that which actually received policy or program benefits—it is the same group. Consider, for example, the problem of assessing the impact of a crime policy on state crime rates. In an experimental design an analyst would randomly assign these policies to states and observe the crime rate differences between states with and without this particularly policy. No central authority—let alone any single policy analyst—has the power to randomly assign policies to sovereign governments, so the experimental design is impractical. A quasi-experimental option is to use a time trend on crime rates that is bisected, or interrupted, by introduction of the policy. So you get a time series of crime rates over, say, forty years, when the policy is adopted at year twenty. The counterfactual is estimated using the measures before the policy, the resultant using the measures after its introduction.

This approach is attractive because impact analyses can take advantage of the fact that outcome of interest measures exist for many public policies and programs before and after they were adopted. The big problem, of course, is that the world is not static, and outcomes of interest like crime rates can vary considerably across time for a lot of reasons beyond the introduction of policy. An interrupted time series design as just described would likely take the form of a multiple regression analysis that included controls for other causes of crime rates. This shifts the design away from a quasi-experimental design, where equivalency is achieved through careful selection of the group or unit of analysis used to estimate the counterfactual, to a purely correlational design, where there are no real control or comparison groups. Technically a correlational design is one where there is no centralized selection on who does or does not receive program benefits; individuals (or social aggregates) decide themselves whether to adopt or take advantage of the policy. There are no consciously selected control or comparison groups; all an analyst can do is observe and try to create equivalency by statistically controlling for alternate causes of the outcome of interest. Because there is no conscious selection underlying the estimate of the counterfactual and no real manipulation of the key independent variable—just observations of variance— the correlational design has the weakest claim to generating valid estimates of the counterfactual.

Assuming equivalence can be achieved statistically, correlational designs do provide valid estimates of a counterfactual (see Mohr 1995). However, in most cases correlational designs practically translate into garden variety multiple regression analyses, which are always vulnerable to specification debates. In other words, there is usually some basis for claiming that equivalency has not been achieved because some important cause of the outcome of interest has been excluded from the model, or because some irrelevant variable has been included. As the preceding discussion suggests, the line between quasi-experimental and correlational designs is not clear-cut. Impact analysis routinely makes use of statistical control techniques even in experimental designs (randomized field trials of school vouchers, for example, have used statistical controls to control for attrition in the experimental or control groups). This makes the counterfactual concept of causality vulnerable to post-positivist criticisms that values can readily creep into even a well-intentioned and executed impact analysis; because inferred impacts are critically dependent on these controls, the choice of controls can determine the conclusions of an impact analysis. Proponents of straightforward quantitative impact analysis acknowledge such possibilities but argue that "normative creep" can be reduced (if not eliminated) by subjecting ex post conclusions to the same sorts of sensitivity analysis that is common to ex ante prescriptive studies. In short, if choice of statistical controls can manipulate the estimate of the counterfactual, then the analysis should be run with different sets of controls to make their influence clear (see Smith and Granberg-Rademaker 2003).

Assuming that, regardless of research design approach, a valid estimate of the counterfactual is obtained, an impact analysis will provide a precise estimate of the effect of a program or policy: impact equals resultant minus counterfactual ($I = R - C$). If the goal(s) of the policy can be expressed as a point estimate of the outcome of interest, the effectiveness of the policy can also be quantitatively assessed through an effectiveness ratio: effectiveness = $R - C / P - C$ (where "P" is the planned or projected level of the outcome of interest). An effectiveness ratio is intuitive; it represents the proportion of the policy's goal that has been achieved on a given outcome of interest. A policy with an effectiveness ratio greater than one has exceeded its goals (it is more than 100 percent effective), one that is less than one is short of the planned level of the outcome of interest (see Mohr 1995 for an in-depth discussion of these measures).

This, ultimately, is what impact analysis strives for—"honest numbers." More formally, it seeks a precise, quantitative answer to the question of "what have we done?" The utility and validity of that answer is tied to a number of issues, but most critical are the counterfactual notion of causality and the strength of the research design. Without a valid estimate of the counterfactual, R − C, regardless of the sophistication of the methods and measures, is at best an educated guess.

Conclusion

A central focus of ex post facto policy studies is the impact of a public policy or program. Public policies are purposive social mechanisms; they are designed to change the existing state of the world. Exactly what policy is directed toward and what it is expected to change are all issues that can be considered ex ante, but adopting and implementing a program even on the basis of careful policy analysis is no guarantee it will actually achieve its objectives. The fundamental question of ex post policy studies, then, boils down to this: what have we done?

Impact analysis offers a systematic framework to provide answers to this question. Impact analysis is useful because it is not tied to any single causal theory; rather, it is based on a logical understanding of causality. Impact analysis does not require a universal theory, or even a universal normative yardstick like efficiency as a basis for judging policy. What it needs is some notion of the causal beliefs linking a policy activity and an outcome of interest. These beliefs do not even have to be correct; they simply have to provide an explanation of why X is expected to change Y. This does not require a general theory such as rational choice; the causal beliefs linking X and Y can just as easily be drawn from ideology or broader political expectations. What impact analysis seeks to test is the empirical validity of these causal claims, regardless of their origin.

To do this, impact analysis relies on the counterfactual notion of causality. This is why research design is such a critical element of impact analysis; a research design constitutes the means to estimate the counterfactual, and a valid estimate requires less of a perfect theory but more of a robust research design. Impact analysis is subject to a broad set of objections from post-positivist critics. These criticisms have some merit. An impact analysis is wholly dependent upon generating a valid estimate of the counterfactual, and this is only possible if the correct activity and outcome of interest have been identified and accurately measured, if the causal link connecting them is accurately understood, and if these elements are brought together in a robust and well-thought-out research design. This constitutes a lot of "ifs."

Still, impact analysis is unusual in the field of policy studies in that it offers a comparatively clear and clean systematic framework, one supported by well-thought-out internal logic, and readily amenable to a wide variety of theories and quantitative methods. As such, impact analysis offers a compelling epistemological framework for generating and defending answers to the core question of ex post policy studies: what have we done?

Notes

1. That said, there are a number of field-specific policy evaluation journals, the most prominent of which is the *American Journal of Evaluation* (AJE), published under the auspices of the American Evaluation Association. The AJE publishes a broad variety of papers on the methods, theory, and applications of evaluation, many of them academic. The intended audience of the AJE, though, is intended to be as broad as possible, certainly far beyond the realms of academia. Currently there are easily a dozen or more professional journals dedicated to evaluation studies, including *Evaluation and Program Planning, Evaluation Practice, Evaluation Review,* and *Evaluation Quarterly.* Some of these journals are devoted solely to evaluation in specific policy areas, such as the *Studies in Educational Evaluation.*

2. Similar sorts of examples are found through well-known program evaluation texts such as Weiss (1998) and Mohr (1995).

3. Virtually every experimental design has a direct quasi-experimental analog (see Mohr 1995).

4. Although less common than interrupted time series designs, regression discontinuity designs are similar conceptually and methodologically. They arguably produce more valid estimates of the counterfactual but require an analyst (or some other central authority) to exercise assignment control, though in regression discontinuity this is on the basis of an assignment variable (e.g., the neediest get the program) rather than randomization. For a good overview of the pros and cons of experimental versus quasi-experimental designs, and also the pros and cons of various quasi-experimental approaches, see Shadish, Cook, and Campbell (2002).

CHAPTER SEVEN

How Does It Work?
Policy Implementation

The previous two chapters have focused on separate ends of a policy chain. On one end is the problem of deciding what should be done. On the other is the problem of figuring what has been done. In between are a lot of decisions and actions that causally connect one end of this chain to the other. Implementation research seeks to make sense of this space between government intention and policy impact.

This is a complicated and muddled piece of political geography that replicates the entire policy cycle, often more than once. From an implementation perspective, policy begins rather than ends with a formal declaration of what government is going to do. When Congress passes a law to, say, decrease pollutants in public waterways, the legislature does not adjourn to carry water filters down to the bank of the Potomac. The declaration of intent—the passage of a law—has to somehow be translated into reality.

That translation job is typically assigned to an executive branch agency (or agencies; implementation is often plural bureaucracy-wise). Under ideal circumstances, that agency has a two-stage challenge in implementing the policy intentions of the elected branches of government. First, it has to figure out exactly what the elected branch wants to do. Second, it has to figure out a way to do it.

Even under these ideal circumstances, implementation is not easy. Even a law that is fairly unambiguous about what should be done tends to be light on the specifics of how to do it. Agencies formally fill in these details through the process of formulating rules. Rules state the specific actions government will take, and formulating them involves a quasi-legislative process whose machinery mirrors the broader legislative process; hearings are held, lobbying is conducted, and there is give and take among interested parties with competing agendas (see Kerwin 1999). Assuming the rules are realistic and have practical enough guidelines for line-level bureaucrats to follow, and that these same bureaucrats are committed to putting them into action, there still remain coordination issues. Different units within agencies may interpret the rules differently, and even the most detailed set of rules cannot cover all contingencies likely to arise in the running of public programs of policies.

Ideal circumstances are fairly rare. More common are vague laws, overlapping jurisdictions, competing priorities for agency attention, and a thousand-and-one decisions that have to be made a long way from the formal rule-making process (not to mention the formal legislative process).

Surprisingly, policy scholars were relatively slow to recognize the importance of this bureaucracy-dominated gap between policy adoption and policy outcome. The conventional wisdom (not entirely correct, as we shall see) is that the systematic study of policy implementation did not begin until Jeffrey Pressman and Aaron Wildavsky's seminal study (1973)—in other words, a couple of decades after Lasswell called for a separate discipline of policy studies, and well after the laying of formal foundations for the rationalist project in policy evaluation and analysis. Once policy scholars turned to implementation, however, they were immediately clear about its importance.

The key issue for implementation studies is figuring out how a policy works, or more accurately given the often noted failure bias of implementation studies, how a policy does not work.

Three Generations of Implementation Studies

Though one of the most complex areas in policy studies, the field of implementation's definitional issues over the core concept are perhaps more straightforward. Widely cited definitions include those suggested by Mazmanian and Sabatier (1983, 5), Ferman (1990), and O'Toole (1995), all of which focus on the gap between policy intent and policy outcomes. O'Toole's (1995, 42) definition serves as a good representative example, saying that policy implementation "refers to the connection between the expression of governmental intention and results." Although numerous scholars proffer more detailed definitions, all are variations on this basic theme. Implementation is what happens after government declares a formal intent to do something and before a policy outcome has been produced.

As mentioned in the previous chapter, the field of policy evaluation overlaps considerably with implementation studies, especially in the sense of taking stock of agency actions to see if they should be adjusted to improve outcomes. Specifically, what we termed as process evaluation in the last chapter is clearly oriented toward assessing programmatic activities that link policy intent and policy outcome. Key questions of process evaluation—do program staff know what they are supposed to be doing? Are they qualified to do it? Do they have the necessary resources to carry out that task?—are intimately linked to implementation success or failure. As such, our discussion of implementation studies covers much of the same ground as process evaluation, and at least for our purposes the latter should be treated as a subset of the former.

Implementation studies begin with the realization that a formal adoption of a policy goal does not necessarily provide any direction on what should be done to achieve that goal. As Mazmanian and Sabatier put it, "Knowing the [policy] objectives . . . [gives] only a general hint of what will actually be done by the agency responsible for carrying out the program and how successful it will be at winning the cooperation and compliance of the persons affected by it" (1983, 4–5). The key research questions for implementation scholars like Mazmanian and Sabatier are closely linked to process evaluation concerns: "Could the outcome have been different? Can we learn from experience and avoid similar problems in designing future public programs?" (1983, 2).

The importance of implementation to policy success or policy failure is intuitively obvious. It matters little if the government has a clear notion of what should be done if the agency charged with implementing the law lacks the ability to actually do it. Assessing precisely what has been done provides important information, but understanding why outcomes were (or were not) achieved is critical if policy success is to be replicated or policy failure to be avoided. Given the obvious importance of implementation to policy success or failure, it is somewhat surprising to find that implementation studies (at least in mainstream political science) were relatively rare creatures until the late 1970s and early 1980s. When they did begin to appear, however, implementation studies made a big splash. The potential value of implementation studies was clear: a systematic understanding of what connected policy intent to a successful policy outcome would go a long way to fulfilling Lasswellian notions of what the policy sciences were all about. A systematic understanding of implementation could make democratic policymaking work better.

Unfortunately, as we shall see, such a systematic understanding remains a long way off. Following Goggin et al. (1990), the field of implementation studies is traditionally divided into three generations (and, perhaps, an emerging fourth generation). The story of implementation research across these generations starts with excitement over the possibility of breaking new intellectual ground, maturity and with it a more sober assessment of the intellectual challenges, to an ongoing debate over whether implementation studies are poised to move forward and fulfill their original promise or constitute an intellectual dead end and should be abandoned altogether (see Lester and Goggin 1998).

First-Generation Implementation Studies: Understanding Implementation Is Important

The first generation of implementation studies began, undoubtedly, with a seminal book by Jeffrey Pressman and Aaron Wildavsky (1973): *Implementation: How Great Expectations in Washington Are Dashed in Oakland.* The focus of the book was the federal government's attempt to create 3,000 jobs in inner-city Oakland. What really motivated Pressman and Wildavsky was not this particular policy per se, but rather its spectacular failure to achieve its policy objectives. What was surprising, at least initially, about the inability of the government to achieve its policy objectives was that context seemed to, if not preordain, then at least favor success.

Pressman and Wildavksy (1973) argued that the focus of their case study was, in effect, a best-case scenario for policy implementation. To start with, there was general agreement on the objectives of the policy; no organized constituency sought to stymie its success. There was a reasonably unambiguous objective (create jobs in inner-city Oakland), and broad agreement that this objective was a worthwhile undertaking, especially in the particular political context of the time. Jobs had followed "white flight" out of the cities in the 1960s, and high unemployment and lack of economic opportunities had triggered civil unrest. Creating inner-city jobs was seen as a reasonable answer to the "what should we do?" question.

The policy was also focused—it targeted a single city, Oakland, California—and it was (at least in theory) under the control of a single federal agency, the Economic Development Agency (EDA), that was committed to its success. Resources were not a problem; ample funds were available to support the program, and a lot of money was spent. Yet the policy failed miserably, producing few jobs and leaving much frustration in its wake. Pressman and Wildavsky wanted to know why policies like this, best-case scenarios with the stars seemingly aligned for success, failed. Their intensive case study brought the complex world between policy intention and policy outcome to the attention of a broad audience in political science. What they found set the foundation for an explosive growth in implementation studies, for what they found wasn't pretty.

The central lesson to be taken from Pressman and Wildvasky was that complexity of joint action is a central obstacle for effective implementation. The federal system of the United States means that virtually any domestic policy is dependent upon multiple layers of government and its agencies. Interactions among these various government entities are complex, and coordination difficult. Potential roadblocks to implementation range from jurisdictional turf battles, to resource constraints, to clashing management styles.

For example, Pressman and Wildavsky (1973) found that broad agreement on ends does not necessarily translate into agreement on means. Just because all parties support the same policy outcome does not mean they agree on the best way to go about achieving that goal. Each government agency can have its own perspective, not just on how things should be done, but on who should do them. Different levels of government, and different government agencies at the same level of government, may also have very different priorities. Whereas all may generally agree that a particular policy objective is worthwhile, they may prioritize that objective differently. Government agencies tend to be committed to multiple programs and policies, and the level of commitment to a specific program or policy is driven by agency perspective. Getting all of these agencies to adopt a general plan on means, to synchronize their priorities, and to generally share the same vision of a policy or program turned out to be the governmental equivalent of herding cats.

Perhaps the most cited lesson from Pressman and Wildavsky's (1973) study was their insight into decision points and the importance of control and coordination. Creating jobs through public works and other programs in Oakland required the involvement of state and local authorities; and other federal agencies inevitably become involved too. To get anything substantive done thus required getting a wide range of agencies at different governmental levels to approve key implementation decisions. Pressman and Wildavsky found that the more approvals that have to be granted for an action to be taken, the higher the likelihood that that action would *not* be taken. To quantify this point, Pressman and Wildavsky provided an example where thirty decision points have to be cleared, involving seventy separate required agreements before an action can be approved and undertaken. Assuming a .95 probability of approval at each agreement point, Pressman and Wildavsky calculated that the probability of a particular proposal running this bureaucratic gauntlet and actually being implemented is .000395 (1973, 106–107). In other words, when dealing with a dispersed decision-making system, one's chances of getting anything done are low—often astonishingly low—even when most people want to do it. Even if the odds are overcome, getting anything done is going to take a long time. Pressman and Wildavsky estimated that each of those seventy agreements would require one to six weeks to secure, which resulted in an estimate that the Oakland project would face four-and-a-half years' worth of delays. Their estimate proved to be fairly accurate (1973, 106–107).

A contemporary first-generation study that is still widely cited in the implementation literature is Martha Derthick's (1972) examination of a federal program to build model communities on federally owned land in urban areas. This was a project that grew out of President Lyndon Johnson's administration in the late 1960s and was designed to address the social and economic problems that developed in the wake of urban sprawl, which created low-density suburbs surrounding a socioeconomically depressed urban center. The program began with lofty ideals and goals, to address a growing metropolitan crisis by building self-contained centrally planned "new towns" that would be socially and racially integrated. Like the EDA's attempt to generate jobs in Oakland, the program was a spectacular failure, and Derthick's examination of the implementation process echoes the lamentations of Pressman and Wildavsky.

Derthick was particularly attuned to the opposing perspectives at different governmental levels and to the difficulties of centralized coordination over implementation. What looked like a good idea from the federal level encountered stiff opposition at the local level. Conservationist groups wanted to protect the open lands, and neighborhood associations feared the new housing plans would bring racial imbalance. This led to intense opposition and conflict at the local level, which translated into strong local government resistance to the federal plans. This opposition had really not been accounted for in the federal government's vision of the policy, and it had trouble adjusting to the reality on the ground (Derthick 1972, 98). What began with noble and idealized hopes sputtered and sank because of the difficulties of implementation.

Though Derthick's and Pressman and Wildavsky's studies reflected some important differences in context, they shared some key takeaway points. First and foremost was that not enough thought and attention was devoted to implementation given its importance to policy success. While planners and academics lavished attention on how to decide what to do and how to assess what had been done, there were too many assumptions and not enough knowledge about what happened between these two points in the policy change. The overwhelming impression from reading Derthick and Pressman and Wildavsky was that the real surprise wasn't that public policies failed, it was that they ever worked at all. These studies threw a spotlight on implementation as a key reason for policy failure, and they also offered prescriptive advice on how to increase the odds of policy success: cut down on decision points, and push control and authority downward to allow those closest to the project to make important decisions quickly and effectively.

More important for a book on the theories of public policy, Derthick, and especially Pressman and Wildvasky, hinted that a systematic understanding of cause and effect in implementation might be possible. This suggested that general frameworks of implementation could be constructed, and a more valuable contribution of the policy sciences to successful democratic policymaking would not be hard to imagine. A general theory of implementation could help avoid repeats of the Oakland and new towns policy failures by laying out detailed steps for executing a particular policy or program, making democratic policymaking more effective. This was just the sort of contribution the Lasswellian ideal envisioned for the field of policy studies. By the end of the 1970s the race was on to construct a general framework of implementation, a systematic understanding of how policies worked.

Second-Generation Studies: Understanding Implementation Is Complex

First-generation implementation studies made important contributions, but they suffered a number of critical drawbacks. Most important, as case studies they were bound by time and space. They provided many details and a depth of understanding about what worked (or more often, did not work) for a particular program at a particular time, but not much could be systematically generalized to other programs in other contexts. The conclusions and prescriptions drawn from studies such as Pressman and Wildavsky provided motivation for constructing a theory of implementation, rather than an actual framework of cause and effect.

Noting these drawbacks, and with the attention of policy studies fully engaged with the problems of implementation, a second generation of implementation studies shifted focus from the examination of specific policies to the construction of general theories of the implementation process. One of the first notable attempts to construct such a framework was Eugene Bardach's *The Implementation Game* (1977). This study took an extended critique of Derthick and Pressman and Wildavsky as a jumping-off point for building a general understanding of implementation.

Bardach (1977) sought to make sense of implementation by classifying implementation into a series of games. He used the metaphor of games because it focused analysts' attention on the actors involved in implementation; the stakes they played for; the rules they played by; and the tactics, strategies, and resources each brought to the table. Using these as raw materials, Bardach sought to create a basic typology of implementation games. Like Derthick and Pressman and Wildavsky, Bardach was focused on what in implementation caused policy failure. He argued there are four basic "adverse effects" that can occur in the implementation process: 1) the diversion of resources; 2) the deflection of policy goals; 3) resistance to control; and 4) the dissipation of personal and political energy

(1977, 66). He categorized his description of games according to each of these adverse effects.

For example, the "budget game" diverted resources. The budget game springs from the incentives government agencies have to "move money." Unlike tangible policy outcomes, which can take years to show up, expenditures can be used as short-term assessment measures. Spending money shows that something is being done, even if it is not exactly clear what, why, or how it will support the ultimate policy objectives. Bardach pointed out in the Oakland jobs project studied by Pressman and Wildavsky (1973) that the EDA put resources into specific job-creating projects not because they were systematically assessed to be the best for these purposes, but because they were the projects that were ready to go. There was political pressure to be seen as doing something, and funneling money in jobs projects created the impression of purposive action, even if not many jobs ended up being created. Bardach saw this as one example of a general game played by all government agencies that serve as conduits of public money: "moving money somehow, somewhere, and fast, even at the price of programmatic objectives, is the characteristic strategy of virtually every government agency that channels grants to other levels of government or to nonprofit institutions" (1977, 72). Other games Bardach identified included "piling on" (deflecting goals by using new programs as Trojan horses for an agency's preferred goals), "tokenism" (resisting control by making only token efforts to programmatic goals), and "tenacity" (dissipating political energy by blocking progress of a program in an attempt to extract self-interested terms or concessions that may or may not be related to policy goals).

Bardach, in short, saw implementation as an extension of politics. He sought to impose theoretical order on this complex world of negotiation, scheming and jockeying for favor by classifying behavioral patterns that had been repeatedly observed within and between the actors given primary responsibility for implementation, i.e., government bureaucracies. Other frameworks shared the basic perspective that implementation was an extension of politics but expanded the cast of actors. Giandomenico Majone and Aaron Wildavsky (1979), for example, argued that implementation should be viewed as an evolutionary process. Implementation is shaped by general policy that is formally adopted but encompasses a wide range of goals, interactions, and dispositions, all of which are complexly connected. Rather than an agency treating formal policy adoption as a set of marching orders, they saw agencies, the target populations of policy, and even policymakers as having to adapt to the goals and expectations created by policy. For studies like Bardach's and Majone and Wildavsky's, the key explanatory target is the behavior of implementers. This makes sense as a dependent variable because as Pressman and Wildavsky amply demonstrated, the behavior of the implementers is absolutely critical to success.

Other approaches to theory construction, however, targeted policy outputs and outcomes as the key dependent variable. A quite different approach to Bardach's was taken by Daniel Mazmanian and Paul Sabatier, whose *Implementation and Public Policy* (1983) sought to lay down a series of empirically testable causal hypotheses about implementation. Mazmanian and Sabatier argued that there are three basic perspectives on the implementation of any program or policy. First there is the perspective of what they term the "center," or the perspective of the initial policymaker. Second is the perspective of the "periphery," or the lower-level bureaucrats whose behavior actually translates the policy into action. Finally, there is the perspective of the "target group," or the people at whom the policy or program is aimed.

Implementation, Mazmanian and Sabatier argued, looked very different depending on perspective. From the center, implementation is a top-down phenomenon. The objective of implementation is to achieve official policy objectives, to translate the intent of a formally adopted policy into action. From the perspective of higher-level officials or institutions, then, the key issue is how to get lower-level officials and institutions to act in a manner consistent with that intent. From the periphery—the basic perspective taken by Bardach—implementation is all about how lower-level officials and institutions adapt to the shocks to their environment caused by higher-levels introducing new policies and programs. From the target group perspective, implementation is about how the policy affects their lives (e.g., do the services provided by, say, a jobs training program actually increase the target population's employment prospects?). Mazmanian and Sabatier recognized considerable overlap in these perspectives; if the official goal is to get jobs for the unemployed, then the perspectives of the center and target population will obviously have much in common. However, they also recognized the difficulty in combining all three perspectives simultaneously into a single study or theory. Accordingly, Mazmanian and Sabatier's framework tended to reflect a center perspective (1983, 12–13).

Mazmanian and Sabatier's framework took a distinct center-perspective bias for the simple reason that they viewed the achievement of formal policy objectives as the key dependent variable, not the behavior of the implementers: "In our view, the crucial role of implementation analysis is the identification of the variables which affect the achievement of legal objectives" (1983, 21). Accordingly, the explanatory goal of their framework reflected the desired outcomes of the implementation process. These outcomes were subdivided into five distinct elements: the outputs of implementing agencies, the target population's compliance with these policy outputs, the actual impacts of policy outputs, the perceived impacts of policy outputs, and major revision in the statute (1983, 22). These constituted the dependent variables the framework sought to explain. Even a casual consideration of these five dependent variables should give some notion of the complex task undertaken by Mazmanian and Sabatier, and by extension the whole project of constructing a generalizable theory of the implementation process. Embedded within those dependent variables, for example, is arguably the whole field of policy evaluation (assessing actual policy impacts), as well as large areas of policy analysis (major statute revisions raise the question of "what should we do?" or at least "what should we do differently?").

Mazmanian and Sabatier created systematic sense of the independent variables driving the implementation process by categorizing them into three broad categories: the tractability of the problem, the ability of statute to structure implementation, and non-statutory variables that affected implementation (1983, 20–42). The tractability of the problem referred to the social problem the policy officially targeted. The bottom line is that some social problems are easier to deal with than others. The problems may be persistent social ills that any single program or policy is unlikely to cure (e.g., poverty), the technology to address the problem may be imperfect or nonexistent (e.g., replacing polluting fossil fuels with renewable alternatives), and the behavior required of the target population to achieve official policy objectives may be unrealistic (e.g., getting drivers to obey a uniform national speed limit of 55 mph).

The ability of statute to structure implementation depended on another set of key variables independent of the tractability of the problem.

First and foremost was the transmission of clear and consistent objectives; it is impossible to implement a formal policy objective if no one is sure what that objective is. Second, there must be a real causal theory connecting the actions of policy to the desired policy objectives. It is unrealistic to achieve policy objectives without a basic understanding of what will cause the desired outcomes. Other variables included in this category were allocation of adequate financial resources, recruitment of the right set of implementing agencies, and laying down clear lines of coordination and control among the implementing actors. Collectively, these elements constituted the "statutory coherence" hypothesis, which posited that the outcomes of the implementation process were partially determined by how (or if) the statute clarified objectives, understood what needed to be done to realize those objectives, identified the actors qualified to take these actions, allocated them adequate resources, and established a system of control and accountability.

Non-statutory variables included public support and the leadership and competence of implementing officials. A good program with a realistic objective can still fail if its managers are incompetent, disinterested, or distracted by other priorities. Even committed and competent managers have a hard time achieving policy objectives that are resisted by the public. Prohibition, for example, was a spectacular failure not because the federal government was incompetent but because the public refused to stop consuming alcohol.

Mazmanian and Sabatier's (1983) theory is notable not just for being one of the first comprehensive theoretical frameworks of the implementation process, but because it highlights two critical issues that second-generation implementation studies never fully resolved: perspective and complexity. It was, and is, not clear what perspective—center, periphery, target population, or some combination—provides the best starting point for building implementation theory. Mazmanian and Sabatier and others seeking to propose systematic and testable causal relationships tended to favor the top-down approach that came with a center perspective (e.g., Berman 1980; Nakamura and Smallwood 1980).

Others, however, made a strong case for a "bottom-up" starting point, using the periphery or the target population as the best platform for understanding implementation. One of the best-known advocates of the bottom-up approach is Michael Lipsky (1971, 1980), whose notion of the street-level bureaucrat created a powerful case that Mazmanian and Sabatier's periphery was anything but peripheral when it came to determining what happened in implementation. For Lipsky, the key actors in implementation were the people who actually did the implementing.

Street-level bureaucrats represent the primary interface between citizens and government: "Most citizens encounter government (if they encounter it all) not through letters to congressmen [sic] or by attendance at school board meetings but through their teachers and their children's teachers and through the policeman on the corner or in the patrol car. Each encounter of this kind represents an instance of policy delivery" (1980, 3). These individuals, argued Lipsky, are primary shapers of policy delivery because of the simple fact that they make the decisions on the spot. Lipsky went even further, arguing that they are primary policy*makers*, not just implementers. A legislature may pass a speed limit of 55 mph, but that policy is utterly dependent upon diligent enforcement by a traffic cop. If that individual police officer only stops cars traveling in excess of 60 mph, then that officer has effectively set a speed limit—a public policy—different from that set by the legislature.

Lipsky also noted that a natural tension exists between policy actors closer to the center and those closer to the periphery. The street-level bureaucrat is frequently dealing not just with ambiguous policy but also with the ambiguous nature of day-to-day reality. Policy and rules dictated from the center may seem unclear, unfair, or impractical to the street-level bureaucrat charged with implementing them. Those serving on the front lines of policy delivery are often short of resources, understaffed, and required to deal with an endless series of decisions (stop the car going 57 mph?) that in effect are policymaking decisions. This creates friction between the center, which seeks compliance with formal policy objectives, and the periphery, which seeks the autonomy to deal as they see fit with the day-to-day dilemmas of the job.

For the "bottom-uppers," it is down at the street level where implementation really happens, and to favor a center over a periphery perspective is to ignore the practical realities of delivering public services. A number of scholars pitched the argument that because implementation was ultimately dependent on street-level bureaucrats, they had to take center stage in any theory of the implementation process (e.g., Hjern 1982; Hjern and Hull 1983). Actually, the bottom-uppers' argument went even further. Given that street-level bureaucrats were clearly making policy, and given that compliance issues with the center were virtually inevitable, it made sense to start thinking of implementation as an important stage of the policy formulation process. From the bottom-up perspective, it made sense to make the periphery's implementation perspective (and the target population's) a key issue in the process of resolving questions of "what should we do?" The conclusions of, say, a traditional cost-benefit analysis could change radically depending on the periphery's perspective of how (or if) a policy option could/should be put into practice. As the street-level bureaucrats ultimately made these decisions in practice, it made sense to include them in policy formulation discussions for the simple reason that any policy was doomed to failure if they could not adapt its objectives to local conditions.

This latter point was not entirely new. One of the key lessons drawn from studies like Derthick's and Pressman and Wildavsky's was that there should be a lot more attention paid to the practicalities of implementation in the policy formulation debate. The key question for policy scholars was how to provide a framework for doing that in a manner that was reasonably generalizable and systematic.

While the top-downers generally acknowledged the points of the bottom-uppers, there remained resistance to swapping one perspective for the other. The top-downers were trying to figure out how to translate formal policy objectives into reality; their focus was on how to translate the intent of policy into action *after* the formal policy objective had been decided. Bottom-uppers did not want implementation so confined; they wanted the periphery and the target population perspective incorporated into all stages of the policy process; they argued that implementation had to be considered holistically. Top-downers were more focused on outcomes, bottom-uppers on the behavior and choices of implementers. We also see something of a split between the rationalist and the post-positivist camps in policy studies. Top-downers, with their focus on empirically testable causal relationships, tended to fit comfortably within the rationalist project. Bottom-uppers, with their desire to bring traditionally unrepresented viewpoints into the entire policy process, tended to use more of a post-positivist lens to look at policy (deLeon 1999a).

The top-down versus bottom-up debate has never been fully resolved, though both sides acknowledge the validity of the opposing perspective, and something of a truce has been declared. A number of attempts have been made to synthesize the two approaches, notably by Sabatier (1988, 1997; see also Elmore 1985; Matland 1995). Yet a full reconciliation of the two viewpoints has not been made. The "correct" or "best" dependent variable for implementation studies—policy outcome or implementer behavior—is still a matter of some disagreement, as is the best epistemological approach (rationalist or post-positivist; see discussion below). Many ended up viewing the whole debate as an unfortunate distraction, claiming the underlying issue was more one of degree than kind. Few top-downers rejected the notion that street-level bureaucrats played a key role in implementation, just as few bottom-uppers rejected the notion that achieving formally adopted policy objectives was an important driver of implementation. O'Toole described the whole debate as more about how to look at implementation rather than a disagreement about what is or is not important, arguing (perhaps optimistically) that policy scholars had "moved past the rather sterile top-down, bottom-up dispute" (2000, 267).

While the top-down/bottom-up controversy sputtered, if not to a reconciliation, at least to an amicable cohabitation, the second big issue raised by theory-building efforts like Mazmanian and Sabatier's has remained stubbornly at the forefront of implementation studies. Basically, by organizing the wide range of variables critical to implementation into a causal framework, second-generation research made crystal clear the enormous complexity of implementation. In their framework, for example, Mazmanian and Sabatier (1983, 22) specified five dependent variables. Under the three broad categories of causal determinants of these dependent variables (problem tractability, ability of statute to structure implementation, and non-statutory variables affecting implementation) were a total of sixteen broadly described independent variables. None of the latter specified a clear, generalizable measure. Indeed, as their own empirical work demonstrated, operationalizing the concepts at the heart of their framework was a formidable measurement challenge, and bringing them together for parsimonious quantitative analysis created research design and methodological issues.

If building generalizable frameworks of implementation was the central challenge of second-generation studies, testing them would prove to be the central challenge of third-generation studies.

Third-Generation Studies: Understanding
Implementation Is ... Impossible?

Dividing the evolution of implementation studies into three distinct generations is usually attributed to Malcolm Goggin and his colleagues (1990), who saw the decades straddling the turn of the twenty-first century as ripe for a fruitful maturation of the field. Writing at the tail end of the 1980s, they foresaw a third generation of implementation studies that would be empirically oriented, the focus not just on developing causal hypotheses but on rigorously testing them. Third-generation studies so focused held out the possibility of separating the theoretical wheat from the chaff and clarifying a generalizable understanding of successful implementation: in other words, a theory of how policy actually works (or does not). The central aim of third-generation studies, they argued, "is simply to be more scientific than the previous two (generations) in its approach to the study of implementation" (Goggin et al. 1990, 18).

Needless to say, this reflected high hopes for the trajectory of implementation studies. Goggin et al. believed public policy studies during the 1990s would "very likely be defined by its focus on implementation. The nineties are likely to be the implementation era" (1990, 9). This did not exactly turn out to be the case. Indeed, within a decade, several leading figures in the field—including Goggin and his colleagues—were publishing laments for the demise of implementation studies and urging its reconsideration to scholars who had more or less declared the enterprise dead (see Lester and Goggin 1998; deLeon 1999a; deLeon and deLeon 2002). What happened?

The central problem, if not fully recognized at the time, had already been discovered by Mazmanian and Sabatier (1983). Once the distraction of the top-down/bottom-up controversy was set aside, the sheer complexity of the implementation process emerged as a major stumbling block to any parsimonious and generalizable framework. It was not just the issue of research design and concept measurement (though these were hard enough); it was the sheer number of variables. Frameworks such as those proposed by Mazmanian and Sabatier (1983), and third-generation follow-ups such as those proposed by Goggin et al. (1990), struggled to make parsimonious sense of implementation. To encompass all the apparently essential elements of implementation, theoretical frameworks had to carry so much causal water that they sprang leaks at the seams.

Good examples of this come from a number of studies that in spirit, if not chronologically, fit with Goggin et al.'s notion of third-generation implementation studies. There were a number of attempts in the 1980s and 1990s to test Mazmanian and Sabatier's framework on various policy issues (e.g., Bullock 1981; Rosenbaum 1981). These generally found support for the framework, but all faced significant difficulties in operationalizing concepts and in executing a comprehensive test.

A good example is Deborah McFarlane's (1989) work. Rather than test the entire framework, McFarlane focused on the statutory coherence hypothesis. In the Mazmanian and Sabatier framework, the ability of a statute to structure implementation specified seven specific elements of statutory coherence: 1) clear goals; 2) adequate causal theory; 3) adequate resources; 4) hierarchical integration of implementing agencies; 5) decision rules for agencies that supported implementation; 6) commitment of implementing agencies to the policy objectives; and 7) formal participation by constituencies supporting the policy objectives. What McFarlane sought to do was operationalize each of these concepts and empirically assess their ability to predict the policy outputs of implementing agencies.

In brief, the findings were supportive of the statutory coherence hypothesis, and thus of the Mazmanian and Sabatier framework. Of more interest for present purposes, however, were the caveats McFarlane carefully placed on her findings. Notably, the choice of dependent variables was driven in no small part by the practicalities of data availability and served as a proxy for just one of the five dependent variables in the framework (1989, 417). The operationalization of independent variables "was problematic . . . the measures utilized were crude . . . there is considerable distance between the measures employed and the broad concepts embodied in the statutory variables" (McFarlane 1989, 418–419). In other words, even a limited test of the framework posed significant conceptual, measurement, and methodological issues. McFarlane expressed hope that future refinements could improve the tractability of the framework for comprehensive empirical studies, but follow-ups ran into very similar issues (e.g., Meier and McFarlane 1996).

The third generation certainly did not fail because of lack of effort. Considerable energy was expended on rigorous theory development and empirical testing, not just in the sense of testing implementation frameworks developed in second-generation studies, but in using other frameworks—especially economic-based frameworks like game theory and principal agent theory. At least in a formal sense, none seemed to satisfactorily offer a general understanding of implementation. As O'Toole (1995, 54) put it, "implementation networks contain complications that modeling can neither ignore nor fully address." That serves as an apt epitaph for the high hopes of third-generation implementation research.

Third-generation studies did not die because their core research agenda was falsified; they in large part simply stuttered to a crawl because implementation resisted parsimonious explanation. In a much-cited review of more than one hundred studies, O'Toole (1986), discovered more than three hundred key variables being forwarded as key determinants of implementation process and outcomes. Creating coherent structure out of those materials is, to put it mildly, a daunting task. In this sort of context, the ambiguity in frameworks such as Mazmanian and Sabatier's is remarkable not for its presence but for the fact that it has been corralled to such a minimal level. The third generation could not find a way to parse the extensive network of causal relationships captured within such frameworks down to a generally accepted, irreducible minimum. As Peter deLeon put it, "What the contemporary policy implementation community is seemingly confronted with is an acknowledgement . . . of what the early implementation scholars apparently knew best, as reflected in their case study approach: that the complexity of the implementation process is more than daunting, it is apparently impenetrable" (1999a, 319).

Third-generation studies ultimately ended up with a less-than-satisfying answer to the core question of "how does it work?" The consensus response seemed to be, "we're not really sure." Sometimes it was even worse than that. Lin (1996) suggested not only that the difference between implementation working and not working was more about luck than design but that careful design might do more harm than good: "successful implementation is often accidental, while failed implementation is the result of design" (4).

Implementation studies, needless to say, did not develop into the central focus of policy studies as Goggin et al. (1990) had hopefully forecast. Indeed, in the years following this prediction, numerous policy scholars expressed skepticism about the ability of implementation studies to move significantly beyond the achievements of the second generation. Implementation studies were seen as failing to achieve conceptual clarity (Goggin et al. 1990, 462), unlikely to reach a comprehensive rational explanation of implementation in the foreseeable future (Garrett 1993, 1249), or "an intellectual dead end" (deLeon 1999a, 313).

A Fourth Generation?

Implementation studies did not entirely founder on the difficulties encountered in the third-generation project. In many ways, implementation studies simply returned to a more second- (or even first-) generation perspective. Richard Matland (1995), for example, sought to rethink the whole notion of how to assemble a comprehensive explanation of implementation. Rather than specifying causal relationships between specific variables, he took an approach more similar to Bardach by seeking to classify implementation. Rather than describing a series of games, however, Matland sought a true typology, seeking to do for implementation what Theodore Lowi (1964) had sought to do for policy as a whole.

Matland's conceptual starting point was a central focus of second-generation studies: the still-lingering top-down/bottom-up debate. Rather than trying to resolve the question of what should be the appropriate dependent variable (or the appropriate method), Matland took a step back and looked at the substantive policy focus of the two camps. He argued that top-downers and bottom-uppers tended to study two different sorts of polices. Bottom-uppers were drawn to policies with high levels of ambiguity and conflict; such policies had the natural effect of delegating key policy decisions to street-level bureaucrats. Top-downers were more attracted to policies with less ambiguity and less conflict; this had the natural effect of clarifying what needed to be done and freeing researchers to concentrate on the covariates of successful (or unsuccessful) implementation. Rather than take a side, Matland synthesized the two approaches and conceptualized different implementation approaches as being driven by relative levels of conflict and ambiguity.

This approach led to a two-by-two matrix of implementation approaches: four cells, each representing a type of implementation based on levels of conflict and ambiguity. For example, a policy with low ambiguity and low conflict was ripe for a prototypical top-down approach to implementation (Matland termed this "administrative implementation"). Implementing agencies knew clearly what had to be done and how to do it, and there was little disagreement about the means or the ends of the policy. The important variable in administrative implementation was resources; given the resources, a competent, top-down approach would achieve policy success. Matland's exemplar of this type of policy was smallpox eradication. In this case, policy outcome was the readily justifiable dependent variable and identifying its causal determinants the natural focus of an implementation study.

On the other extreme were policies of high ambiguity and high conflict, which was more suited to a bottom-up perspective. In these situations, it is what Matland (1995) termed "coalitional strength" at the local level that determines policy outcomes. With high ambiguity and high conflict, different groups have very different notions of what the policy objectives are (or should be). Whichever group perspective prevails at the local level will drive the implementation process, meaning there will be considerable variation in policy outcomes across different cites. In this case, policy outcome is less important as a dependent variable because it is a plural rather than a singular. The key factor is the behavior of implementers; it is their behavior that drives variation in policy outcomes, and thus variation in behavior is the critical element to understand.

Matland's work provides an example that theoretical advances were being made in the midst of what many perceived to be a serious wane in implementation studies. And Matland was far from alone. James Lester and Malcolm Goggin (1998) proposed a similar matrix approach, arguing that successful implementation was driven by government commitment, and institutional capacity. Laurence O'Toole (1995), as already mentioned, used a rational choice lens to examine implementation with some success. Denise Scheberle (1997) sought to create a systematic framework based on the levels of trust among and involvement by implementing officials. A number of scholars, however, saw these efforts as not adding up to a cumulative advance. Theoretical insights kept piling up on each other, but they were not hanging together in anything approaching a parsimonious general understanding of implementation. Around the turn of the century, a number of the leading names in implementation research were seeking to revive what they saw as an increasingly flagging research agenda.

The latter included Peter and Linda deLeon (deLeon and deLeon 2002), who posed the question of "what ever happened to policy implementation?" and Lester and Goggin (1998), who sought to reenergize implementation studies with a provocative essay that replanted the third-generation flag under the title of "Back to the Future." Lester and Goggin divided implementation scholars into four distinct camps based on whether they had a positive or negative view of the continuation of implementation research and on whether they believed significant modifications were needed in implementation theory.

Those with negative views about the continuation were divided into "skeptics," who believed that to go forward, implementation research needed major theoretical and conceptual changes and the "terminators," who wanted to discontinue implementation research as currently conceived and reenvision this entire sector of the policy process. Those with positive views were divided into "testers," those who wanted to continue rigorous empirical testing of existing frameworks like Mazmanian and Sabatier's; and the "reformers," those still committed to the earlier high promise of implementation research, but also seeing the need for theoretical formulation and more empirical work.

Lester and Goggin (1998) put themselves squarely in the reformers camp and sought to rally the third-generation troops for another sustained intellectual assault. Specifically, they called for organizing research around the dependent variable of implementer behavior, which meant dropping implementation's traditional focus on policy outcome as the key explanatory target. "The essential characteristic of the implementation process," Lester and Goggin argued, "is the timely and satisfactory performance of certain necessary tasks related to carrying out the intents of the law. This means rejecting a dichotomous conceptualization of implementation as simply success or failure" (1998, 5). Having clarified the dependent variable, they called for the development of a "parsimonious, yet complete, theory of policy implementation and a set of testable hypotheses that explain variations in the way implementers behave" (1998, 6). That theory, they strongly suggested, would most likely come from a synthesis of theoretical efforts by people like Matland, O'Toole, and others, the raw materials of this meta-theory coming from insights of communications theory, regime theory, contingency theory, and rational choice theory.

Response to Lester and Goggin's essay provides a fascinating insight into the contemporary state of implementation research. Some responded to the call. Winter (1999), for example, seconded the call to make behavior the central dependent variable of implementation research, especially variation in implementer behavior. Winter also called for a strong emphasis on quantitative methods compared to traditional case studies. This constitutes an endorsement of the third-generation manifesto. Others, however, were more reluctant to follow this lead.

Meier (1999) said he was not really the tester Lester and Goggin had described but was more of a "stealth terminator." He expressed a strong skepticism about implementation theory, describing it as "forty-seven variables that completely explain five case studies," and suggested a fresh start. He disagreed with shifting the dependent variable to behavior, arguing policy outcomes were the natural target for implementation research. The most important issues for explaining how a policy does (or does not) work boil down to knowing whether manipulating variable X will result in the desired policy outcome Y. The behavior in between is undoubtedly important, but it is the outcome that theoretically and practically is the most important. He also cast doubt on the prospects of combining insights from a range of theoretical frameworks into a better causal model of implementation. Part of the existing problem, Meier argued, is that implementation theory already was trying to include too many insights and in the process was reflecting the complexity of implementation rather than actually explaining it. The only real hope for implementation studies was to expand its scope to include anything that happens in the policy process after formal adoption. This meant recognizing a lot of, for example, public management and public administration studies as implementation research.

Finally, and perhaps confirming Lester and Goggin's tester label, Meier called for much more empirical work. The real job of the testers, at least from Meier's perspective, was to start trimming the lengthy list of variables clogging up the already insight-heavy implementation frameworks. In short, Meier staked the case that the top-downers remained the best hope for generating cumulative knowledge about implementation.

Peter deLeon (1999c) had a mixed reaction to his Lester and Goggin–issued label as a skeptic. In one sense he was not a skeptic; he viewed implementation studies as of central importance to the policy process, both in practical and theoretical terms. In that way, he was squarely on the side of those who saw implementation as worthy of attracting the efforts of the best and brightest in policy studies. However, he admitted this positive view was more about the potential of implementation research rather than its current practice: "one need not go much beyond [the Lester and Goggin article] to see the vast and amoebic array of policy implementation essays and books that, to most observers, would comprise a largely aimless wandering in search of some consensus" (deLeon 1999c, 7). That consensus, deLeon argued, is not likely to come from plucking the insights of disparate theoretical frameworks, which was akin to prescribing "the planting and blooming of a thousand flowers (on the assumption that one of the thousand might indeed be the genuine article)" (1999c, 7).

Rather than follow the third-generation vision of Lester and Goggin, and in contrast to the arguments of the more traditional top-downers, deLeon opted for remaking the case for the bottom-up approach (1999a, 2002). He argued that implementation research was indeed headed for an intellectual dead end if it proceeded on a third-generation and/or top-down path, but that at the same time the vital importance of implementation to the effective delivery of public goods and services demanded the serious attention of policy scholars. Rather than the methods of the rationalist project à la Winter or Meier, however, he championed a more post-positivist approach and a greater emphasis on inclusion and democratic values (deLeon 1999a, 330).

These differing responses give a reasonable insight into the contemporary state of implementation research. Everyone agrees that better theory is sorely needed, but there is little agreement on what that theory is supposed to explain (implementer behavior? policy outputs? policy outcomes?), whether such a theory is possible, or how it is likely to be discovered (synthesis? adoption of post-positivism? a complete field-wide "do over"?). What seems to have emerged from the third-generation push is something very similar to what we have already seen in our examination of policy analysis and policy evaluation—an emergent division between the rationalist project and its post-positivist critics. In implementation the rationalists are mostly top-downers in theoretical perspective and testers or skeptics in methodological practice. When they seek to understand how a policy works, what they are talking about is the causal connection between some post-adoption variable that can be manipulated by the center and a policy outcome. The post-positivists are bottom-uppers. When they seek to understand how a policy works, what they are talking about is how implementation reflects inclusive, democratic practices and how it impacts the periphery and the target population. Despite the best efforts of those, like Matland, who seek to stitch the two sides together, the underlying differences in rationalist and post-positivist epistemologies keep wary distance between the two camps.

Conclusion

The conventional wisdom on implementation studies is that it began with Pressman and Wildavsky, flowered with second-generation studies like Mazmanian and Sabatier's, and lost the spotlight at some point during the third generation because key issues that bubbled up in the first two generations seemed to be intractable. The end result was a series of implementation camps that can be categorized in a number of ways but that ultimately reflect the tensions of the rationalist and post-positivist disagreements discussed in previous chapters.

There is an argument that conventional wisdom is mistaken and far too pessimistic, at least in its contemporary take on things. For one thing, the classic story on the beginnings of implementation theory is almost certainly wrong. Implementation research certainly did not begin with Pressman and Wildavsky or with Derthick. In a detailed intellectual history of the field, Harald Saetren (2005) found that systematic implementation research predates Pressman and Wildavsky by at least four decades. Certainly public administration was paying attention to implementation long before the "first" generation of implementation studies showed up in political science. Scholars such as Emmette Redford (1969) spent their entire careers trying to reconcile the principles of democracy with the seemingly hierarchical and authoritarian nature of the agencies implementing public policies, and the decisions bureaucrats made within these agencies that were inevitably political choices. Though not self-promoted as "implementation," at least from the publication of Dwight Waldo's (1946) *The Administrative State*, public administration scholars have been systematically assessing the democratic implications of the government's implementation machinery. Redford (1969, 134) argued that "administration in practice"—what in this chapter has been called "implementation"—should be guided above all by a "democratic morality" whose core value was the humane treatment of people. In Redford's conception, the key question of implementation was whether it reflected core democratic principles such as majority rule (balanced with minority rights) and the right of universal participation in deciding the ultimate outcome.

Just as conventional wisdom on the beginning of implementation studies has a questionable starting point, the "end" of implementation research is likewise greatly exaggerated; there is a vibrant, ongoing implementation research literature that is simultaneously cutting new theoretical ground and making significant contributions to the practical delivery of public goods and services. It is managing to do this without getting tangled in endless debate on the pros and cons of top-down/bottom-up or rationalist/post-positivist arguments. This research is simply out of view of mainstream policy studies because it is too narrowly focused (primarily in the fields of public policy, political science, and public administration).

The real action in implementation studies, Saetren argued, is in policy-oriented fields in general and education in particular (by Saetren's estimate, nearly 40 percent of the systematic research on implementation is related to education). Whereas implementation studies have trailed off in policy, political science, and public administration journals, implementation studies in more policy-specific fields—health, education, the environment—are going stronger than ever. There were more than 1,600 implementation dissertations written between 1985 and 2003; that constitutes two younger generations of scholars whose research interests would seemingly secure the foreseeable future of implementation as a key research focus.

Yet while providing plenty of evidence that rumors of the death of implementation research are greatly exaggerated, Saetren's numbers also circled back to the central issues at the heart of the debate triggered by Lester and Goggin. There is plenty of research out there; the key problem is extracting from it a parsimonious understanding of the entire process. We are accumulating a lot of studies, Saetren suggested, but this does not mean we are accumulating a lot of knowledge. Certainly, we have learned some things in the four decades since Pressman and Wildavsky launched implementation to the top of the policy studies research agenda. Given the initial promise of first- and second-generation studies, however, it is perhaps fair to say that by now we were expecting to know a lot more.

CHAPTER EIGHT

Whose Values? Policy Design

The tension between the rationalist project and its post-positivist critics is, as previous chapters have highlighted, a consistent theme in policy studies. Yet whereas there is considerable debate over the appropriate role of values in the method and epistemology of policy studies, there is general agreement that public policy itself is value-based. If politics is defined as the authoritative allocation of values, then public policy represents the means of allocating and distributing those values (Easton 1953; A. Schneider and Ingram 1997, 2). But exactly whose values are sanctioned by the coercive powers of the state? This is a central question of policy studies that cuts to the heart of power relationships within society.

Policy design is an umbrella term for the field of policy studies devoted to the systematic examination of the substantive content of policy. From a rationalist perspective, policy is purposive—it is a means to achieve a desired end, a solution to a problem. Policy design scholars readily accept the notion that policy is purposive, but they argue that the substance of policy is much more complex and nuanced than the instrumental assumption of rationalists. Rather than identifying the goal (or problem) and trying to assess what to do or what should be done, policy design scholars look for the "blueprint" or "architecture" of policy. Policy from this perspective is more than an instrumental means to a desired end; it symbolizes what, and who, society values. Policy design scholars recognize the instrumental dimension of policy but are more focused on identifying and interpreting the symbolic elements. Policy design, and the design process, can shed information on why particular outcomes of interest were or were not achieved, but it is more revealing for what it says about who does, and who does not, have political power, i.e., the ability to have a preferred set of values backed by the coercive powers of the state.

A wholly rationalist view of the policy process suggests that decisions about policy design are made on the basis of comparing potential solutions to defined problems and that policy actors and citizens react to such decisions using similar criteria. The policy design perspective sees such assumptions as naive and incomplete. In the political arena, even the most scientific ("objective") evidence tends to be used subjectively and selectively, championed and accepted when it supports preexisting assumptions about the world and how it works, and rejected when it counters these assumptions (A. Schneider and Ingram 1997). And objective, or at least falsifiable, claims about policy often tend to be secondary considerations even when they do enter the political arena; it is often the symbolic cues stemming from policy that tend to be more appealing than policy facts (Edelman 1990). The decision over policy such as, say, the Patriot Act, tends to be structured not by objective analysis of its expected impact on a particular set of problems but rather by the symbolic and emotional freight of what it means to be a patriot in a time of grave threat to national security.

These symbolic and emotional dimensions are, according to the policy design perspective, highly revealing about the real purposes of public policy, which may be some distance from the putative goals actually expressed by the policy. Indeed, policy design scholars argue that the values embedded in policy design reflect what political struggle is all about. For example, rational actor models of political participation indicate citizens engage in politics to express their policy preferences and, accordingly, will vote out those officials with policy preferences that are different from their own. The field of policy design flips this argument on its head. Values are embedded in policy design, and elected officials and policymakers use these values to secure or maintain political power. Citizens, in turn, tend to be more responsive to value-based arguments than arguments highlighting the costs and benefits of a particular policy program.

The ability of elected officials to use values and symbols to their advantage when crafting public policy has attracted numerous scholars to the study of policy design. Some are interested in explaining political, social, and economic disparities and see the underlying structure of policymaking as contributing to these inequities. Others are interested in trying to bring certain values (egalitarianism, diversity, participation) to the policymaking process. Still others are interested in exploring the conflict between the values they see in mainstream social science methods and theories and the democratic values they believe should be central to public policy. What ties all of this together is a core research question: Whose values does public policy promote? This chapter will explore their contributions as well as what values are inherent in policy design and how those values are believed to affect the targets of public policy.

Objective Policy Design?

Policy design refers to the content of public policy. Empirically, the content of public policy includes the following observable characteristics: target population (the citizens who receive the benefits or bear the costs of the policy), the values being distributed by the policy, the rules governing or constraining action, rationales (the justification for policy), and the assumptions that logically tie all these elements together (A. Schneider and Ingram 1997, 2). Though observable, the content of public policy is not viewed objectively by citizens and policymakers, nor is it based on rational considerations. Instead, the process of assembling policy content is based on highly subjective interpretations: interpretations of who justifiably deserves the costs or benefits of a policy, what values should be backed by the coercive powers of the state, and who (or what) should have their freedom of action promoted or constrained to uphold those values. Common to the group of scholars adopting this framework is the notion that value-laden interpretations are inherent in the policy process because language is used as a means for justifying and rationalizing actions or outcomes.

In *Constructing the Political Spectacle* (1990), Murray Edelman made the claim that there is no one way to view policy. Nothing in the political world is objective; all facts are subjective. Edelman's "political spectacle" is suggestive of a political and policy process that is highly subjective and highly manipulative. Instead of policy design reflecting the needs of society, Edelman presented a political world in which governmental action is not based on a rational response to societal problems. Rather, symbols and language are used to perpetuate political status and ideology. As Edelman wrote, language is a means of evoking "favorable interpretations" (1990, 103). What does this mean for the study of policy design? According to Edelman, actions taken by the government are based on alternatives and explanations that promote favorable measures but maintain unresolved problems (18). The construction of the political spectacle is intended to protect immediate interests in an unpredictable world. By defining problems according to self-serving solutions, policymakers preserve the status quo.

Edelman first picked up the theme of the intersubjective nature of policy and politics in his 1964 book *The Symbolic Uses of Politics*. It is here where Edelman first wrote of the deliberate way in which policymakers use symbols and narratives to craft public policy. Since that time, other scholars have also noted the ability of policymakers to manipulate the policy process. Most notable of this research is the work of Frank Fischer. In *Politics, Values, and Public Policy* (1980), Fischer argued that values are embedded in the policy process and policymakers appeal to certain values when designing public policy. Decisions about problem definition, alternative selection, and policy evaluation are based on the deliberate use of values and the subjective interpretation of those values. For Fischer, the process of policy evaluation is best described as one of "political evaluation" (1980, 71). Policymakers construct realities that minimize political costs and maximize political gain.

Edelman and Fischer have painted a very nuanced and chaotic picture of how the content of public policy is assembled, one in which debates between policymakers over who should receive policy benefits are based on subjective, rather than "rational," arguments. This fits well with Frank Fischer and John Forester's (1993) work on the "argumentative" turn in policy analysis. Similar to Edelman's work on the intersubjectivity of public policymaking, Fischer and Forester argued that language shapes reality. Politics is based on arguments over who gets what, when, and how. Fischer and Forester wrote that these arguments spill over to the policy process and affect the way policymakers define a problem and select solutions to problems. Policymakers and analysts use language to craft a reality that fits with their policy design rather than crafting policy design that

fits with reality. Like Edelman, these authors argued that problem definition is subject to framing and the deliberate use of narratives, symbols,
and stories to shape reality (see also Hajer and Laws 2006).

Put simply, policymakers tend to make "political" rather than rational
or objective evaluations of public policy (Fischer 1980). In other words,
they approach the content of public policy from the value-laden perspective, from a notion of what the world should look like, and not from a
hard-nosed, objective notion of a societal problem and a systematic
analysis of its potential policy solutions. Like Fischer and Forester,
Charles Anderson (1979) argued that policy evaluation is highly subjective and highly normative, and that language is the key to understanding
the policy process. Writing at roughly the same time as Fischer, Anderson
argued that "policy analysis has less to do with problem solving than with
the process of argument" (1979, 712). This resonates with Fischer's description of "political evaluation" as well as Fischer and Forester's (1993)
notion of the argumentative nature of public policy analysis.

For Edelman, Fischer, Forester, and Anderson, the policy process is
clearly not rational. Policy design is an instrumental, cost-benefit exercise, but it is based on the deliberate use of values and symbols to achieve
a particular outcome. In other words, policy outcomes are judged in a relative context; there is no one objective way to view policy design. This has
serious practical implications in terms of judging whether a policy is effective. If Edelman is correct, and all reality is constructed, that nothing is
"verifiable or falsifiable" (1990, 111), then how do we know what policies
to maintain and what policies to discard? What do Edelman's, Fischer and
Forester's, and Anderson's arguments mean for policy evaluation? If policymakers make political or normative instead of rational judgments
about public policy, how do we effectively evaluate public policy? Or,
more simply, how do we know if a policy is "good" or "bad"?

The underlying similarity between all the aforementioned scholars is
their resolve about moving away from strict, empirical analyses of public
policy. Policy analysts should instead embrace theoretical approaches
ranging from post-positivism to critical theory, to deconstructionism, to
hermeneutics. Edelman (1990) offered a prescription for the future that
calls for an "awareness" and understanding of conflicting perspectives in
the decision-making process (130). Such awareness calls for a focus on
what serves an individual's and a community's long-term self-interest, as
well as a need to recognize that reality is constructed through "art,

science, and culture" (Edelman 1990, 130). As Fischer noted, policymakers make political decisions about whether a policy is good or bad. To understand the political nature of such decisions, Fischer argued for a methodology that extends beyond traditional costs/benefit or rational analyses. Instead, policy scholars must employ a "multimethodological" approach (Fischer 1980, 11). Cost-benefit analyses assume policy design can be viewed through a single, objective lens. To accurately study policy design, a methodology that accounts for multiple perspectives is required. For Fischer, the multimethodological approach, an approach that accounts for intersubjectivity and the deliberate use of symbols and language, is the most comprehensive and realistic means for analyzing public policy. Fischer and Forester's (1993) argumentative model rests on similar assumptions. The only way to capture the constructed realities of the policy process is through methodologies that account for intersubjectivity.

Like Edelman and Fischer, Anderson argued that policy evaluation is best understood through an intersubjective or dialectical framework. Whether a policy is judged as good or bad depends on the view of the individual policymaker. Policymakers come from diverse backgrounds, and that training ultimately affects whether a condition in society is viewed as a problem requiring action or a simply a condition. Whereas an economist might describe a particular policy as successful or efficient, an analyst trained in sociology might view it as inequitable or damaging to the fabric of a community (C. Anderson 1979, 714). To circumvent this dilemma, Anderson advocated for a broader notion of policy rationality similar to that of Fischer. Of this new conception of rationality, Anderson wrote "policy making is understood as a process of reasoned deliberation, argument and criticism rather than pragmatic calculus" (1979, 722). In short, because the policy process is inundated with values, the methodology required to study the policy process must account for such intersubjectivity.

In the title of this chapter we posed the question: "whose values?" For Edelman, Fischer, and others, this is the critical question, both in terms of whose values are being supported or distributed by the policy, and whose values are being used to judge the relative success or worth of the public policy. Values permeate the policy process, and what values are important will vary according to the observer. Reality is constructed by each observer (Edelman 1990, 101). For some, distributing benefits to low-income families may be perceived as perpetuating shoddy lifestyle habits; for others, such benefits are seen as a corrective measure for poorly designed institutions. As Edelman (1990) wrote, "reason and rationalization are intertwined" (105). Put another way, "political language is political reality" (Edelman 1990, 104). To sum up, these early policy design scholars were simply pointing out what is most likely obvious to any policymaker—policy design is a messy, political, value-laden process.

The "Paradox" of Policy Design

Edelman, Fischer, and Anderson have provided a basic conceptual platform for studying policy design. The key assumptions of this framework are that policy design is based on intersubjective meanings and the use of symbolic cues, that the content of public policy is designed to fit within policymakers' constructed realities, and that the content of policy will be viewed differently by different groups in society. This framework, as already alluded to in our discussion of policy analysis and evaluation, is not well suited to mainstream rationalist methodologies. Indeed, some scholars such as Deborah Stone (2002) have contended that rational evaluation of policy design and the policy process is simply not possible. For Stone, the "policy paradox" represents the ambiguous nature of the policy process. Nothing in the policy process is clear-cut; all policies present a "double-edged sword" (Stone 2002, 169). Rational, market-based approaches to policymaking are insufficient and inaccurate because they treat the policymaking process like an "assembly line" (Stone 2002, 10).

Discounting the rational decision-making model as too narrow, Stone argued that policy decision making is more accurately represented by a model based on political reason. Stone's framework is based on two premises: 1) that economic frameworks rooted in rational choice theory (the foundation for analysis and evaluation methods such as cost-benefit analysis) are inadequate for evaluating public policy; and 2) that society should be viewed through the lens of a "polis" and not the market. For Stone, policymaking is defined as "the struggle over ideas" (2002, 11). The policy process is characterized by a combination of rational decision making based on scientific calculations and political goals derived from social interaction and "community life" (Stone 2002, 10). The polis, or political community, allows for both perspectives when evaluating public policy. In this regard, Stone's argument is similar to the work of Edelman and Fischer. Policy design must be viewed through multiple perspectives; there is no one rational or objective way to evaluate public policy.

For Stone, the policy process is irrational at both the agenda-setting and decision-making stages. As other scholars have noted, how a problem is defined affects whether the policy receives a favorable reaction from elected officials and citizens (Baumgartner and Jones 1993; Kingdon 1995). For Stone and Fischer, the use of symbols, images, and narratives most strongly affects the problem-definition stage of the policy process. Indeed, Stone (2002, 133) wrote that problem definition is "the strategic representation of situations." When a policymaker uses the image of a "welfare queen" to talk about equity in distributing welfare benefits, she is clearly pushing for more stringent welfare benefits. However, when a policymaker uses images of families with young children in homeless shelters, she is trying to shift the debate from one based on the in-equitable distribution of benefits to one based on compassion and fair-ness. At the decision-making stage, the policy process is not rational because alternatives are not considered equally. Policymakers tend to use political language and ambiguous goals that do not allow for rational cost-benefit comparisons. Policy problems tend to be written as narra-tives, with numbers being used selectively to support the story line. For example, Stone wrote of the use of metaphors, such as the "war on poverty" or the "war on drugs," as political tools deliberately designed to elicit support for certain policies (2002, 154). Similarly, Stone noted how policymakers often use a synecdoche such as the "welfare queen" to push for tougher restrictions on the distribution of welfare benefits (2002, 146).[1]

Stone's argument extends to policymakers as well as targets of public policy. To determine whether a policy will be effective, Stone argued that policy analysts must understand the target's view point. As Stone noted, contrary to predictions of the rational actor model, behavior does not al-ways change based on monetary costs and benefits. Rewards and sanc-tions tend to have different meanings for different populations, and such populations tend to act strategically. As an example, Stone wrote of how the Clinton administration incorrectly assumed welfare recipients would work more if the penalty for working while receiving benefits was re-duced. Instead, Stone argued it is more likely that such recipients worked as a means of having enough money to put food on the table. Thus, de-creasing the penalty for working while receiving benefits would be an ineffective policy because most welfare recipients work in response to their daily needs rather than existing welfare provisions (Stone 2002, 279).

The paradox of Stone's *Policy Paradox* is that whereas public policy is often justified as adhering to one of five democratic values (equity, efficiency, security, liberty, community), in reality there is widespread disagreement over what is equitable, what is efficient, what is secure, what liberates, and what constitutes community. A rational evaluation of public policy implies a common understanding of these democratic goals. As Stone wrote, such a view is shortsighted and naive. Instead, disagreements arise between citizens, between policymakers, and between citizens and policymakers over the definition of these values.

As an example of the problem of achieving the goal of efficiency, Stone asked the reader to consider the efficiency of a public library (2002, 62–65). How should policymakers (librarians) spend savings resulting from the restaffing of the library? To achieve efficiency there must be an agreement on the goals of the organization. Should the library increase the number of books? If so, what type of books? Should the library seek to reduce the amount of time necessary to locate materials? Should the library focus on the goals as perceived by library staff or the goals as perceived by citizens? As with the values of equity, liberty, and security, efficiency requires an agreement on the goal of the organization. Within the public sector, rarely is there widespread agreement on such goals. Think about any federal agency. What should be the goal of that agency? Is there likely to be agreement on that goal among staffers of the agency? Among policymakers? Among citizens? Moreover, as Stone stated, efficiency requires complete information, a state that is rarely achieved in the polis. Thus, the paradox of using these goals as justification for policy design is that citizens and policymakers are most likely to disagree on how best to achieve these goals. People want these democratic values to guide the policy process; they are simply unable to agree on how they should be reflected in policy design.

What (or whose) values should guide the policy design process? Stone argued that attempts by policy scholars to quantify and create a more scientific approach to policy analysis potentially abrogates democratic values. Equity, efficiency, security, liberty, and community are actually goals and should "serve as the standards we use to evaluate existing situations and policy proposals" (Stone 2002, 12). However, citizens and policymakers have different perspectives on what an equitable or efficient policy looks like. Efficiency is usually defined as inputs over outputs. But for most public organizations, there is disagreement over desired output, and this is exactly Stone's argument. What output should be the focus of the public library in the above example? Expediency of the citizen in finding a particular book, video, magazine, or newspaper? Quality of book collection? Because of this disagreement, the likelihood of achieving consensus regarding efficiency is small. There will always be disagreement as to what constitutes a good outcome.[2]

The problems with efficiency are also seen with the democratic values of equity, security, and liberty. In her discussion on equity, Stone used the example of school board elections to demonstrate the difficulty of designing policy that allows for equitable participation by all interested actors. The most equitable policy regarding school board elections would be to allow all citizens to vote. But others may disagree by arguing that only those affected by the decision should be allowed to vote. Still others may argue that only those citizens with school-age children can vote (Stone 2002, 43). Again, while most people agree on the need for equity in policy decision making for public organizations, what constitutes equity is an open question. As Stone wrote, "every policy involves the distribution of something" (2002, 53). Welfare policy, Social Security, Medicare, Medicaid, and student financial aid are all policies designed to distribute resources to particular groups. The question arises as to what is the most appropriate (i.e., equitable) way of distributing such resources. Stone summed up this point nicely when she wrote:

> Equality may in fact mean inequality; equal treatment may require unequal treatment; and the same distribution may be seen as equal or unequal, depending on one's point of view. (2002, 42)

The contribution of Stone is that she has raised awareness of the competing perspectives over seemingly agreeable goals. The market model, according to Stone, indicates a zero-sum relationship between equity and efficiency. To efficiently distribute welfare benefits means that not all of those who qualify for such benefits will receive them. Stone rejected this model in favor of the polis model, which states that policymakers use symbols when designing policy to perpetuate existing stereotypes. According to Stone, the democratic values of equity, efficiency, security, liberty, and community not only guide policy design but also serve as goals and benchmarks. Policymakers and citizens want the content of public policy to reflect democratic values, but agreement on whether such values are reflected in policy content is rare. Other scholars have also picked up on Stone's paradox. H. George Frederickson (2007) wrote that "results-driven management" approaches are naive because they ignore the very problem identified by Stone. As Frederickson wrote,

> public administrators catch criminals, put out fires and even try to prevent them, teach children, supply pure water, fight battles, distribute social security checks, and carry out a thousand other activities—all outputs. (2007, 11)

Applying the value of efficiency, however, how do we analyze such outputs? For a local fire department, should efficiency be defined by response time to fires, the number of fires put out per month, or the number of complaints by local citizens? These choices are important because they can determine whether a policy is judged as efficient or not, and more generally whether the policy is judged as good or bad. Frederickson also applied this notion to breast cancer research by medical research organizations. Should such organizations be held accountable according to "the percentage of women of a certain age receiving mammograms or the percentage of women of a certain age with breast cancer" (2007, 11)? In this case the organization must choose between "agency outputs" and "social outcomes" (Frederickson 2007, 11). Although Frederickson focused on the problem of achieving consensus on accountability, the problem could just as easily be applied to the concept of efficiency. The point is that attaching too much weight to specific measures of policy output overlooks the diversity of outputs produced by public organizations and the different values citizens and policymakers attach to such outputs.

At the heart of Stone's argument is the notion that public policy should be accountable to a diverse set of interests. However, as Frederickson's argument suggests, the value of accountability suffers from the same problems as those of equity, efficiency, security, and liberty. In January 2002, President George W. Bush signed into law the No Child Left Behind Act as a means of increasing the accountability of K–12 education. Since that time, administrators and parents have clashed over how accountability should be defined. For some, any measurable improvement is a sign of success; for others, test scores are the only appropriate measure. Making the problem even more difficult is the fact that schools tend to face what economists label "economies of scope." A school that focuses its resources on increasing graduation rates may see a subsequent decrease in test scores as marginal students are kept in school. Similarly, schools interested in increasing test scores may see a rise in truancy rates as marginal students are not encouraged to stay in school, particularly on test days (see Wenger 2000; Smith and Larimer 2004). Although policymakers, school administrators, and parents agree on the need to increase school efficiency and effectiveness, all three groups tend to define such values differently.

Scholars from other subfields have also recognized the dilemma in attempting to implement objective means for evaluating public policy. Going back to the work of Woodrow Wilson, public administration scholars have long argued that the dichotomy between politics and administration is a false one. Instead, administration is infused with political battles. As many public administration scholars have noted, this creates problems when attempting to evaluate the efficiency of public policies. An exchange in *Public Administration Review*, the leading journal in public administration, highlighted Stone's interdisciplinary contribution.

Scholars were invited to contribute on the topic of "Looking at the Efficiency Concept in Our Time." In this exchange, Schachter (2007) argued for a more democratic form of efficiency:

> In a democracy, efficient administration requires a polity with a democratic underpinning so elected officials and administrators get a sense of the outcomes communities want. (807)

In other words, citizens should be involved in the policymaking process. Like Stone, Schachter was making a normative argument about what values should guide the policy process. For policy design to reflect the preferences of citizens, they must be involved in the policy process. Implicit in Schachter's argument are Edelman's and Stone's claims that policy design is subject to interpretation. There is no one objective way to define efficiency for a particular policy. Instead, policymakers need to recognize that citizens value processes and outcomes differently. Reacting to Schachter's argument, Bohte (2007) agreed that citizens and policymakers are likely to disagree over the importance of policy outcomes. In fact, Bohte wrote that disagreement is "probably the rule rather than the exception" (2007, 812).

Because there is no one agreed-upon definition of efficiency or equity, policymakers are free to use symbols and to craft language in such a way as to create certain policy images. These policy images then serve as representations of the policy generally. What values guide the policy process? For Edelman, Fischer, and Stone, the answer to this question is "it depends." Whether a policy is judged as good or bad or is considered a success or failure is ultimately a value choice. Normative or value judgments, in addition to rational judgments, influence public policy decisions. Although efficiency arguments tend to guide policy analysis, Stone made a strong case that what constitutes efficiency, as well as other democratic values, is also a value choice.

Social Constructions and Target Populations

To understand and analyze the policy process requires an understanding of the way in which policymakers create and use measures for policy evaluation. How we characterize groups of individuals is based on multiple perspectives of the problem, as well as symbolism and the strategic framing of interests. Peter May (1991) wrote of such a strategy when distinguishing between "policies with publics" and "policies without publics." Policies with publics, i.e., policies with established constituencies, face a different set of design constraints than policies without publics. Whereas policies without publics do not have to adhere to the expectations of interested advocacy groups, such policies must also avoid inciting conflict that gets the attention of previously uninterested groups. The point is that policy design does not operate independently of politics. The process of policy design requires an acute awareness of how the public and the political world will respond to policy proposals.

As we have indicated, Stone's primary argument countered the "unambiguous" model of rational decision making; essentially, nothing is "value-free." What to include or exclude from the policy process is based on individual interpretation and contrasting worldviews. Although Stone did not completely discount rational decision making, she argued that the political community has a profound impact on the policy process. Key to Stone's argument is the notion that policy design is based on the politics of categorization: "what needs are legitimate" (2002, 98) and "how we do and should categorize in a world where categories are not given" (2002, 380).

Anne L. Schneider and Helen Ingram (1997) picked up on Stone's (1988) original notion of the politics of categorization. However, unlike scholars in the previous two sections who primarily focused on values of policymakers, Schneider and Ingram focused both on the deliberate use of values by policymakers as well as how such values are translated and interpreted by citizens. We turn first to their discussion of the actions of policymakers.

Schneider and Ingram began by arguing that only by evaluating policy content and substance is it possible to discern how and why policies are constructed. Using "policy design" as the dependent variable and "social construction" as the independent variable, the authors characterized the policymaking process as "degenerative" (1997, 11). Policies are designed by public officials to reinforce social constructions of various groups in society, described as "target populations." In addition, science is often used to further stigmatize these groups as "deserving" or "undeserving." As the authors noted, science is exploited as a means for justifying policy, not verifying specifics as the most appropriate means available as would be expected in the rational actor model. Science is used only when it is convergent with favorable policy options (A. Schneider and Ingram 1997, 12).

Policy designs are constructed and interpreted according to favorable meanings based on societal perspectives of target populations. Schneider and Ingram divided target populations into four main groups based on political power and perceived social constructions of deserving and undeserving groups. The four groups are advantaged, contenders, dependents, and deviants (1997, 109). Advantaged groups include scientists, business owners, senior citizens, and the military. Contenders, like advantaged groups, have a lot of political power but are perceived as less deserving than advantaged groups. Examples include labor unions, gun owners, and CEOs. Dependents are those groups that lack political power but are positively socially constructed (i.e., mothers, children, the poor, the mentally handicapped). For example, whereas individuals with disabilities seeking public education would fall under the heading of "dependents," distributive policies to this group have lacked sufficient resources because special education advocates are "weakly represented," thus yielding few political opportunities (A. Schneider and Ingram 1997,

126). Finally, deviants lack both political power and a positive social construction; thus they are perceived as politically weak and undeserving. Welfare mothers, criminals, terrorists, gangs, and the homeless tend to fall within this classification (examples are from A. Schneider and Ingram 1997, 109; Ingram, A. Schneider, and P. deLeon 2007, 102).

Importantly, these four categories are fluid and subject to change. Ingram, Schneider, and deLeon (2007) later distinguished between big business and small business, with the former being classified as contenders and the latter as advantaged. Advocacy groups tend to be the most fluid. For example, environmentalists in Schneider and Ingram's early classification are classified as having moderate political power and perceived as deserving, resulting in a classification somewhere between contenders and deviants. Later revisions by Ingram, Schneider, and deLeon (2007) placed environmentalists clearly in the contender grouping. Even within categories, groups can affect how other groups are socially constructed. Tracing the history of the social construction of welfare recipients, Sanford Schram (2005) wrote that because welfare was constructed in such a way as being synonymous with African Americans, the social construction of African Americans suffered. This had significant repercussions because African Americans suffered in terms of political power. Because welfare recipients were categorized as dependents, African Americans were initially socially constructed as a dependent population.

According to Schneider and Ingram, public officials purposefully construct policy designs based on a "burden/benefit" analysis of political opportunities and risks of the four categories of target populations (1997, 114). Advantaged groups tend to be targets for distributive policies that allocate benefits with little or no costs. Because advantaged groups are high in political power, policymakers benefit by minimizing policy costs and maximizing policy benefits to such groups. Contender groups also tend to receive policy benefits, but these benefits are not as explicit as for advantaged groups. Contenders tend to be perceived as "selfish, untrustworthy, and morally suspect" (Ingram, Schneider, and deLeon 2007, 102) and thus less deserving than advantaged groups. As a result, policy burdens tend to be more publicized than policy benefits. Indeed, as Ingram, Schneider, and deLeon wrote (2007), "benefits to contenders are hidden because no legislators want to openly do good things for shady people" (102).

Both advantaged groups and contenders tend to have a high degree of political power; the only difference is that the former are perceived as deserving whereas the latter are perceived as undeserving. Unlike these two groups, the other two groups in Schneider and Ingram's framework lack political power. Dependent groups such as the poor or handicapped are those groups that lack political power but are socially constructed as deserving. Although benefits distributed to dependent groups tend to be more explicit than those distributed to contenders, dependents' lack of political power prevents such groups from receiving maximum policy benefits. The problems of dependent groups are perceived as the result of individual failings rather than social problems. Doling out benefits to the poor or people on welfare is politically risky because such benefits are perceived as addressing individual problems at the expense of the public good. Dependent groups also tend to be the first to see their benefits cut in times of fiscal crisis (Schneider and Ingram 1993, 345; Ingram, Schneider, and deLeon 2007, 103). Finally, deviants, as would be expected, receive few if any policy benefits. Instead, policymakers tend to be more interested in ensuring "burdens" are distributed to such groups. Deviants "deserve to punished," and any policies that deviate from such expectations are likely to lead to negative consequences for the policymaker (Schneider and Ingram 1997, 130).

Schneider and Ingram's research is unique for the two-stage research process it employs. In the first stage, the researchers treat policy design as the dependent variable and social constructions as the key independent variable. As we have discussed, how groups are socially constructed (deserving or undeserving) ultimately affects policy design (the distribution of policy benefits and burdens). The second stage of Schneider and Ingram's work is to treat policy design as the independent variable and test for any effects on perceptions of citizenship and democratic efficacy. The authors posited that individuals placed in politically powerless groups (dependents and deviants) have a negative view of the political system, resulting in political apathy and low levels of political participation. Target populations learn their position in society as deserving or undeserving (Schneider and Ingram 1997, 103), and this has real implications for attitudes toward government.

Joe Soss (2005) provided a direct test of the second stage of Schneider and Ingram's framework. To conduct his research, Soss drew on interviews with recipients of Aid to Families with Dependent Children (AFDC). Because AFDC recipients depend on caseworkers for benefits, Soss argued that these individuals lack a sense of self-worth, resulting in negative or apathetic views about the political system. Soss found that recipients tend to sense that they have been categorized as members of a negative or "stigmatized" group (2005, 316). As a result, these recipients tend to be less likely to participate in government and are less likely to view such participation as meaningful. Earlier work by Soss (1999) also found that perceptions regarding policy designs directly influence perceptions of political efficacy. As Soss wrote, "policy designs teach lessons about citizenship status and government" (1999, 376).

By distributing costs and benefits to target populations according to whether they are perceived as deserving or undeserving, elites reinforce power relationships. In turn, this shapes political participation as the targets of specific policies develop positive or negative attitudes toward government and the ability to effectively influence governmental activity. Take a real-life example from a college community: following a homecoming football game, several hundred college students rioted in the streets, burning cars and causing significant property damage. In the years following that event, the local police department rightly placed riot barricades along the street where the most rioting occurred. This first riot, however, proved to be the exception rather than the rule. Nonetheless, in the ten years since that initial and singular event, the police of the local community have placed riot police on the streets during homecoming weekend in anticipation of a violent demonstration by college students. Adopting the first phase of Schneider and Ingram's framework, the image conveyed to those citizens is that they are deviant and uncivil citizens. The target population is college students, and this group is socially constructed as a deviant and undeserving population. The second phase of Schneider and Ingram's framework would suggest that these students are likely to have, on average, more negative attitudes toward government and, on average, perceive government as less likely to respond to their interests.

The work by Soss, as well as early work by Schneider and Ingram, clearly implicates the connection between the study of policy design and the study of democratic citizenship and whether the actions of government fulfill democratic values. Ingram and Schneider (2005b, 6) later argued that the "degenerative" nature of public policy is worsened by the path-dependent nature of social constructions. Social constructions become embedded in society, rarely questioned and rarely subject to change. Implicit in this reasoning is the notion that any policy proposals xisting social constructions will be passed unanimously by a legislative body. But can social constructions change? Can the targets of public policies expand or contract?

According to Peter May, the answer is yes. Social constructions are not static; instead, policymakers adjust beliefs about policy problems in response to incoming stimuli, evidence of what May (1992, 332) described as "social learning." Social learning is different from instrumental learning. Although both entail forms of what May has described as "policy learning," instrumental learning is more reflective of the rationalist approach to policy analysis, emphasizing the means for solving policy problems and learning through policy evaluation. Social learning is more goal-oriented, focusing on the cause of the problem and beliefs about target populations. May has cited evidence of social policy learning as cases in which the targets of policy proposals change or beliefs about the goals of the policy change (1992, 351). Policy learning is considerably more likely for "policies with publics" (May 1991) because such policies allow for a give and take and an updating of beliefs about established groups.

Learning, however, is not limited to policy content. Unlike policy learning, "political learning" concerns the ability of policy elites to craft politically feasible policy proposals. Political learning and policy learning are distinct but interrelated concepts; with a change in beliefs about the goals of a policy, policy elites may adopt new strategies for pushing a particular policy. Although May has admitted that evidence of policy and political learning is difficult to systematically and empirically assess, his model provides a theoretical basis as to how target populations are socially constructed and also that such social constructions are subject to change.

Nicholson-Crotty and Meier (2005) picked up on this issue. Whereas Nicholson-Crotty and Meier agreed that policymakers deliberately use social constructions to craft public policy, they contended that the process is more complex than suggested by Ingram and Schneider. At issue is the notion that policy proposals designed to burden deviant groups will have little or no resistance in becoming public policy. Nicholson-Crotty and Meier instead have argued that three conditions must be met before this transition takes place. First, the group must be perceived as "marginal" by those who hold political power. Second, there must be a "moral entrepreneur" who actively seeks to link the actions of the group to larger societal problems. This individual must possess political power or be a well-respected expert. Nicholson-Crotty and Meier discussed the role of James Q. Wilson as a moral entrepreneur in assisting the passage of crime legislation in 1984. Wilson, because of his role as a well-respected academic, was able to shape the discussion in such a way that linked criminal behavior with the decline of community values (Nicholson-Crotty and Meier 2005, 237). Finally, the third component is the "political entrepreneur." This individual is similar to Kingdon's (1995) policy entrepreneur in that this person attempts to convince other policymakers that the proposal represents sound public policy. In short, policymakers use social constructions to design public policy, but the link is more nuanced than originally argued by Schneider and Ingram.

Despite the preconditions outlined by Nicholson-Crotty and Meier (2005), most policy design scholars agree on the intersubjective nature of policy design as well as the potential for degenerative politics. Edelman, Fischer, and Stone have all argued that values have infused the policy process; that policy decisions are based on the deliberate use of symbols, narratives, and stories; and that the study of public policy requires postpositivist methodology, which accounts for intersubjectivity and constructed realities. Anne Schneider and Helen Ingram took this a step further by asking whether such intersubjectivity is deleterious to democracy. As should be apparent by our discussion, they found strong evidence that socially constructed realities do in fact create unequal groups. Some groups are targeted for policy benefits whereas others are targeted for policy burdens. These decisions are not based on rational cost-benefit analyses but instead on socially constructed realities. Although "policy learning" does occur (May 1992), so too does political learning, thus there is no guarantee that policymakers will make decisions on the basis of what is good public policy. And even though it may be more practical and logical to design policy that redistributes benefits to groups that are rationally justified as suffering from societal problems, political risks often dissuade rational officials from pursuing such action (Schneider and Ingram 1997, 115). The lack of democratic values and the subsequent lack of interest in politics also have real practical implications for democracy.

"Democratic" Values and Policy Design

In liberal democracies, the normative underpinning of public policy should be democratic values. As a normative claim, this is a supportable argument. But how do we test it? Do public policies indeed reflect democratic ideals? Stone's (2002) work has questioned whether there can ever be agreement on what constitutes such democratic values as equity or liberty. Schneider and Ingram have also stressed that the values inherent in policy symbols are inherently undemocratic. Unique to all of these scholars is an explicit call for a more democratic policymaking process; from problem definition to policy design, democratic values should be inherent in the policy process. So, if democratic values should guide the policy process, but clearly do not, how do we correct this?

As we discussed earlier in the chapter, many scholars agree that quantitative approaches to the study of public policy such as cost-benefit analyses ignore the intersubjectivity guiding the policy process (see Fischer 1980; Edelman 1990). Up to this point, we have emphasized the theoretical solutions to this dilemma, most notably post-positivist methodology such as constructionism and hermeneutics. For Peter deLeon, however, this intersubjectivity and deliberate use of value and symbols has resulted in a growing separation between government and its citizens, requiring a more practical response.

Drawing on Harold Lasswell's notion of the "policy sciences of democracy," deLeon (1995, 1997) argued that the policymaking process has shifted away from core democratic values. For deLeon, the move toward a more positivist approach to the study of public policy resulted in a shift away from Lasswell's policy sciences of democracy. Ultimately, deLeon saw the policy sciences as captured by two dominant approaches, utilitarianism and liberal-rationalism, both of which have increased the distance between citizens and their government. Utilitarianism, because it advocates a strong role for the market and relies heavily on data, ignores "human factors" (P. deLeon 1997, 53). The utilitarian approach ignores the wishes of ordinary citizens and ignores how citizens interpret policy messages sent by governing elites. As deLeon (1997) wrote, this leads to policy research that is "methodologically rich and results poor" (55). The solution? According to deLeon, a more involved citizenry. As deLeon has written, "individual values are just as open to analysis as are the relative 'facts,' and must similarly be open to public discourse" (P. deLeon 1997, 79).

On a theoretical level, deLeon called for post-positivist methodology, particularly the use of deconstructionism and hermeneutics to more appropriately link the policy sciences with democratic values. DeLeon, however, also offered a practical solution for more democratic policy design.

For deLeon, the current state of policy research is detrimental to democracy. The lack of democratic values creates an apathetic public, and, as deLeon (1997) wrote, democracy cannot "cope with the contemporary civic malaise and political frustration" (100). DeLeon's main concern was that policy science has become disconnected from its primary "clientele, the citizenry" (1997, 98). To correct this, the study of public policy must be characterized by open discourse between citizens and policymakers. The solution: participatory policy analysis (PPA). PPA refers to the notion of directly engaging citizens in public policymaking. DeLeon has cited numerous examples in which citizen panels have been constructed to assist in policy design and in which the result has been a more satisfied citizenry. The underlying assumption of PPA is that citizens want more involvement in the policymaking process and that such involvement will ameliorate growing disenchantment with government institutions and government elite.

For policy design scholars such as Schneider and Ingram (1997) and Soss (1999, 2006) apathy breeds disinterest and the desire to withdraw from political life, further perpetuating a cycle of undemocratic policymaking. Participatory policy analysis moves the citizen from a passive, reactionary role in the policy process to an active, decision-making role. Paraphrasing John Dewey, deLeon wrote: "The cure for the ailments of democracy is more civic participation" (1997, 43). More citizen participation in the policy process increases citizen satisfaction with the political process *and* creates better public policy.[3] Only through citizen engagement will the policy sciences truly reflect democratic values. DeLeon's (1997) call for PPA has fueled research examining the effects of citizen participation on improving policy responsiveness and overall citizen satisfaction with the policymaking process (see also Fung and Wright 2003a; Macedo 2005). Even public administration scholars have advocated for a more citizen-oriented approach to policy design. For example, Schachter (2007) has argued that the only way for an organization to agree on efficiency is through input from stakeholders. Although Schachter does not cite deLeon, her policy prescriptions are certainly in line with those of deLeon.

The manner in which target populations identify with and engage in society speaks volumes about the state of democracy. In their seminal work, *Policy Design for Democracy*, Schneider and Ingram concluded that the social construction of target populations challenges pluralist ideals, threatening to further the crisis of democracy (1997, 198). Policy designs are based on the construction and maintenance of power through target populations. Policy design determines the social construction of target population and, in turn, affects how those target populations view their role in society. Designs that favor the status quo are favorable because they represent political opportunity. As a result, certain groups have maintained relatively permanent status as positive target populations, with a significant amount of political power.

Refining their earlier work, Ingram and Schneider (2006) later called for a more explicit and active role for citizens. Like Peter deLeon, Ingram and Schneider (2006) view the study of public policy as a normative exercise: "The public must become more directly involved in holding government structures accountable" (Ingram and Schneider 2006, 182). Ingram and Schneider have explicitly argued that policy design should serve democracy and policy analysts should "design policy that will better serve democracy" (2006, 172). Not only should policy design serve democracy, but, according to Ingram and Schneider, "citizens ought to view their role as citizens as important" (2006, 172). For deLeon, Ingram, and Schneider, policy design shapes the connection between citizens and government. Thus, the primary means for improving policy design and increasing citizen satisfaction with government is through citizen engagement in the policy process. Similar to deLeon's PPA approach, Ingram and Schneider (2006) have contended that when citizens are given a voice in the policy process, they will "be encouraged through this policy change to engage in discourse" (176).

The policy process rarely fits with the market model of economics in which goals are clearly defined and alternatives considered comprehensively in an objective costs-and-benefits manner. Instead, it is a battle over what values should guide the policy process. Schneider and Ingram have made a strong case that democratic values should be involved in policy design. However, in their view, policy design tends to be based on constructed realities that benefit advantaged groups. The result is undemocratic policy design and a self-perpetuating system of "degenerative politics." Not only are values and symbols present in the policy process, they are used deliberately by policymakers. For Schneider and Ingram, the current state of policy design is both undemocratic and non-pluralist. Policy designs impart messages to target populations of their status and how others think of them, and current policy designs teach powerless groups (dependents and deviants) that mobilization and participation are useless. As Ingram, Schneider, and deLeon stated, "Messages convey who belongs, whose interests are important, what kind of 'game' politics is, and whether one has a place at the table" (2007, 100). For deLeon, the only way to change such messages is through a more policy active citizenry. When citizens participate in the policymaking process, their sense of efficacy and trust in government increases, making the policy process more democratic as well as improving the overall quality of policy design.

Testing Policy Design Theories?

In one sense, the claims that emerge from the field of policy design draw universal agreement. Most policy scholars agree with Edelman, Fischer, and Stone that policymakers make deliberate and selective use of facts, stories, and images to support particular policies. Most policy scholars agree with Schneider and Ingram that policymakers distribute policy burdens and benefits in such a way as to maximize political gain. Political scientists have long noted that elected officials are driven primarily by the desire for reelection (see Mayhew 1974). So it is no surprise that elites will attempt to embed certain values within policy designs that reinforce existing perceptions and avoid negative repercussions. Yet for positivist social scientists, the frameworks discussed throughout this chapter are viewed with skepticism—the concepts too amorphous to systematically guide research and the methods lacking the empirical rigor associated with the rationalist project.

Testing the policy design theories discussed in this chapter, like the theories themselves, is a messy process. To be considered a legitimate subfield, policy design needs to offer some predictability to the policy process. Thus far we have broken the field down into three stages: the values scholars (Edelman, Fischer and Forester, C. Anderson), the politics-of-categorization scholars (Stone, Schneider, and Ingram), and the participatory scholars (deLeon, Schneider, and Ingram). All three sets of scholars agree on the need for diverse methodology when studying policy design, but to be considered a legitimate subfield (i.e., one that generates testable hypotheses), many questions still need to be answered.

As has been discussed, early policy design scholars argued that policymakers craft stories to fit with existing policies. Can we predict what values, stories, narratives, and images will resonate with citizens? Are post-positivist methods such as constructionism or hermeneutics more appro-priate for certain stages of the policy process? Schneider and Ingram have argued that social constructions and policy design reduce democratic participation. Perhaps, but by how much? What type of participation? Soss (2005) has provided a solid first cut at these questions using survey research, but questions still remain. How much variation in participation levels is there between deviants and dependents, between contenders and advantaged groups? What causes a group to change from deviant to de-pendent? Can a group ever move from dependent to contender to advan-taged, and vice versa? From Kingdon (1995) we know that focusing events significantly shape how we view societal problems. Does this hold for the classification of target groups? Why do some social constructions fade over time? What constitutes evidence of "social learning" or "politi-cal learning"? A central problem for the policy design project is that its conceptual frameworks do not generate clean, empirically testable hy-potheses; ultimately its empirical claims are not particularly empirical. This is not wholly surprising given its emphasis on the subjective nature of reality, but it provides no clear basis for sorting out which claims or perspectives are the best basis for judging policy. The rationalist project, for all of its shortcomings, offers a steady platform for generating com-parative judgments of public policy and has a central notion of the value to guide such judgments: efficiency. Policy design has no equivalent inter-nal conceptual gyroscope.

Consider deLeon, Schneider, and Ingram's call for PPA. Does this not fly directly in the face of Stone's argument about the difficulties of ensur-ing equity? Who participates? How much participation? At what stage of the policy process? About what decisions? The assumption underlying this solution is that citizens, if given the chance, want to be involved in policymaking. However, research on public attitudes toward government suggest otherwise. Drawing from extensive survey and focus group re-search, Hibbing and Theiss-Morse (1995, 2002) found that in fact most citizens do *not* want to be involved in the policy process. What they want is the comfort in knowing that policymakers are looking out for their best interests. As Hibbing and Theiss-Morse found, most citizens are not com-forted by what they see in the policy process. As a result, they feel forced to pay attention to politics, not out of a desire to participate but out of a desire to keep policymakers in check. Joining groups is not the answer to increased satisfaction with government because homogenous groups tend to reinforce the perception of a commonality of interest where one does not exist (Hibbing and Theiss-Morse 2005). Thus, whereas deLeon has argued that increased levels of citizen participation will improve satisfaction with government, Hibbing and Theiss-Morse argued that rarely do citizens want to participate, only when they feel it is necessary to prevent self-interested behavior on the part of elites. Even Deborah Stone (2002) would most likely take issue with deLeon's recommendation for more citizen involvement. As her discussion of ensuring equity in school board elections demonstrates, even when most parties are in agreement on the need to be inclusive, conflict arises over what constitutes equitable public participation. On a more practical level, Bohte (2007, 813) cautioned against too much citizen involvement because citizens tend to lack the knowledge regarding how policies will be implemented.

Conclusion

Policy design scholars have made a series of important contributions to the field of policy studies. Edelman, Fischer, Stone, and others make a convincing case that the content of public policy is normatively driven and that policymakers symbolically manipulate the policy process to achieve value-based ends. Moreover, they make an equally convincing case that rational actor models of political behavior and policy evaluation are unlikely to catch the key policy implications of this normative perspective.

Although their descriptions of the policy process and policy design are not neat and clean, they do move us closer to understanding the content of public policy and what it means for understanding power relationships in society. One of the clear lessons of policy design research is that those who wield political power are those who are able to construct a reality that fits with their proposed policies. Policy design is perhaps best understood as the politics of defining goals or the politics of categorization. Stone (2005) has summed up this argument quite nicely by writing: "policy is precisely this deliberate ordering of the world according to the principle of different treatment for different categories" (ix).

The field of policy design has also contributed significantly to the study of how citizens form perceptions in relation to their government. Policy designs are often utilized to reinforce existing power relationships and perceptions regarding the appropriate role of government. As Schneider and Ingram (1997) and Soss (2005) noted, values are often embedded in policy designs, and these values have important implications regarding democratic participation. In fact, most policy design scholars agree that the study of policy design provides evidence of nondemocratic values in the policymaking process and non-pluralistic competition, and that policy is often used to reinforce nondemocratic values (see Schneider and Ingram 2005). Stone and Fischer have both agreed that policy evaluations are based on political evaluations. Schneider and Ingram have provided a framework for testing whether these political evaluations have damaging effects on political participation and attitudes toward government.

If the policy process is based on constructed realities and intersubjective interpretations, the obvious question is: How does one determine whether a policy is effective? Edelman, Fischer, and Stone have laid the groundwork for a theory of policy design and policy analysis based on post-positivist methodology. Their primary interest is accounting for "constructed" realities when conducting policy evaluations. Even though Stone and Fischer paint a picture of the policy process that is based on a constructed reality, this does not necessarily mean the policy process is unpredictable (see also Kingdon 1995). Rather, predictability increases once one recognizes the intersubjective nature of policymaking. Schneider and Ingram take this a step further by asking, given that policy design is infused with values, symbols, and stories, what effect does this have on the targets of such policy? Under this framework, "policy design" is treated as both the dependent variable and an important independent variable. We originally asked whose values are inherent in the policy process. As this chapter has made clear, a number of policy scholars see the content of public policies as undemocratic. Scholars describe the process of policy design as deliberate and manipulative, not a rational response to public problems. Policymakers use symbols and language to craft policy in such a way as to perpetuate existing stereotypes. For most of these scholars, policymakers, analysts, and even scholars should be more involved in accounting for the diversity of views shared by citizens affected by particular policies. One practical solution to this dilemma is the notion of more citizen involvement. By allowing for direct citizen participation in the policy process, policy design will reflect the values of the citizenry and avoid unintended or intended messages that deter citizen involvement or deter citizen efficacy. However, as noted in the previous section, there are serious empirical roadblocks regarding this solution.

Notes

1. See also Gilens (2000) for a discussion of the way symbolic language such as "welfare queen" has been used to perpetuate existing stereotypes of welfare recipients and to decrease public support for increasing welfare benefits.

2. Bohte (2007, 812) also used Stone's library example as an example of the difficulty of achieving efficiency in a public organization.

3. Other scholars (L. deLeon and Denhardt 2000) also express criticism at approaches that appear to strengthen the role of policymakers, such as bureaucrats, at the expense of citizens.

CHAPTER NINE

New Directions in Policy Research

In this chapter we present alternative approaches to the study of public policy that are being developed in fields such as experimental and behavioral economics, evolutionary psychology, and even neuroscience. The driving force behind these developments is the claim that rational choice in both its classical and bounded variants has problems explaining a large portion of human behavior. As these two general models of human behavior underpin a good deal of the most important conceptual frameworks in public policy (e.g., incrementalism, new institutionalism, the Tiebout model, punctuated equilibrium, and virtually all of the applied analysis frameworks originating in economics, such as cost-benefit analysis and welfare economics), their development obviously has the potential to significantly shape the field of policy studies. The central research question at the heart of these new theoretical approaches is this: Why do people do what they do? This is a question that strikes to the heart of all the social sciences. Is it important to public policy? The literature is at a relatively early stage of development, but the answer thus far clearly seems to be yes.

The field of policy studies, like other social sciences, has long held the view that people tend to deviate from models of complete rationality.

Where other fields such as behavioral economics, neuroscience, and experimental psychology have surpassed policy studies, however, is in building a theoretical framework for explaining such deviations. That people do not conform to traditional models of rationality is taken as a given in what are considered to be some of the most prominent policy models, e.g., incrementalism, new institutionalism, and punctuated equilibrium. What is missing is a theory for explaining such "irrational" behavior.

A quickly emerging and powerful tool for explaining deviations from the rational-comprehensive model comes from outside mainstream policy studies. For this group of scholars, people are still capable of making rational decisions, it is just that the type of rationality is more in line with what evolutionary psychologists refer to as "adaptive rationality." The basic premise of models of adaptive rationality is that the human mind evolved in an environment of scarce resources, in which group cooperation was critical to survival. Because of this environment, humans developed a strong sense of fairness and concern for what others think. Importantly, and unlike classical rationality often used in policy studies, adaptive rationality makes room for emotional considerations and cognitive shortcuts. Some scholars question whether these shortcuts are in fact "adaptive." Following Herbert Simon's (1947) initial emphasis on the limitations of human rationality, Newell and Simon (1972) documented the inability of people to adapt their decision-making heuristics to new situations. Cognitive shortcuts often resulted in suboptimal decisions. More recently, Bryan Jones has also picked up on the limitations of decision-making heuristics. While accepting the premise that people are incapable of making completely rational decisions, Jones (2001) has contended that cognitive limitations prevent people from adapting appropriately to current situations. Instead, people tend to "adapt in disjointed ways" (B. Jones 2001, ix). The inability of human beings to process information in a rational manner leads to a heavy reliance on decision-making shortcuts or heuristics. For Jones, these heuristics not only represent deviations from the rational actor model but also potentially bad policy decisions. Institutions offer the key to correcting for such heuristics, and the best way to conceptualize institutional design is through an interdisciplinary approach to human behavior. For scholars such as Jones, heuristics are not adaptive, and in fact require well-structured institutions to prevent maladaptive decisions. For evolutionary psychologists, the question is not whether these heuristics are adaptive but that such heuristics developed in response to evolutionary pressures.

Other scholars have placed strong emphasis on categorizing decision-making heuristics under the umbrella of bounded rationality. Scholars in the ABC Research Group at the Max Planck Institute for Human Development have devoted two edited volumes to the research and development of the concepts of "Simple Heuristics That Make Us Smart" and bounded rationality (Gigerenzer and Selton 2002; Gigerenzer and Todd 1999b).

Whether it is adaptive rationality or reasoning through heuristics, the point is that the rational-comprehensive model of decision making is unrealistic and incomplete. In the remainder of this chapter we discuss several heuristics, or what might better be considered well-established patterns in human decision making, that we believe have the most relevance for explaining change in the policy process and policy decision making. The list is by no means complete, nor is it exhaustive. Rather, we believe they provide good starting points for retesting existing theories as well as building new conceptual frameworks. Following this section, we discuss the role of evolutionary psychology as a potentially fruitful avenue for theory building, with a specific application to crime policy. Theoretical and empirical developments being made outside mainstream political and policy science offer important insights for understanding the policy process; we believe it would behoove policy scholars to pay attention to such developments.

Policy Change and Social Utility

To become an issue, an idea must reach the governmental agenda. In Chapter 2 we discussed theories put forth by policy scholars about how an idea becomes an issue. For Baumgartner and Jones (1993), agenda setting is a relatively stable process, with an occasional punctuation usually sparked by a change in policy image. More recent work by True, Jones, and Baumgartner (1999; B. Jones, Baumgartner, and True 1998) has suggested that such punctuations are more widespread and occur more frequently than originally thought. For Kingdon (1995), policy change is the result of the merging of the three "streams." At the heart of each of these explanations is a focus on policy definition. As issues are redefined, they increase or decrease the likelihood of policymakers picking up on the issue (see Stone 2002). Despite the explanatory power of these frameworks, questions remain: What causes people to pay attention to particular issues? Why do people tend to react strongly to some policy images rather than others? Why do issues that are defined as social dilemmas do better than issues defined purely in instrumental terms?

Baumgartner and Jones's punctuated equilibrium and Kingdon's streams approach do not address these questions. Instead, their interest is in describing macro-level policy change (Wood and Vedlitz 2007). What is needed is a micro-level model of policy change that focuses on how individuals process policy information, particularly information relating to policy image. B. Dan Wood and his colleagues have offered an attempt at such a model. Of particular interest is the finding that people tend to conform to the majority opinion. When presented with information about the predominant view of others on a particular issue, people tend to adjust their views to match those of their peers (Wood and Vedlitz 2007; see also Wood and Doan 2003). From a rationalist perspective, this seems illogical. Why should the views of others matter when evaluating public policy? From the standpoint of social psychology and neuroscience, however, it makes perfect sense. People tend to be hypersensitive to what others think of them (Cialdini and Goldstein 2004). Indeed, evidence from neuroscience indicates that social exclusion results in neural activity similar to that which is experienced during physical pain (Eisenberger, Lieberman, and Williams 2003). That is, the brain processes sensations experienced by social exclusion as being analogous to those experienced during physical trauma. Repercussions stemming from the loss of an existing social bond are likely to be perceived as damaging to individual fitness as are decisions to forego immediate tangible incentives (Panksepp 2003). As such, we would expect people to moderate their individual policy attitudes to match those of their surroundings. For models of policy change, this suggests policy proposals often gain traction not because of their policy appeal but rather because others find them appealing. Policymakers who are able to craft proposals perceived as enjoying mass support are therefore at a distinct advantage.

The "policy sciences" were intended to improve upon the quality of public policy as a way of improving upon the human condition. To understand the human condition, however, requires an understanding of what makes people happy. Reviewing the extant literature in neuroscience, Rose McDermott (2004) wrote that it is not material well-being or "economic indicators" such as income that produces happiness. Instead, happiness is related to what McDermott described as "social support" (2004, 701). What does this mean for public policy? McDermott wrote,

> if happiness derives from social support, government should place less emphasis on incomes and more on employment and job programs, encouraging leisure activities . . . by supporting after-school programs and public parks—and supporting marriage and other family relationships. (701)

Humans are social creatures, deriving satisfaction from interactions with others. People tend to shy away from expressing preferences that are at odds with the rest of the group. In fact, people will often incur material costs to maximize social benefits. A simple way to maximize social benefits is fitting within the group. The result is often that revealed preferences are at odds with private preferences. Kuran (1995) described this tendency as "preference falsification." Particularly in public settings, people tend to withhold their true preferences to maintain a favorable reputation and avoid social ostracism.

Kuran's notion of preference falsification is significant when considered in the context of Baumgartner and Jones's punctuated equilibrium. Kuran's basic argument was that people tend to have an intrinsic utility (their true preference), a reputational utility (the result of how others will react to one's true preference), and an expressive utility (the utility of expressing one's true preference publicly). In a public setting, the choice between maximizing reputational utility versus expressive utility tends toward the former. However, Kuran noted that this tendency leads to "hidden opposition to positions that enjoy vast public support" (1995, 335). As more people express an opinion, the pressure to maximize one's reputational utility, at the expense of intrinsic utility, increases.[1] However, if it is revealed that what most people prefer in private is shared by others, there exists the potential for a "social explosion" (335). The premise behind punctuated equilibrium is that a change in policy image can cause a sudden change in policy. The theoretical basis for this sudden change most likely rests with people's willingness to maximize their expressive utility. Baumgartner and Jones gave the example of nuclear scientists who privately held skepticism about the safety standards of nuclear power.

Only after the Three Mile Island accident were they willing to express these reservations publicly. In other words, once the majority opinion shifted to be more in line with their private preferences, they were willing to maximize their intrinsic utility.

Kuran's work also speaks to Kingdon's (1995) model of policy change. To achieve significant policy change, policy specialists working in the policy stream must be able to recognize the opening of a policy window in the problem or political stream. The latter stream is determined in large part by public opinion, or what Kingdon has called the "national mood." Preference falsification is potentially problematic for policy specialists in two ways: 1) the national mood may not reflect the public's true preference for policy change, leading to unwanted policy (reputational utility is more beneficial than expressive utility); and 2) the national mood is highly volatile and can change without any action on the part of the policy specialist (a focusing event increases the costs of reputational utility allowing for maximization of expressive utility).

For evolutionary psychologists and neuroscientists, the tendency to engage in preference falsification is hardwired into our brains. People tend to value being part of a group as much or more than tangible benefits they may receive from a particular policy. Existing models of policy change, however, tend to rely solely on such benefits or environmental causes. Recognizing that preference falsification is endogenous to policy change will improve our understanding of why sudden and rapid policy change occurs.

Policy Decision Making Is Emotional

Joseph LeDoux (1996, 2002), a leading neuroscientist, has argued that neural connections in the brain point to a significant role for emotions in decision-making processes. Focusing on the amygdala as the emotional center for affects associated with fear, LeDoux finds that neural connections flowing from the cortical areas to the amygdala are weaker than connections flowing from the amygdala to the cortical regions of the brain. In other words, whereas the cortex and neocortex are assumed to represent the cognitive, reasoning portion of the brain—serving as a filter to guide rational decision making—the amygdala, representing a focal point for affective motivations, is capable of overriding conscious, rational processes.

Stated differently, emotional processes exert a stronger influence over the process of discerning the context of external stimuli than rational processes. Indeed, as LeDoux and others (see Damasio 1994; Fessler 2002) have observed, this process often occurs unconsciously, furthering the argument that emotions serve as powerful behavioral motivations in human decision-making processes.

The two dominant frameworks of policy analysis, cost-benefit analysis and welfare economics, are designed with the explicit intent of removing emotion from the decision-making processes. Policy decisions should be made according to the estimated costs and benefits of available alternatives, with the most efficient decision (the one that minimizes costs and maximizes benefits) being implemented. From a rationalist perspective, cost-benefit analysis makes perfect sense. From a neurological perspective, this is at odds with how the brain actually works. Rather than focusing on costs and benefits, or economic rationality, the brain processes information in such a way that is more line with "emotional rationality" (McDermott 2004).[2] Not only do emotions affect decision making, they tend to guide decision making, often with improvements in the overall outcome. The basic assumption of welfare economics, institutional rational choice, the Tiebout model, and their prescriptive policy derivatives such as school choice is that people are rational actors and will behave in ways that maximize their own economic self-interest. The theory of emotional rationality suggests this is the exception rather than the norm.

In short, emotional triggers drown out rational considerations. McDermott wrote, "emotion remains endogenous to rationality itself" (2004, 693). A purely rationalist approach to policy analysis is essentially asking the human brain to override itself. If emotions result in bad policy decisions, such an approach might be warranted. But, as it turns out, this is not the case. Humans are capable of making intelligent decisions. As Damasio's (1994) research on patients with acute brain damage has demonstrated, people lacking areas of the brain associated with emotional responses are unable to engage in favorable social interactions— often exhibiting higher levels of unemployment and divorce.

That emotions guide decision making casts considerable doubt on the assumptions of "classic" policy models. Take, for example, the Tiebout model. The assumption of the Tiebout model is that people make mobility decisions based on the quality of service being provided—that people make rational decisions based on policy outputs. The same argument holds for proponents of school choice—parental decisions about which school to send their children are based on school outputs such as test scores. As we discussed at length in Chapter 3, the assumptions of the Tiebout model and school choice models break down when subjected to empirical scrutiny. But what is the theoretical and empirical basis for this disconnect? The neurological role of emotions gives policy scholars an endogenous variable that will boost the explanatory power of policy decision models. Policy specialists that position alternatives in the context of emotional appeals are more likely to find receptive venues than if such alternatives are discussed in purely instrumental or rational terms. In fact, there is now evidence that politicians who cater to emotions have more electoral success than those who focus on policy details, or what would be considered the "rational" part of public policy (Weston 2007). We do not deny that emotional rationality opens the door for demagoguery on the part of politicians and policy specialists. But understanding that the potential for such demagoguery exists is likely the first step in understanding ways to correct for it. To do so requires a neurological understanding of how the brain processes incoming information, whether that information is policy related or not.

People do not make decisions based on policy outputs; they make decisions on the basis of emotions and the preferences of their group, however they define "group." For some, this might mean conforming to the preferences of their neighbors; for others the group might be the local PTA, a bowling club, or a reading group. That emotions guide the decision-making process has important implications for at least two major areas of policy scholarship: 1) agenda setting; and 2) policy analysis. Models of policy change continue to be critiqued on the grounds that they are not predictive. Yes, significant policy change can occur because of a focusing event or the merging of the three streams, but when is this likely to happen? The problem is that these models tend to be couched in a rationalist framework. If the frame of reference were shifted from economic rationality to emotional rationality, we argue, the predictive power of such models would increase. People make decisions not devoid of emotions or in a vacuum but rather with a very strong awareness of what those around them will think about their decision and with a very powerful emotional base.

Merging Policy Studies with Evolutionary Psychology

Why is the brain wired in such a way as to give social pressure and a concern for reputation within a group such prominence in decision making? Why are people so sensitive to the perceptions of others? The basic assumption of evolutionary psychology is that the human mind is a product of evolutionary pressures. The brain evolved to solve adaptive problems faced by our hunter-gatherer ancestors in the Environment of Evolutionary Adaptation or EEA (Cosmides and Tooby 1992). A main problem of the EEA was a reliable source of food. The scarcity of food resources required group cooperation and sharing to survive. A cognitive by-product of this environment was a strong tendency toward cooperation with one's in-group and a desire to maintain a favorable reputation among other group members. Scarcity of resources also created a hypersensitivity to fairness norms. A group member who hoarded food in the EEA was essentially trading a public good for his or her own selfish ends. Because such behavior likely meant death for another group member, people developed a strong disposition for detecting cheaters in social situations. According to Cosmides and Tooby, the EEA led to the development of a "cheater detection module"—a behavioral predisposition for detecting cheaters in instances of social exchange.

Evolutionary psychology posits that individual preferences are a function of *both* the environment and what Cosmides and Tooby have called evolved "psychological mechanisms" (1992, 165). Within political science, the assumptions of evolutionary psychology are gaining traction as a useful framework for explaining political behavior. Alford and Hibbing (2004) have proposed that people are actually "wary cooperators." People will cooperate when others cooperate but will cease cooperation when others defect and will incur a cost to punish others for noncooperation. Alford and Hibbing argued that the model of the wary cooperator has important policy implications. Take, for example, compliance with tax policy. The wary cooperator model posits that we pay our taxes only because we assume others are doing the same (Alford and Hibbing 2004, 711). If it is revealed that others are cheating on their taxes by not paying, and getting away with it, the result is likely to be widespread disgust with government (this also fits with Kuran's model of preference falsification). The same holds for perceptions of welfare policy. Why does an image of a welfare recipient not actively seeking employment provoke such strong public reactions? Because such an image sets off our cheater detection sensor—this is someone who is accepting benefits without incurring a cost. The "welfare to work" motto of the 1996 Welfare Reform Act passed by the federal government was most likely an attempt to allay fears that the policy was simply benefiting free riders (Rubin 2002, 196); the motto served to ease the reaction of our cheater detection module. Humans seem to possess a strong disposition toward cooperation but also a high level of skepticism toward others. From an evolutionary perspective, this is a highly adaptive strategy (Orbell et al. 2004). On the one hand, it leads to optimal outcomes while at the same time preventing suboptimal outcomes as a result of being played for a sucker. In fact, the cheater detection module allows humans to remember cheaters at a higher rate than altruists (Chiappe et al. 2004), suggesting that strong reactions to the image of the lazy welfare recipient or the non-taxpayer are likely to be long-lasting.

If adaptive pressures on the mind produced similar behavioral outcomes and expressed preferences as those predicted by the rational actor model, this research could be ignored. Similarly, if adaptive rationality led to suboptimal outcomes, the evolutionary psychology framework could be dismissed. But, as Cosmides and Tooby (1994, 329) have discussed, evolved modules, such as the cheater detection module, actually lead to decisions that are "better than rational." For example, Gerd Gigerenzer and his colleagues have repeatedly demonstrated that people using "fast and frugal" decision-making heuristics are quite capable of making optimal decisions (Gigerenzer and Todd 1999a; see also Gigerenzer and Selton 2002). The reason: adaptive pressures have selected for optimal cognitive mechanisms, mechanisms that deviate sharply from the assumption of complete information in the rational-comprehensive model. These mechanisms are designed to efficiently and effectively solve social dilemmas, and they have important relevance for solving policy problems.

A prime example of adaptive rationality in action comes from the work of Elinor Ostrom and her colleagues on common-pool resource dilemmas. In the case of a common-pool resource, the rational actor model would predict an overuse of the resource. From a welfare economics perspective, to correct for such inefficiency requires external intervention. As we discussed at length in Chapter 3, these dilemmas can actually be solved through mechanisms other than those predicted by welfare economics or cost-benefit analyses; simple solutions such as face-to-face communication and the threat of punishment are enough to prevent overuse and ensure cooperation (Ostrom, Walker, and Gardner 1992, 1994; see also E. Ostrom 2005). The question that is left unanswered, however, is: Why are such mechanisms so effective? The theory of the "wary" cooperator and "emotional rationality" provide an answer to this question. Face-to-face communication creates a sense of group identity, which if violated, is likely to lead to social ostracism. Adaptive psychological mechanisms have created behavioral predispositions that guard against ostracism-type behavior.

As an example ingrained in the minds of policy scholars, take March's (1994) "logic of appropriateness." According to March's theory, people tend to do what is perceived as appropriate for the situation. That is, people tend to base their behavior on existing institutional culture and norms. Essential to this argument is an ability to read others' expectations and gauge what is acceptable and not acceptable within an organization. At a very basic level this is about the ability to fit within a group and identify with other group members. Evolutionary psychology and the theory of the "wary cooperator" indicate humans possess a strong capacity for doing just that. In fact, the ability to mind-read has been found to be evolutionarily adaptive and fits within the broader framework of "Machiavellian intelligence" (Orbell et al. 2004, 14; see also Whiten and Byrne 1997). The EEA mandated an ability to join groups and sustain group membership. A failure to conform to group norms meant social ostracism and most likely death. Doing what is appropriate is about figuring out how to be part of the in-group and successfully navigating in-group relationships.

Biological and cognitive factors also provide enormous explanatory power to everyday policy decisions. To take one example, consider the decision to contribute to a public good such as National Public Radio (NPR). From a purely rational perspective, at the individual level, no one should contribute; they should free ride off others' contributions. But if everyone free rides, no one will contribute. The reality is that people do contribute, and often can be cajoled into contributing through emotional appeals or social pressure. Why? The pressure to conform with the majority opinion, the fear of being labeled a "free rider," or not conforming to social norms in a public setting all increase the likelihood of a negative reaction from one's peers.[3] Consider other donation drives that attempt to prime the emotion of shame by asking for donations over the phone or in person at the local grocery store. The idea is to put people in a situation that favors an emotional response, and most likely a generous response. Behavioral predispositions against violating group norms are the result of evolutionary pressures and exert a strong influence on public preferences.

Knowing that people are more adept at solving social dilemmas could also help to explain why people react to certain policy images in the way that they do. For example, Nelson (1984) found that child abuse was able to reach the policy agenda only after it was redefined as a social dilemma. Similarly, the issue of providing education to children with disabilities only reached the national agenda after it was defined as a social issue (Cremins 1983). From a rationalist perspective, the framing of the issue is irrelevant. Redefined as social issues, however, people are better able to understand the issues and are more open to addressing them. Although we acknowledge that policymakers can use this information to manipulate policy images in such a way as to trick citizens, we believe such an approach is still useful. In fact, as Paul Rubin (2002, 164–165) wrote, this social element is built into policy decision making. Rather than relying on policy details, elected officials regularly bring in individuals affected by a policy or issue to give their personal testimony. As Rubin noted, from a rationalist perspective this does not make sense nor should it affect the final decision. The details of the policy have not changed. Personal testimony, however, particularly on highly salient issues, gives people "identifiable" individuals who are affected by the policy (2002, 164). For those watching, the policy image has changed from an abstract problem to one with social and emotional implications. The result is that people will give more weight to one side of the argument even though the details have not changed. Consider the effect of Ryan White on the image of AIDS as a national problem, or the effect of Michael J. Fox testifying before Congress on the need for stem-cell research to help cure Parkinson's and other diseases. These "identifiable" individuals caused a change in policy image, which, according to Baumgartner and Jones (1993), will cause a change in policy venue and the potential for a policy punctuation. When viewed through the lens of evolutionary psychology and the neuroscience of emotion, this potential makes perfect sense.

That policy images can be manipulated to serve selfish ends also has roots in behavioral economics, specifically prospect theory, the theoretical underpinnings of which are rooted in evolutionary psychology (Mc-

Dermott, Fowler, and Smirnov 2008). Tversky and Kahneman's (1981) widely cited paper on this topic essentially gives policy advocates a blueprint for manipulating policy images in such a way as to promote or hinder policy success. Prospect theory states that people will be risk-averse when faced with gains and risk-seeking when faced with losses. What Kahneman and Tversky demonstrated is that preference for a particular policy solution depends on whether that solution is framed in terms of gains or losses. When presented with a health crisis, subjects in their study favored a solution that minimized risk when the solution was framed in terms of "saving" lives, but favored a riskier approach when the solution was framed in terms of the number of people who would die. Although mathematically the outcome of each solution set was the same, subjects reversed their preferences due to the framing of the solutions.[4]

When the risks and benefits of a particular policy are defined in social terms, they tend to be given more weight than in statistical models. The result is potentially inefficient policy. A story depicting the ability of a single individual to cheat the system is most likely to lead to calls for more oversight mechanisms, despite the fact that the costs of such mechanisms are likely to outweigh the benefits. Such biases in decision making have important policy implications. Rubin (2002, 175) has documented the fact that during the 2000 U.S. presidential election, Vice President Al Gore attempted to counter then governor George Bush's argument to privatize Social Security by appealing to people's general tendency toward the status quo and loss aversion. Since the publication of Rubin's book, President Bush again made a similar push for privatizing Social Security, and again, the tendency to overvalue loss and a preference for the status quo seems to have prevented such an overhaul, regardless of the potential benefits. In short, the adaptive rationality framework provides important insights for both policy scholars and policy elites seeking to better understand the way in which people react to policy proposals and solutions.

Putting It All Together

Public policy is an aggregation of human decisions. But what do we know about the human decision-making process? From a public policy perspective, not much. We assume policymakers have preferences and will act on those preferences. The dominant theoretical paradigms within public policy (e.g., public choice, bounded rationality, welfare economics) tend to take preferences as a given; policymakers are assumed to be self-interested decision makers. Deviations from such predictions are assumed to be the result of environmental constraints such as institutional rules and norms. The last few decades have seen widespread rejection of the rational choice model on multiple grounds: 1) it generates untestable assumptions (Green and Shapiro 1994); 2) observed behavior in social dilemmas deviates widely from economic rationality (see Camerer, Lowenstein, and Rabin 2004), and 3) what is viewed as "overcooperation" in social dilemmas makes sense from an evolutionary psychology perspective (Field 2004). And though attempts have been made to discard the rational actor model from public policy, such attempts tend not to stray too far from rationalist assumptions.

More notably, Bryan Jones (2001, 2003) has pushed for a renewed emphasis on bounded rationality as a model for human decision making. Although Jones agrees with evolutionary psychologists that bounded rationality is a product of human evolution, he seems less interested in explaining why people tend to deviate from the rational actor model than in redesigning institutions to account for such deviations. For Jones, preferences are taken as given, whether they conform to bounded rationality or complete rationality, and the means for achieving more efficient policy is through the manipulation of the "task environment." The task environment is akin to institutional rules and norms. Scant attention is given to the manner in which people are "bounded." Instead, the focus is on how institutional design can correct for cognitive limitations. As Jones (2001) wrote, "People can make better decisions, individually and collectively, because of institutions" (190).

Political scientist John Orbell and his colleagues (2004) have distinguished between "rationality in action" and "rationality in design." Rationality is action grounded in the assumptions of the rational-comprehensive model, whereas rationality in design is based on the assumption that natural selection favored the development of certain cognitive mechanisms that improve the prospect of group living. Although Jones departs from rationality in action, he is unwilling to accept the premise of rationality in design, or adaptive rationality. The "task" environment is essentially an argument that decision making is the result of exogenous factors. Endogenous factors are taken as a given. Evolutionary psychology starts from a different premise. People are not bounded; rather, the human mind evolved certain mechanisms for solving adaptive problems. These mechanisms allow people to make good or appropriate decisions when faced with a social dilemma, decisions not normally predicted by rationalist models. Unfortunately, little effort has been made toward incorporating endogenous variables relating to cognitive and biological mechanisms into models of policy change.

Even though policy scholars have long been critical of the rational actor model (see Stone 2002), these critiques often fail to provide theoretical justification for why the rational framework should be rejected or what should replace it. Bryan Jones deserves credit for taking a more interdisciplinary approach to understanding organizational behavior and policy decision making. In fact, from our reading of the literature, Jones is the first major policy scholar not only to advocate but to utilize empirical and theoretical models based in biology and cognitive psychology. Other policy approaches, however, have been less successful than Jones. For example, post-positivist approaches seem less interested in developing a unifying framework than in preserving the notion that reality, or at least political reality, is socially constructed. Such an approach does little to advance our understanding of how people process policy information. In fact, constructivism, hermeneutics, and intersubjectivity deny that any unifying framework is possible. Under these models, humans lack any universal preferences or tendencies. As the discussion in this chapter has demonstrated, people do not come to a policy problem with an empty set of preferences. Rather, human cognitive capacities are a product of human evolution. The theory of the wary cooperator and findings from neuroscience give policy scholars a solid theoretical and empirical foundation for how the public will react to certain variations in issue definition.

To be sure, cognitive approaches to policy change are creeping into the field of policy studies. Work by Leach and Sabatier (2005) holds promise for moving beyond strictly rational or environmental explanations of policy change. Utilizing both rational choice and social psychology, Leach and Sabatier identify factors that are critical to fostering and maintaining trust among policy elites. Theoretical predictions from social psychology are more appropriate for explaining interpersonal trust than rational-choice theory. In particular, perceptions of fairness and legitimacy are better able to explain interpersonal trust than past policy outcomes. As a whole, however, policy studies appears stuck in what Cosmides and Tooby have described as the "Standard Social Science Model." Exogenous factors dominate models of the policy process; no attention is given to endogenous factors such as biological or psychological mechanisms. As such, the current state of policy decision-making research is largely descriptive, with little predictive power. Leach and Sabatier's work is important because it attempts to provide a testable theory regarding the formation and disintegration of policy subsystems—one that is balanced between exogenous and endogenous variables.

One of the main drawbacks of policy research is that it lacks coherent theory-building (Sabatier 2007). When theory is criticized, such as policy stages or policy typologies, rarely is a replacement theory put forth. The preceding discussion suggests that the raw materials for constructing replacement theories are readily available; they are just located outside of the fields of policy studies and political science. The main critique of punctuated equilibrium and policy streams is that they fail to predict policy change. Emotional rationality or emotional intelligence completely reverses past models of decision making founded on rationalist assumptions. Emotions do matter, and they tend to operate a priori to rational thought. Public policies require the support of the electorate to be changed, maintained, or even adopted. Taking preferences as a given as is done with rationalist approaches leads to incorrect inferences about public policy preferences. Moreover, it is limited to a single set of covariates. Environmental variables such as institutional rules do explain a lot of what is known about policy change, but they give only one side of the explanation. If we open the "black box," it is likely that we will increase the explanatory power of existing models of policy change as well as other policy-related models. For example, compliance with public policy tends to be grounded in perceptions of trust (Tyler 1990, 2001; Scholz 1998). Perceptions of trust are in large part based on perceptions of fairness, which, according to evolutionary psychology, are a function of evolutionary pressures in the EEA. Only by including nonrational, endogenous considerations such as emotions are we able to build a complete model of policy compliance. Simply showing that rationalist approaches are wrong is not enough. What is needed is a theory that can explain and predict how people will respond to policy images and policy outcomes. Such a theory is likely to be interdisciplinary in nature, with a strong emphasis in evolutionary psychology, neuroscience, and behavioral economics.

An Application to Criminal Justice Policy

What the above discussion suggests is that the power of conceptual models in public policy can be significantly improved by accounting for emotions and evolutionary psychology. In this section we attempt to provide a policy-specific example by showing how findings from behavioral economics and evolutionary psychology have real implications for criminal justice policy. We discuss below three important insights from this research: 1) a tendency to seek retribution for unfair behavior, 2) the occurrence of criminal behavior, and 3) the inefficiency of jury trials.

Social norms have a strong effect on individual behavior (Cialdini and Trost 1998; Cialdini and Goldstein 2004). People tend to conform to the expectations of others. The strength of a particular norm can be assessed by the level of compliance, particularly in the absence of others, as well as the degree to which others are willing to punish others for failure to comply with the norm. We noted earlier that evolutionary pressures support the development of a mental module for detecting cheaters, particularly violators of fairness norms. Experimental and neurological evidence also indicates a strong desire to punish such cheaters.

In laboratory settings, people tend to exhibit a strong desire to punish others for unfair behavior, even at substantial costs to themselves.[5] In fact, this tendency is so strong that it is evident for third parties, or individuals unaffected by the outcome (Fehr and Fischbacher 2004), persists even when allowing for a substantial increase in monetary stakes (Cameron 1999; Fehr, Fischbacher, and Tougareva 2002), and extends across cultures (Henrich et al. 2001). The latter point suggests punishment for unfair behavior is a universal behavioral characteristic. The desire to punish also has strong biological roots. Brain activity associated with unfair offers in two-person bargaining scenarios tends to be located in the anterior insula, an area of the brain considered to be the source of negative emotional states (Sanfey et al. 2003, 1756). The decision to punish, however, is reflected in areas of the brain commonly associated with anticipated satisfaction (de Quervain et al. 2004). Notably, this brain activity occurs only when subjects are allowed to "effectively punish," where punishment reduces the payoff of the noncooperator (de Quervain et al. 2004, 1254). In short, people tend to have a very negative emotional reaction to unfair behavior but a very positive reaction to punishment. Such anticipated satisfaction explains why individuals are willing to incur the short-term costs of punishing free riders with full knowledge that there will be no future payoffs for the punishing individual.[6]

This extreme sensitivity, both behaviorally and neurologically, to injustice begins to explain why people are quite willing to file grievances for even the smallest deviation from what they perceive as fair, perhaps also explaining why people are willing to go to court over what may seem like trivial matters. Others have also noted that despite its ineffectiveness as a deterrent mechanism, the public remains quite supportive of the death penalty, a position that defies rational explanations based on outcomes or efficiency but fits with evolutionary theory favoring a strong preference for swift and immediate justice (Alford and Hibbing 2004, 711). The desire to punish for violation of fairness norms can also be an efficient policy mechanism because it is able to solve common-pool-resource dilemmas in the absence of an external authority (Ostrom, Gardner, and Walker 1994).

That evolutionary pressures favor a cheater detection module is suggestive of a long lineage of cheater or criminal-type behavior. Criminologists are now beginning to accept evolutionary explanations for the occurrence of criminal behavior. In the EEA, high status was a means to reproductive success. One way to gain status was to dominate other group members. That status-seeking is particularly prominent among males suggests males will be more prone to dominating tendencies such as physical aggression. Anthony Walsh (2006, 255), a criminologist, has written that "Non-evolutionary theories cannot account for why men everywhere and always commit far more criminal and antisocial acts than females." On a less extreme scale, that people tend to cooperate in social dilemmas also presents an opportunity for deception (Walsh 2006). In fact, in laboratory settings people tend to be more concerned with appearing fair than actually behaving fairly (Smith 2006b), what some have labeled "Machiavellian intelligence" (see Whiten and Byrne 1997; Orbell et al. 2004). Humans possess a strong tendency to cooperate, but also a strong tendency to exploit others' cooperation if such exploitation can go undetected, a strategy that would have been advantageous in an environment of small groups and scarce resources.

Finally, consider the method in which justice is delivered. Jury trials are the essence of incorporating "identifiable" individuals. We noted earlier in the chapter that biases in information processing result in more weight being given to social or emotional cues, particularly when policies are associated with identifiable individuals (Rubin 2002). In a jury setting the identifiable individual is sitting in the same room as the jury and in relatively close proximity. Such a setting essentially ensures that less weight will be given to statistical models, with an overreliance placed on personal testimonies. In a sense, jurors are put to the ultimate test; they are placed in an environment that stimulates neurological activity shaped by evolutionary pressures to be the best response to social dilemmas, and they are asked to ignore such influences. Indeed, Rubin (2002, 176–180) finds evidence that such jury bias may in fact lead to overcompensation in damage payments. Because jury settings ignore social and biological pressures, they create an environment ripe for bad policy decisions.

Conclusion: Answering the Call for New Theory

Theoretical developments being made outside mainstream political and policy science offer important insights for understanding the policy process. Over the last twenty years, numerous scholars have written of the need for better policy theory (Sabatier 1991b, 1999b, 2007; Hill 1997). Though progress has been made in terms of criticizing initial attempts at theory, such as policy stages and policy typologies (see Chapter 2), a unifying approach to policy change is still lacking. In this chapter we suggest several new directions for policy theory, especially for human decision-making models that make use of insights from neuroscience, behavioral economics, and evolutionary psychology.[7] Several consistent themes emerging from these fields seem to have clear implications for policy theory. First, perceptions of others matters. The human brain evolved in an environment of scarce resources that necessitated group living for survival. As such, people tend to be highly sensitive to fairness norms and highly cognizant of their reputations with others. This translates into a strong desire to conform to the majority opinion as well as a strong skepticism toward policies perceived to favor cheaters. Second, people do not process information in a manner consistent with the rational actor model that serves as the basis for many existing theories of public policy. Instead, people rely on heuristics and particularly emotions. Despite rationalists' fear that emotions result in suboptimal decision making, physiological and experimental evidence indicates that people do reason using emotional and other heuristics, and that such reasoning tends to result in outcomes that are "better than rational." Third, an overreliance on exogenous or environmental variables ignores the powerful influence of endogenous variables on information processing. Advances made in the fields of neuroscience, cognitive psychology, behavioral economics, and evolutionary psychology contribute to our understanding of how the public reacts to policy processes and policy outcomes. They also give policymakers insight into how to increase public awareness of an issue. For example, images that activate the cheater detection module can potentially be utilized by policymakers seeking to increase opposition to a particular policy.

An interdisciplinary approach to public policy theory is not new. Simon (1985) advocated for a more psychological understanding of policymaking theory, and more than fifty years ago, Harold Lasswell (1951b) argued that the "policy sciences" should be grounded in interdisciplinary theory. More recently, in his 2008 presidential address to the American Political Science Association, Robert Axelrod advocated the need for more interdisciplinary research. Policy scientists have relied too heavily on environmental explanations of policy change. Bryan Jones's (2001) intended rationality model, despite borrowing from cognitive psychology and biology, gives disproportionate weight to institutional rules. We are not calling for discarding such variables; rather, we ask that psychological and biological variables be given equal weight. Without straying too far into the nature versus nurture debate, we argue that the field of policy studies is ready for more nature to balance with the nurture. Despite physiological evidence, social scientists have been reluctant to include emotions as primary influences on human behavior. Indeed, the debate between rational, cognitive processes and emotional, or affective, influences has assumed multiple forms: "passions vs. reason" (Frank 1988), "emotion vs. reason" (Damasio 1994), and "emotional vs. rational" (Marcus, Neuman, MacKuen 2000), to name a few. However, as scholars have recognized the value of interdisciplinary findings, particularly those from evolutionary biology and neuroscience, models of human behavior are increasingly being advanced that theoretically and empirically account for the role of emotions in decision-making processes.

The field of public policy makes a lot of assumptions about human decision making. Policy scholars, however, are not experts on the way humans process information. To compensate, assumptions are built into policymaking models about how policymakers *should* make policy decisions. Not only are those assumptions about human decision making wrong, they are at complete odds with how the brain actually works. To make accurate policy prescriptions requires broad knowledge of human behavior. Great strides have been made over the last couple of decades in understanding the human decision-making process. In particular, neuroscience, behavioral economics, and evolutionary psychology are at the forefront of answering the question: Why do people do what they do? These disciplines have already made great advances toward developing theories for replacing the rational actor model as an answer to this question. Policy scholars ignore these advances at their own peril. Future work in policy theory would be wise to heed Lasswell's advice for a truly interdisciplinary approach to the field of policy studies.

Notes

1. That people respond to social pressure has been known in the field of political behavior for some time (see Huckfeldt and Sprague 1987; Kenny 1992; Schram and Sonnemans 1996). Yet, there have been few attempts to incorporate this theoretical framework into models of policy change.

2. Daniel Goleman (1995) has referred to the primacy of emotions and its role in optimal decision making as "emotional intelligence."

3. For example, publicly revealing violators of the norm of voting has been found to significantly increase voter turnout (Gerber, Green, and Larimer 2008).

4. Research in behavioral economics also points to problems with attempting to make policy evaluation decisions on the basis of consistent preferences. As it turns out, people assign different utilities to decisions on the basis of whether they have experience with the decision. Known as "experienced utility," people who have experience with a decision or policy are more likely to avoid errors in assigning utility than people who have no such experience (Kahneman and Sugden 2005; Kahneman and Thaler 2006). Because of such cognitive biases, Kahneman and Sugden (2005, 175) have advocated for a "day reconstruction method" for assessing utility in which preferences are deliberately recalled on an "episodic" basis. This is done to avoid the tendency to focus on a particularly salient experience with the policy in question, a tendency known as "focusing illusion." Like the theory of preference falsification, experienced utility demonstrates the weakness of assuming consistent preferences as is done in the rational-comprehensive model.

5. See Nowak, Page, and Sigmund (2000) and Guth and Tietz (1990) for evidence in two-person bargaining scenarios. See Fehr and Gächter (2000) for evidence in a public goods game.

6. See Smirnov (2007) for a discussion of this literature as it relates to political science.

7. See Crawford and Salmon (2004) for an initial attempt at bridging public policy and evolutionary psychology.

CHAPTER TEN

Do the Policy Sciences Exist?

This book's central goal was to explore the core research questions of public policy scholarship with an eye toward gaining the tools necessary to make a decision on whether there really is, or ever can be, such a thing as an academic field of policy studies. The preceding chapters, we believe, marshal considerable evidence supporting an integrationist conception of the field of public policy studies.

In Chapter 1 we identified the basic characteristics that identify an academic discipline as things like a core research question or a central problem, a unifying theoretical framework, a common methodological framework, and a general agreement on epistemology. Some of these characteristics clearly apply to the field of policy studies. True, the field does not have a central research question, nor is it oriented to a single overarching problem. Still, given what's been presented in the preceding chapters, we believe there is a strong argument that public policy does have a set of clearly identified research questions, and that these questions roughly define distinct scholarly domains. We do not always see a dominant theoretical framework within these domains, but we do see considerable evidence of theory construction. In areas such as policy process and implementation, there are general notions of what a conceptual framework needs to do, even if no one has—yet—figured out how to perfect that framework. At a minimum, we see lively debate over theory-building, and constructing explanatory frameworks is progressing at least episodically.

But what connects these domains? What stitches them together into something that can be defined and defended as a distinct field? Perhaps the best answer to this question is that whereas policy studies is not oriented toward *a* particular problem, there is a legitimate case that policy studies has anchored itself using the problem orientation foundational to the Lasswellian vision of the policy sciences. What can be drawn from all areas of policy studies is a deeper applied understanding of how democracies deal with, have dealt with, or might deal with whatever problems society or a group within society believes is worth addressing. This is the common thread that connects all areas of policy studies, even in areas such as the policy process literature, which to the novice can seem an overwhelmingly academic exercise where knowledge is pursued for its own sake. At a minimum, work such as Kingdon's (1995) and Baumgartner and Jones's (1993) can be mined for a wealth of practical advice on how to get a democratic system to pursue a particular solution to a particular problem. Have a solution ready, be ready to attach it to another problem, change indicators, be alert to focusing events, breach the subsystem monopoly, and seek a shift in venue—though not written as how-to manuals for policy advocates, these sort of works can be mined for exactly that sort of systematic advice.

Although the problem orientation is arguably a pretty thin way to connect the disparate research questions that orient different policy domains, it is no weaker (and perhaps a good deal stronger) than the bonds that hold together varied subfields in disciplines like political science, public administration, or sociology. The same defense can be made for public policy's lack of distinct methodology or its running epistemological battle between the rationalist project and its post-positivist critics. Whatever balkanizing influences such issues have on the field of public policy, they are not so different from those in related social science disciplines.

This same line of argument, however, also advances the perspective that policy studies do not add up to a coherent academic field. If the primary claim for policy studies as a distinct discipline boils down to "we're no worse than political science or public administration," then the field is in trouble. To stand on its own it must make a positive claim to be making unique conceptual, theoretical, methodological, epistemological, and empirical contributions; the negative defense that public policy is not any better or worse than related fields is ultimately not only unsatisfying but condemning. If the field of policy studies conceives of itself as a decentralized patchwork of a discipline, content to be borrowing bits and pieces of whatever is useful or fashionable in other social sciences, it deserves its already-commented-on inferiority complex. The core case against treating public policy as a unique discipline boils down to this basic critique: What has the field of policy studies done that adds to the cumulative store of knowledge that has not been borrowed from some other academic home? We believe the contents of this book suggest a reasonable answer to this question is "quite a lot."

The Theoretical Contributions of Policy Studies

As detailed in Chapter 1, policy studies are viewed as a taker and user of theory rather than a producer. It is bad enough that this view is broadly shared among those outside of policy studies, but it is accepted and affirmed by many within the field as well. The lament for better theories comes from those identified with the rationalist project (Sabatier 1999a) and its post-positivist critics (Stone 1988, 3). The inability to construct general conceptual frameworks is blamed for the lack of progress in areas like implementation, and the reliance on theories adapted and taken from other fields is seen as a key reason why policy studies is seen as parasitic to disciplinary hosts like economics and political science. Even in areas where policy studies indisputably generates unique theoretical frameworks, these are seen as too limited and tied to specific times and events to count as a real contribution (program theory being the obvious example).

It is true that policy studies has not yet produced a single generalizable framework that ties together all the causal relationships that fall within its area of interest. Even if we divide the field by central research questions, as we have done in this book, we find little in the way of a guiding conceptual framework within any of them.[1] While ceding this argument, we believe criticisms from this quarter miss the point. No social science, with the potential exception of economics, has managed to establish a central theoretical orthodoxy. And even in economics there is considerable controversy about this theoretical orthodoxy's ability to adequately describe, explain, and predict the phenomena it is supposed to. There is no reason to expect the field of policy studies to be any different in this regard; indeed, given its sprawling subject matter, it is perhaps more expected in this field than any other matter. What is remarkable about policy studies, and what has been a constant theme throughout the preceding chapters, is the astonishing array of theoretical efforts and accomplishments the field has generated.

Consider policy typologies, generally reckoned (as detailed in Chapter 2) to have reached an explanatory dead end because of an inability to overcome the classification problem. What is important to keep in mind about the policy typology project is that it was not simply a theory of public policy, it was (and is) a general theory of politics. It did not borrow from political theory—it was not constructed by adapting preexisting theories from other disciplines—it was an original conception of the political realm that stood on its head the conventional wisdom on causal relationships in politics. Its failure to live up to its tantalizing promise was not due to a failure of logic or an empirical falsification of its key axioms. It failed primarily because of a universal difficulty found in the study of politics, i.e., the inability to separate facts from values or perceptions from objective reality. Though this inability doomed the framework as a predictive theory, for two reasons it is unfair to label typologies as a theoretical failure.

First, typologies continue to provide a useful heuristic for making sense of the political and policy world. Categorizing policy as regulatory, distributive, or redistributive is a quick and intuitive means to make sense not just of policy outputs or outcomes but politics in general. It is conventional wisdom to accept that redistributive policies produce different power relationships than regulatory policies, even if objectively classifying policy into these categories is all but impossible. Second, policy typologies continue to develop as a theoretical construct and have proven to be a remarkably resilient and useful way to conceptualize process, behavior, outputs, and outcomes in a broad swath of the political arena.

To take one example, a significant literature in morality policies developed over a decade or so, beginning in the mid-1990s (e.g., Tatalovich and Daynes 1998; Mooney 2000). Morality policy attracted the attention of scholars because of its increasing centrality to politics at this time; issues such as abortion, gay marriage, and the death penalty became ideological and electoral rallying points. These types of policy issues seemed to produce a particularly virulent form of political conflict, one that mobilized large numbers of people and resisted the sort of compromise typical of the democratic process. Morality policy scholars were interested in whether there was a particular form of policy issue that bred this sort of politics and if so, could it be systematically described, put into a coherent conceptual framework, and used to explain (or even predict) political behavior and policy outputs. At its heart, the morality politics literature is oriented by a classic typology strategy: the attempt to systematically classify policy issues into morality and nonmorality types and to assess whether these classifications had predictive power. Though this literature ultimately stumbled over the same issue as Lowi's (1964) original framework—the problem of objectively classifying policy types—it provided some unique insights into why public policies fail, why public policies orient themselves to some problems over others, why certain policies have such powerful mobilization characteristics and are resistant to compromise—and it even provided some evidence that policies could be classified systematically and empirically if not wholly objectively (e.g. Meier 1994, 1999; Mooney and Lee 1999; Smith 2002). These are significant achievements that drew their conceptual power from a framework developed and refined within the policy field.

Perhaps the classic "failure" of policy theory is the stages heuristic. The harshest critics of the stages approach are almost certainly policy scholars themselves, who argued that the stages theory was not a theory at all (e.g., Sabatier 1991b). As detailed in Chapter 2, these criticisms are not without justification. The stages approach is not predictive and does not generate falsifiable hypotheses; it is descriptive rather than explanatory in any real sense. Yet even if it is only a heuristic guideline to the policy process, it is a remarkably succinct means to impose meaning and order on an incredibly complex undertaking. Understanding public policy in all its dimensions is a daunting task when undertaken as a primary academic career; yet the basic gist can be conveyed to an undergraduate class in ten minutes using the stages framework. Whatever its drawbacks as a grand conceptual theory, this is not an insignificant achievement.

Moreover, the stages heuristic still serves as a useful means to conceptualize what the entire field of policy studies is all about. Figure 10.1 shows how most of the dimensions of policy studies discussed in this book might map onto the stages heuristic. All these dimensions are connected

FIGURE 10.1 **The Stages and Fields of Public Policy**

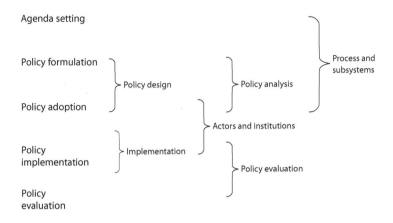

through the larger stages framework, each subfield focused on a particular element or set of elements that together constitute the stages approach. To be sure, there is overlap and redundancy, and no single dimension encompasses every single stage of the policy process, but the stages framework serves as a useful umbrella to demonstrate what the field of policy studies is all about.

Typologies and the stages framework, in short, have made and continue to make useful contributions toward helping scholars understand the complex world of public policy. More to the point, these conceptual frameworks were produced and developed primarily within the policy field; this is hardly the record of an academic discipline as theoretically devoid as policy studies is routinely described to be.

We have taken some pains to point out that the theoretical contributions of policy studies are not limited to these two frameworks. Some policy theories build off conceptual foundations from other disciplines. Notables in this category include Kingdon's (1995) concept of policy windows, which builds from Cohen, March, and Olsen's (1972) garbage can model of organizational behavior. They also include Baumgartner and Jones's punctuated equilibrium framework (1993), which builds from the bounded rationality concepts pioneered by Herbert Simon (1947) in public administration as well as work by Stephen Jay Gould in evolutionary biology.[2] Kingdon and Baumgartner and Jones, however, do considerably more than simply borrow an existing conceptual framework and apply it to a different dependent variable. In both cases, there is considerable theoretical refinement going on. Starting from the fairly raw materials of a new perspective on organizational process (Kingdon) or a well-established notion of how humans make choices (Baumgartner and Jones), these scholars considerably refined the starting concepts and emerged with original contributions to our understanding of where policy comes from, why government pays attention to some problems more than others, and why policy changes.

Even in an area like implementation, where hope of generalizable explanation has been all but abandoned, we still see policy scholars making steady contributions. These range from the basic conceptual tools needed to understand what makes policies work (or not work), things like the complexity of joint action, to full-blown hypothesis-generating, empirically falsifiable theoretical frameworks like the one produced by Mazmanian and Sabatier (1983). The fact that a generalizable theory of implementation has not emerged should not obscure the fact that we know more about what is and is not important in putting a policy into action thanks to three or four decades of implementation research. Pressman and Wildavsky would be hard pressed to make the same lamentations about the lack of research or insight into implementation today that they did when their book first appeared in 1973.

Ironically, it is probably where policy scholars have made the fewest theoretical contributions that policy research has the most settled conceptual frameworks. Policy analysis, at least compared to other areas of the policy studies field, has something approaching a general theoretical gyroscope in the form of welfare economics. Though policy scholars have certainly refined the conceptual materials and made a number of contributions in terms of the methodology, it is reasonable to describe rationalist policy analysis as largely consisting of applied economic analysis (see Munger 2000). Policy evaluation, at least on the rationalist side of the ledger, can appear more concerned with empirically demonstrating causality rather than theoretically explaining it (e.g., Mohr 1995). Evaluation is guided primarily by program theory, which in most cases is a set of beliefs about causality traced to policymaking intentions. As such, program theory tends to be limited to specific programs in specific circumstances and requires no assumptions or fundamental truths about how the world works. Yet policy analysis and evaluation are considerably less likely to be the target of (rationalist) lamentations about the lack of theoretical production in the policy field. This is perhaps because of their more applied nature, which sometimes leads to a focus more on methods and situational tractability rather than grand and universal conceptual frameworks.

Some of the harshest critics of policy theory (or the lack thereof) have come from post-positivist policy scholars, who are either skeptical that theories in the scientific sense are capable of explaining the world of politics and policy, critical that such theories and their associated methods undercut democratic values in the policymaking process, or some combination of both (e.g., P. deLeon 1997; Stone 1988; Fischer 2003). Yet the post-positivists are not antitheory; it's just that as a whole they tend to argue that normative theory (as opposed to the positive theories of the rationalists) should provide the guiding framework for policy studies. Creating normative democratic frameworks for systematically understanding the complex world of public policy is not an undertaking for the fainthearted. Stone's polis model and the epistemological cases made by Fischer and deLeon have nonetheless made a significant impact on policy studies as a field that perceives what it is doing and why. If nothing else, the post-positivists have served to remind the theory-building rationalists that public policy in democracies must ultimately be judged not just by scientific values but also by democratic ones.

Overall, we believe there are plenty of examples to counter the argument that the field of policy studies has contributed little to the systematic understanding of the political world. From our perspective, the real problem is not the field's inability to generate conceptual frameworks that result in genuine insights so much as the field's sprawling subject matter. Policy scholars have made significant advances since Lasswell first envisioned the policy sciences. We know considerably more about agenda setting, decision making, implementation, impact, and evaluation than we did a half-century ago. Much of this book has been devoted to making exactly that point. Yet in the policy field, progress seems to be measured by what we have not done rather than by what we have. We have not produced a robust and generalizable theory of implementation. We have not reconciled the paradox of science and democratic values. We have no overarching framework for the policy process. This list of failures is all true enough. We have, however, provided a decent understanding of the reasons why implementation succeeds or fails. We have been engaged in a serious and long-running debate over how science and democratic values can and should be balanced in policymaking. We have produced a wide array of empirically testable conceptual frameworks (punctuated equilibrium, advocacy coalition frameworks, policy windows) that cover multiple stages of the policy process, even if they do not cover all of them. This list of successes represents important contributions, and any discussion of the policy field's failures should rightly be balanced with an account of its successes.

Key Problems

Although we clearly believe a spirited defense of the policy field's intellectual contributions is more than justified, this should not be used to distract attention from the field's intellectual challenges. The purpose of this book was to demonstrate that policy studies did have a set of core research questions, had constructed useful conceptual frameworks to answer those questions, and had used these to accumulate a useful store of knowledge. Yet our examination has also clearly shown that the policy field consistently stumbles over a set of key conceptual and epistemological challenges.

Conceptual Challenges

The field of policy studies suffers considerably because of the continuing vagueness over what it actually studies. As discussed in some detail in Chapter 1, no precise universal definition of "public policy" exists. A central problem here is making "policy" conceptually distinct from "politics." In languages other than English, "policy" and "politics" are often synonyms. In German, for example, "die Politik" covers policy and politics. In French "politique" does the same.

In English we have fairly precise definitions for politics. In political science the most commonly used are Easton's (1953), "the authoritative allocation of values," and Lasswell's (1936), "who gets what, when and how." Both of these essentially capture the same underlying concept: the process of making society-wide decisions that are binding on everybody. There is little controversy in these definitions or the underlying concept, and they are widely accepted by political scientists as defining the essence of what they study. But if this is politics, what conceptual ground, if any, is left for policy? This is a fundamental question for policy studies—indeed, it is probably *the* fundamental question—and it has never been satisfactorily answered. Astonishingly, the field as a whole seems to have lost all interest in seriously grappling with this question.[3]

If we distill the various definitional approaches summarized in Chapter 1, we end up with a concept that can roughly be thought of as "a purposive action backed by the coercive powers of the state." This definition (and those similar to it) conveys the two basic concepts at the heart of policy studies: 1) public policy is goal-oriented; it is a government response to a perceived problem; 2) public policy, as Lowi (1964, 1972) argued, fundamentally rests upon government's coercive powers. What makes a policy public is the fact that, even if you oppose the purposes of policy, the government can force you to comply with it.

We fully recognize that the validity of this definition is debatable (e.g., what about purposive inaction? Should that not count as policy too?). Our purpose here is not to end the definitional debate but instead to point out its importance to distinguishing policy studies as a distinct academic field. If this definition is, at least for the purposes of argument, accepted as a reasonable expression of the concept at the heart of policy studies, how is it really different from the concept of politics? Does it not simply restate, perhaps in a more narrow and focused way, "the authoritative allocation of values"? Purposive decisions no doubt allocate values—they are expressions of what society considers important and what is going to be done about it. If these decisions are backed by the coercive powers of the state, they are certainly authoritative. Perhaps a key implication of this line of reasoning is that the study of public policy is really the study of the reason for, or the end goals of, politics. If so, it is not at all clear how politics and policy can be conceptually disentangled. Yet there is also the argument that this conceptualization has causal order backward. Lowi (1964) argued that policy begat politics, not the other way around. It is the nature or the type of purposive action that shapes the struggle over whose values get authoritatively allocated.

The larger point here is that the lack of conceptual clarity is a big reason why it is legitimate to question whether the field of policy studies has any legitimate claim to be a distinct academic enterprise. For the past half-century, policy studies has been mostly content to claim the problem orientation á la Lasswell as its raison d'être, or (more commonly) to ignore the issue altogether. Given that the field has never fully or forcefully articulated its reason for being, it is little wonder it is not even sure what to call itself. We have used terms like "policy sciences" as synonyms throughout this book as handy descriptive terms for the general field of policy studies. Yet it is not at all clear that these terms should be treated as interchangeable. A term like "policy sciences," for example, may carry epistemological and philosophical implications that some policy scholars (especially if they are of a post-positivist bent) are at odds with.

Our approach to the conceptual fuzziness lurking at the heart of policy studies is to seek more clarity by looking at key research questions and using these as a basis for defining such terms as "policy analysis" or "policy evaluation." We obviously believe this is at least a partially effective way to impose theoretical and epistemological coherence onto policy studies. Yet these terms are not always used in the way we describe them, and in some ways we have drawn artificially clear conceptual lines. The ex ante and ex post division we use to distinguish analysis and evaluation, for example, is blurred in practice by a considerable amount of in medias res, studies that by definition blur the pre- and post-decision markers we have used. Perhaps if there were a clearer understanding of the core concept of policy, these divisions could be made sharper and with less reliance on the individual perspective of a given researcher or writer.

The bottom line is that public policy must find a way to make the concepts at the heart of the field clearer. At least it must do so if it is ever to justify itself as an academic undertaking distinct from fields such as political science and public administration.

Epistemology

A running theme throughout this book is a central split in philosophy, a difference over how policy should be studied. This split was virtually ordained by Lasswell's original notion of the "policy sciences of democracy." The key problem with that vision, of course, is that science is not particularly democratic, and democratic values seem to leave little room for the positivist leanings of the scientific approach.

The result has been two camps that often imply the two approaches are contradictory and mutually exclusive, camps that we have termed throughout this book as the rationalists and the post-positivists.[4] This is an accurate enough claim within some narrowly defined limits. Rationalists, for the most part, do make assumptions about an objectively knowable state of the world, a world that can be empirically described and analyzed. Post-positivists, for the most part, argue that whatever is objective about the physical world does not imply a similar state of affairs in the political and social world. Reality in those domains is a heavily constructed reality, with "truth" and "fact" varying with perspective and context. These two radically different assumptions about the nature of the political and social world naturally lead to radically different notions of how to go about understanding those worlds.

Yet these differences are sometimes overblown. Many of the self-described post-positivists are not necessarily anti-rationalist in the sense that they see the whole enterprise as pointless (a good example is P. deLeon 1997). Mostly what these scholars are arguing for is epistemological pluralism, a place in policy studies where subjective experience is considered at least as meaningful as a regression coefficient. Similarly, self-proclaimed rationalists have recognized that the failure to account for values is a key weakness of their work and thus have developed methods to incorporate—or at least account for—subjective values in their work (e.g., Meier and Gill 2000; Smith and Granberg-Rademacker 2003; Smith 2005). In practice, then, what we see in public policy is less two warring camps in a fight to the philosophical death than a general recognition by everybody that effectively studying public policy means figuring out ways to combine values and empiricism.

Still, it has to be said that the differences here are significant and deep enough to act as a brake on pushing the field as a whole forward. The harsh truth is that the scientific method that orients the rationalist project is in fundamental ways incompatible with democratic values. Rationalist policy research is not participatory, does not give contradictory outcomes equal weight, and does not submit the validity of its conclusions to a vote. From the post-positivist perspective, this makes the rationalist project misleading (or even dangerous) in democratic terms. Yet in its defense, the rationalist project is enormously informative; it is probably fair to say it has produced more useful knowledge (both in applied and academic senses) than its post-positivist opposite.

Part of the problem for the post-positivists is that the rationalists have a practical and utilitarian epistemology in the scientific method, and the post-positivists simply have no equivalent. The alternate methods of gaining knowledge about public policy pushed from the post-positivist perspective—hermeneutics, discourse theory, and the like—take relativism as virtue. Pile this on top of the conceptual vagueness that characterizes the policy field, and what you tend to end up with is an approach to public policy that confuses as much as it illuminates (at least it is if our experience teaching graduate students is any guide).

Post-positivists recognize this problem and have sought to construct practical approaches to studying public policy. A good example is participatory policy analysis, which springs from the notion of deliberative democracy. The latter is a values-based conception of democracy whose basic premise is that public policy is best legitimated by public deliberation. Participatory policy analysis (PPA) in various forms is championed by scholars such as Fischer (2003), deLeon (1997), and Durning (1993). PPA rests on a fundamental assumption that the problem, the most appropriate policy solution, the impact of the policy, and the relative success of the policy are all at least partially determined by perspective. PPA begins with the basic premise that the perspective of all stakeholders must be given equal consideration if democratic values are going to be taken seriously in the policy realm.

To make this practical, the central component of PPA is to create something like juries: panels of citizens that study a particular policy problem and seek to come to some consensus on what should be done about it. PPA methodology would require policy analysts to select people, "randomly chosen from a broadly defined pool of affected citizens (possibly formulated to take sociocultural variables in account) so as to avoid the stigma of being 'captured' by established interest and stakeholders, to engage in a participatory analytic exercise" (deLeon 1997, 111). PPA has been tried in relatively limited circumstances. For example, deliberative polling, a sort of precursor to full-blown policy analysis, has gained considerable attention worldwide through the work of James Fishkin and Robert Luskin (1999). For the most part, however, neither PPA nor any other post-positivist–championed methodology has come close to providing a widely used alternative to the mostly quantitative tool kit championed by the rationalists.

The reasons for this failure of post-positivist methods to penetrate the mainstream are practical as well as theoretical. Drawing together random samples of citizens is not easy (and not cheap), and it requires a significant investment of time on the part of the analyst. Theoretically, PPA strikes many in the rationalist camp as having internal contradictions.

PPA basically creates mini-legislatures with the aim of forging more consensual policymaking. It is not entirely clear, however, why these groups would be any more or less consensual or reflective of the public's true preferences than the standard-issue legislature of representative democracy. What about the scope of the problem or policy issue? Does PPA work as well for, say, national defense as it does for local traffic problems? What is the mechanism that promotes greater levels of cooperation in PPA? Any decision or policy recommendation that comes out of a PPA process is just as likely to create losers as well as winners; this is an unavoidable characteristic of government decision making. There seems to be a general assumption in PPA that participation itself will promote consensus, or at least greater levels of acceptance. Yet there is considerable evidence that citizens are not yearning to participate, and that when they do, disagreement does not disappear (Hibbing and Theiss-Morse 2002).

It is not even clear that such methods would be more democratic. A panel of citizens that sits for an extended period of time (deLeon 1997, 111, has suggested a year), informing itself about a particular policy issue, distinguishes itself from fellow citizens by the same characteristics post-positivists find troubling about technocratic policy analysts. They become, in effect, policy experts, experts whose informed judgments may differ significantly from those of the public at large (deliberative polling results provide empirical evidence of this possibility). Arguably this leads straight to the very problem that post-positivists are trying to address: elites making decisions on behalf of the public. Beginning with a random sample of citizens does not guarantee its ultimate policy judgment will reflect a consensus that the public will support, anymore than it guarantees its policy recommendations will effectively address the targeted problem.

When it comes to differences between the rationalist and post-positivist camps, there are clearly strengths and weaknesses on both sides. It is our view that the rationalist project, at least thus far, does the better job of identifying problems, probabilistically assessing the likely effects of alternative responses to those problems, identifying the impact of the alternative chosen, and systematically assessing how and why policy changes. It also has the most practical analytical tools. The reasons supporting this perspective are detailed at length in other chapters in this book (but see Chapter 9 for serious limitations). The rationalist project, though, has failed miserably in its effort to separate values from facts, and post-positivists are quite right to point out that any notion that the rationalist project can make political decision making less political is, to put it mildly, highly unlikely. Post-positivist approaches embrace the messy, perspective-driven political realm of policy and use the values of the stakeholders as the lenses to examine problems; the relative worth of proposed solutions; and the process of deciding, changing, or implementing policy; as well as assessing what a policy has actually done. In short, the post-positivists provide a considerably richer picture of politics in policy studies. The problem with this approach is that it is comparatively more difficult to put into practice and it is harder to assess what the end result really means.

Is it possible to find and build from some common ground between these two approaches? Perhaps. Post-positivists, at least for the most part, are not calling for things like the wholesale rejection of regression analysis in the field of policy studies. Rationalists, at least for the most part, recognize the importance of values and perspective. The problem is incorporating these acknowledgments into something that can be practically used as a way to study and understand public policy. Epistemology is something policy studies will struggle with for the foreseeable future. The scientific method and the generally positivist framework of the rationalist project is going to continue to be the primary means of gaining knowledge in the policy field. For all its flaws (and these should not be underestimated), it is still more practical than any alternative. Post-positivist criticisms of the mainstream approach will remain valid because they rightly force the field to continue examining the uneasy paradox of rationalist epistemology and democratic values.

Conclusion: Whither Policy Studies?

The central conclusions reached thus far are that policy studies has made and continues to make important and lasting contributions to our cumulative understanding of how the political and administrative world works, and that policy studies has struggled and continues to struggle with conceptual and epistemological difficulties that are a long way from being resolved. Efforts are also being made to take a more interdisciplinary approach to public policy in the hopes of providing a richer and more powerful way of conceptualizing the way policy decisions are made (see Chapter 9). So where does this leave public policy as a field of study? Does such a thing really exist?

Based on our explorations throughout this book, we believe a strong case can be made for the affirmative. There is such a thing as policy studies and, at least in general terms, we can describe it.

Distilling the message of this book, we propose that the field of policy studies is the systematic search for answers to five core questions: 1) what problems does government pay attention to and why?; 2) what government response represents the most effective response to those problems and why?; 3) how are solutions chosen?; 4) how are those solutions translated into action?; and 5) what impact has policy made on those problems? Out of necessity, these questions demand a theoretical and methodological pluralism; there is no grand theory that ties them altogether (though some policy scholars have given this a pretty good effort, as typologies and the stages heuristic demonstrate). What clearly connects these questions, and the various domains of policy study they generate, is the problem orientation that powered Lasswell's original vision of the policy sciences.

Policy studies is also a field struggling with key conceptual and epistemological issues. Most notably there is a significant philosophical divide between rationalists and post-positivists, the former favoring objectivism and quantitative methodologies and the latter favoring subjectivism and qualitative methodologies. This rift is not really fatal to the field. The differences are no more serious than they are in most other social science fields. As members of both camps recognize the legitimacy of each other's claims, this is less a philosophical fight to the death than a difficult search for common ground.

Policy studies has a strong element of art and craft (as opposed to science), but this is to be expected in a field whose core research questions have such clear applied implications. Public policy is more than a mood, though. Perhaps it is not (yet) a science, but it can stake a legitimate claim to being a field of study.

Notes

1. The one potential exception to this that we can see is the use of the welfare economics paradigm in policy analysis. The welfare economics paradigm, though, is

obviously not a unique product of policy studies. And even here, there is strong resistance to using economics-based frameworks as a primary theoretical vehicle to answer questions of "what should we do?"

2. Kingdon's (1995) framework also owes a significant debt to bounded rationality.

3. We could not find a single citation in any major policy, political science, or public administration journal of the past two decades whose primary subject was defining the concept of public policy, much less one that proposed a conceptual distinction between politics and policy that justified a separate academic discipline to focus on the latter. Such articles may exist, but our search makes us confident that they are not a primary focus of policy scholars.

4. This may be another case of the sloppy and unclear labeling so characteristic of policy studies. We suspect many we have lumped under these classifications have rejected the titles, arguing that, for example, "empiricist" or "deconstructionist" were more accurate and descriptive of their particular perspectives.

REFERENCES

Alford, John R., and John R. Hibbing. 2004. "The Origin of Politics: An Evolutionary Theory of Political Behavior." *Perspectives on Politics* 2: 707–723.

Anderson, Charles. 1979. "The Place of Principle in Policy Analysis." *American Political Science Review* 73: 711–723.

Anderson, James E. 1974. *Public Policy-Making.* New York: Praeger.

———. 1984. *Public Policy-Making.* 3rd ed. New York: Holt, Rinehart, and
Winston.

———. 1994. *Public Policymaking: An Introduction.* 2nd ed. Geneva, IL:
Houghton Mifflin.

Axelrod, Robert. 2008. "Political Science and Beyond: Presidential Address to
the American Political Science Association." *Perspectives on Politics* 6(1):
3–9.

Bachrach, Peter, and Morton Baratz. 1962. "The Two Faces of Power." *American Political Science Review* 56: 947–952.

Bardach, Eugene. 1977. *The Implementation Game: What Happens After a Bill
Becomes Law.* Cambridge, MA: MIT Press.

———. 2005. *A Practical Guide for Policy Analysis: The Eightfold Path to More
Effective Problem Solving.* Washington, DC: CQ Press.

———. 2006. "Policy Dynamics." In *The Oxford Handbook of Public Policy,*
ed. Michael Moran, Martin Rein, and Robert E. Goodin, 336–366. New
York: Oxford University Press.

Baumgartner, Frank R., and Bryan D. Jones. 1993. *Agendas and Instability in
American Politics.* Chicago: University of Chicago Press.

Berman, Paul. 1980. "Thinking About Programmed and Adaptive Implementation: Matching Strategies to Situations." In *Why Policies Succeed or Fail,*
ed. Helen Ingram and Dean Mann, 205–227. Beverly Hills, CA: Sage.

Bingham, Richard D., and Claire Felbinger. 2002. *Evaluation in Practice: A
Methodological Approach.* New York: Seven Bridges Press.

Birkland, Thomas. 2001. *An Introduction to the Policy Process.* Armonk, NY:
M. E. Sharpe.

Boardman, Anthony E., D. H. Greenberg, A. R. Vining, and D. L. Weimer.
2001. *Cost-Benefit Analysis: Concepts and Practice.* Upper Saddle River, NJ:
Prentice Hall.

Boardman, Anthony E., Wendy L. Mallery, and Aidan Vining. 1994. "Learning from *Ex Ante/Ex Post* Cost-Benefit Comparisons: The Coquilhalla Highway Example." *Socio-Economic Planning Sciences* 28: 69–84.

Bobrow, Davis, and John Dryzek. 1987. *Policy Analysis By Design*. Pittsburgh: Pittsburgh University Press.

Bohte, John. 2007. "Governmental Efficiency in Our Times: Is the 'What' Really More Important than the 'How'?" *Public Administration Review* September/October: 811–815.

Brewer, Garry D., and Peter deLeon. 1983. *The Foundations of Policy Analysis*. Homewood, IL: Dorsey Press.

Buchanan, James M., and Gordon Tullock. 1962. *The Calculus of Consent, Logical Foundations of Constitutional Democracy*. Ann Arbor, MI: University of Michigan Press.

Bullock, Charles. 1981. "Implementation of Equal Education Opportunity Programs: A Comparative Analysis." In *Effective Policy Implementation*, ed. Daniel Mazmanian and Paul Sabatier, 89–126. Lexington, MA: D.C. Heath.

Burtless, Gary. 1995. "The Case for Randomized Field Trials in Economic and Policy Research." *Journal of Economic Perspectives* 9: 63–84.

Camerer, Colin F., George Lowenstein, and Matthew Rabin. 2004. *Advances in Behavioral Economics*. Princeton, NJ: Princeton University Press.

Cameron, Lisa. 1999. "Raising the Stakes in the Ultimatum Game: Experimental Evidence from Indonesia." *Economic Inquiry* 37: 47–59.

Campbell, Donald, and Julian Stanley. 1966. *Experimental and Quasi-Experimental Designs for Research*. Chicago: Rand McNally.

Campen, J. T. 1986. *Benefit, Cost, and Beyond: The Political Economy of Benefit-Cost Analysis*. Cambridge, MA: Ballinger.

Carmines, Edward G., and James A. Stimson 1989. *Issue Evolution: Race and the Transformation of American Politics*. Princeton, NJ: Princeton University Press.

Chiappe, Dan, Adam Brown, Brian Dow, Jennifer Koontz, Marisela Rodriguez, and Kelly McCulloch. 2004. "Cheaters Are Looked at Longer and Remembered Better Than Cooperators in Social Exchange Situations." *Evolutionary Psychology* 2: 108–120.

Chubb, John, and Terry Moe. 1988. "Politics, Markets and the Organization of Schools." *American Political Science Review* 82(4): 1065–1087.

———. 1990. *Politics, Markets and America's Schools*. Washington, DC: Brookings Institution Press.

Cialdini, Robert B., and Noah J. Goldstein. 2004. "Social Influence: Compliance and Conformity." *Annual Review of Psychology* 55 (February): 591–621.

Cialdini, Robert B., and Melanie R. Trost. 1998. "Social Influence: Social Norms, Conformity, and Compliance." In *The Handbook of Social Psychol-*

ogy. 4th ed., ed. Daniel T. Gilbert, Susan T. Fiske, and Gardner Lindzey. Boston: McGraw-Hill, 151–192.

Cobb, Roger, and Charles Elder. 1983. *Agenda-Building and Democratic Politics.* Baltimore, MD: Johns Hopkins University Press.

Cohen, Michael, James March, and Johan Olsen. 1972. "A Garbage Can Model of Organizational Choice." *Administrative Science Quarterly* 17: 1–25.

Collingridge, D., and C. Reeves. 1986. *Science Speaks to Power: The Role of Experts in Policymaking.* New York: St. Martin's Press.

Cook, Thomas, and Donald T. Campbell. 1979. *Quasi-Experimentation: Design and Analysis Issues for Field Settings.* Chicago: Rand McNally.

Cook, Thomas, and William Shadish. 1994. "Social Experiments: Some Developments over the Past Fifteen Years." *Annual Review of Psychology* 45: 545–580.

Cosmides, Leda, and John Tooby. 1992. "Cognitive Adaptations for Social Exchange." In *The Adapted Mind,* ed. Jerome H. Barkow, Leda Cosmides, and John Tooby, 163–228. Oxford: Oxford University Press.

———. 1994. "Better Than Rational: Evolutionary Psychology and the Invisible Hand." *American Economic Review* 84(2): 327–332.

Crawford, Charles, and Catherine Salmon. 2004. *Evolutionary Psychology, Public Policy, and Personal Decisions.* Mahwah, NJ: Lawrence Erlbaum Associates.

Cremins, James J. 1983. *Legal and Political Issues in Special Education.* Springfield, IL: Charles C. Thomas.

Damasio, Antonio. 1994. *Descartes' Error: Emotion, Reason, and the Human Brain.* New York: Quill.

Davis, Otto A., M. A. H. Dempster, and Aaron Wildavsky. 1966. "A Theory of the Budgetary Process." *American Political Science Review* 60: 529–547.

Dawes, Robyn M., and Richard H. Thaler. 1988. "Cooperation." *Journal of Economic Perspectives* 2: 187–197.

deLeon, Linda, and Robert B. Denhardt. 2000. "The Political Theory of Reinvention." *Public Administration Review* 60: 89–97.

deLeon, Peter. 1988. *Advice and Consent: The Development of the Policy Sciences.* New York: Russel Sage Foundation.

———. 1995. "Democratic Values and the Policy Sciences." *American Political Science Review* (November): 886–905.

———. 1997. *Democracy and the Policy Sciences.* Albany, NY: State University of New York Press.

———. 1999a. "The Missing Link Revisited: Contemporary Implementation Research." *Policy Studies Review* 16: 311–339.

———. 1999b. "The Stages Approach to the Policy Process." In *Theories of the Policy Process,* ed. Paul A. Sabatier, 19–32. Boulder, CO: Westview Press.

———. 1999c. "Cold Comfort Indeed: A Rejoinder to Lester and Goggin." *Policy Currents* 8: 6–8.

————. 2006. "The Historical Roots of the Field." In *The Oxford Handbook of Public Policy*, ed. Michael Moran, Martin Rein, and Robert E. Goodin, 39–57. New York: Oxford University Press.

deLeon, Peter, and Linda deLeon. 2002. "What Ever Happened to Policy Implementation? An Alternative Approach." *Journal of Public Administration Research and Theory* 12: 467–492.

Deniston, O. Lynn. 1972. "Program Planning for Disease Control Programs." Communicable Disease Center, Health Services and Mental Health Administration, Public Health Service, Department of Health, Education and Welfare.

de Quervain, Dominique J.-F., Urs Fischbacher, Valerie Treyer, Melanie Schellhammer, Ulrich Schnyder, Alfred Buck, and Ernst Fehr. 2004. "The Neural Basis of Altruistic Punishment." *Science* 305: 1254–1258.

Derthick, Martha. 1972. *New Towns In-Town: Why a Federal Program Failed.* Washington, DC: The Urban Institute.

Downs, Anthony. 1957. *An Economic Theory of Democracy.* New York: Harper and Row.

————. 1972. "Up and Down with Ecology—The 'Issue-Attention' Cycle." *Public Interest* 28: 39–41.

Dresang, Dennis. 1983. "Foreword." In *The Logic of Policy Inquiry*, ed. David Paris and James Reynolds. New York: Longman.

Dror, Yehezkel. 1968. *Public Policy Making Reexamined.* Scranton, PA: Chandler Publishing.

Druckman, James N. 2004. "Political Preference Formation: Competition, Deliberation, and the (Ir)relevance of Framing Effects." *American Political Science Review* 98: 671–686.

Dryzek, John. 1989. "Policy Sciences of Democracy." *Polity* 22: 97–118.

Dryzek, John, and Douglas Torgerson. 1993. "Democracy and the Policy Sciences." *Policy Sciences* 26: 127–138.

Dubnick, Mel, and Barbara Bardes. 1983. *Thinking About Public Policy.* New York: John Wiley and Sons.

Dunn, William N. 1981. *Public Policy Analysis.* Englewood Cliffs, NJ: Prentice Hall.

Durning, Dan. 1993. "Participatory Policy Analysis in a Social Service Agency: A Case Study." *Journal of Policy Analysis and Management* 12: 231–257.

Dye, Thomas R. 1976. *Policy Analysis: What Governments Do, Why They Do It, and What Difference It Makes.* Tuscaloosa, AL: The University of Alabama Press.

————. 1987. *Understanding Public Policy.* Upper Saddle River, NJ: Prentice Hall.

Easton, David. 1953. *The Political System.* New York: Knopf.

————. 1965. *A Systems Analysis of Political Life.* New York: Wiley.

Edelman, Murray. 1964. *The Symbolic Uses of Politics.* Urbana, IL: University of Illinois Press.

———. 1990. *Constructing the Political Spectacle.* Chicago: University of Chicago Press.

Eisenberger, Naomi I., Matthew D. Lieberman, and Kipling D. Williams. 2003. "Does Rejection Hurt? An fMRI Study of Social Exclusion." *Science* 302: 290–292.

Elmore, Richard. 1985. "Forward and Backward Mapping." In *Policy Implementation in Federal and Unitary Systems,* ed. K. Hanf and T. Toonen. Dordrecht, The Netherlands: Marinus Nijhoff.

Etzioni, Amitai. 2006. "The Unique Methodology of Policy Research." In *The Oxford Handbook of Public Policy,* ed. Michael Moran, Martin Rein, and Robert E. Goodin, 833–843. New York: Oxford University Press.

Eulau, Heinz. 1977. "The Workshop: The Place of Policy Analysis in Political Science: Five Perspectives." *American Journal of Political Science* 23: 415–433.

Eyestone, Robert. 1971. *The Threads of Public Policy: A Study in Policy Leadership.* Indianapolis: Bobbs-Merrill.

Farr, James, Jacob Hacker, and Nicole Kazee. 2006. "The Policy Scientist of Democracy: The Discipline of Harold D. Lasswell." *American Political Science Review* 100: 579-587.

Fehr, Ernst, and Urs Fischbacher. 2004. "Third-Party Punishment and Social Norms." *Evolution and Human Behavior* 25: 63–87.

Fehr, Ernst, Urs Fischbacher, and Elena Tougareva. 2002. "Do High Stakes Competition Undermine Fairness? Evidence from Russia." *Institute for Empirical Research in Economics.* University of Zurich: Working Paper No. 120.

Fehr, Ernst, and Simon Gächter. 2000. "Cooperation and Punishment in Public Goods Experiments." *American Economic Review* 90: 980–994.

Ferman, Barbara. 1990. "When Failure Is Success: Implementation and Madisonian Government." In *Implementation and the Policy Process: Opening Up the Black Box,* ed. Dennis Palumbo and Donald Calista, 39–50. Westport, CT: Greenwood Press.

Fessler, Daniel T. 2002. "Emotions and Cost-Benefit Assessment: The Role of Shame and Self-Esteem in Risk Taking." In *Bounded Rationality: The Adaptive Toolbox,* ed. Gerd Gigerenzer and Reinhard Selton, 191–214. Cambridge, MA: MIT Press.

Field, Alexander J. 2004. *Altruistically Inclined? The Behavioral Sciences, Evolutionary Theory, and the Origins of Reciprocity.* Ann Arbor, MI: The University of Michigan Press.

Fischer, Frank. 1980. *Politics, Values, and Public Policy: The Problem of Methodology.* Boulder, CO: Westview Press.

———. 1995. *Evaluating Public Policy.* Chicago: Nelson Hall.

———. 2003. *Reframing Public Policy: Discursive Politics and Deliberative Practices.* New York: Oxford University Press.

Fischer, Frank, and John Forester. 1993. *The Argumentative Turn in Policy Analysis and Planning*. Durham, NC: Duke University Press.

Fishkin, James S. 1991. *Democracy and Deliberation*. New Haven: Yale University Press.

Fishkin, James, and Peter Laslett. 2003. *Debating Deliberative Democracy*. Malden, MA: Blackwell.

Fishkin, James, and Robert Luskin. 1999. "Bringing Deliberation to the Democratic Dialogue." In *The Poll with a Human Face*, ed. Amy Reynolds and Maxwell McCombs, 3–38. Philadelphia: Lawrence Erlbaum.

Fitzpatrick, Jody L., James R. Sanders, and Blaine Worthen. 2004. *Program Evaluation: Alternative Approaches and Practical Guidelines*. Boston: Pearson.

Frank, Robert H. 1988. *Passions within Reason: The Strategic Role of Emotions*. New York: W.W. Norton.

Frederickson, H. George. 2007. "Vulgar Accountability." *PA Times* (August): 11.

Frederickson, H. George, and Kevin B. Smith. 2003. *The Public Administration Theory Primer*. Boulder, CO: Westview Press.

Freeman, J. Leiper. 1965. *The Political Process: Executive Bureau-Legislative Committee Relations*. Rev. ed. New York: Random House.

Friedman, Jeffrey. 1996. *The Rational Choice Controversy: Economic Models of Politics Reconsidered*. New Haven: Yale University Press.

Fuguitt, Diana, and Shanton Wilcox. 1999. *Cost-Benefit Analysis for Public Sector Decision Makers*. Westport, CT: Quorum Books.

Fung, Archon, and Erik O. Wright. 2003a. *Deepening Democracy: Institutional Innovations in Empowered Participatory Governance*. London: Verso.

———. 2003b. "Thinking About Empowered Participatory Governance." In *Deepening Democracy: Institutional Innovations in Empowered Participatory Governance*, ed. Archon Fung and Erik O Wright. London: Verso.

Garrett, James E. 1993. "Public Administration and Policy Implementation— A Social Work Perspective." *International Journal of Public Administration* 16: 1247–1263.

George, A. L., and T. J. McKeown. 1985. "Case Studies and Theories of Organizational Decision Making." In *Research on Public Organizations*, ed. R. F. Coulam and R. A. Smith. Greenwich, CT: JAI Press.

Gerber, Alan S., Donald P. Green, and Christopher W. Larimer. 2008. "Social Pressure and Voter Turnout: Evidence from a Large Scale Field Experiment." *American Political Science Review* 102 (February): 33–48.

Gigerenzer, Gerd, and Reinhard Selton. 2002. *Bounded Rationality: The Adaptive Toolbox*. Cambridge, MA: MIT Press.

Gigerenzer, Gerd, and Peter M. Todd. 1999a. "Fast and Frugal Heuristics." In *Simple Heuristics That Make Us Smart*, ed. Gerd Gigerenzer and Peter M. Todd, 3–34. New York: Oxford University Press.

———. 1999b. *Simple Heuristics That Make Us Smart*. New York: Oxford University Press.

Gilens, Martin. 2000. *Why Americans Hate Welfare: Race, Media, and the Politics of Antipoverty Policy*. Chicago: University of Chicago Press.

Goggin, Malcolm, Ann O'M. Bowman, James Lester, and Laurence O'Toole Jr. 1990. *Implementation Theory and Practice: Towards a Third Generation*. Glenview, IL: Scott, Foresman/Little, Brown.

Goleman, Daniel. 1995. *Emotional Intelligence: Why It Can Matter More Than IQ*. New York: Bantam.

Goodin, Robert. 1999. "Rationality Redux: Reflections on Herbert A. Simon's Vision of Politics." In *Competition and Cooperation: Conversations with Nobelists About Economics and Political Science*, ed. James E. Alt, Margaret Levi, and Elinor Ostrom, 60–84. New York: Russell Sage Foundation.

Goodin, Robert, Martin Rein, and Michael Moran. 2006. "The Public and Its Policies." In *The Oxford Handbook of Public Policy*, ed. Michael Moran, Martin Rein, and Robert E. Goodin, 3–35. New York: Oxford University Press.

Gormley, William. 1986. "Regulatory Issue Networks in a Federal System." *Polity* 18 (Summer): 595–620.

Government Accountability Office (GAO). 2001. *School Vouchers: Publicly Funded Programs in Cleveland and Milwaukee*. Washington, DC: USGAO.

———. 2002. *School Vouchers: Characteristics of Privately Funded Programs*. Washington, D.C.: USGAO.

Gravetter, Frederick, and Larry Wallnau. 2004. *Statistics for the Behavioral Sciences*, 6th ed. Belmont, CA: Wadsworth.

Green, Donald P., and Ian Shapiro. 1994. *Pathologies of Rational Choice Theory: A Critique of Applications in Political Science*. New Haven: Yale University Press.

Greenberg, George, Jeffrey Miller, Lawrence Mohr, and Bruce Vladeck. 1977. "Developing Public Policy Theory: Perspectives from Empirical Research." *American Political Science Review* 71(4): 1532–1543.

Gupta, Dipak. 2001. *Analyzing Public Policy: Concepts, Tools, and Techniques*. Washington, DC: CQ Press.

Guth, Werner, and Reinhard Tietz. 1990. "Ultimatum Bargaining Behavior: A Survey and Comparison of Experimental Results." *Journal of Economic Psychology* 11: 417–449.

Hajer, Maarten, and David Laws. 2006. "Ordering Through Discourse." In *The Oxford Handbook of Public Policy*, ed. Michael Moran, Martin Rein, and Robert E. Goodin, 251–268. New York: Oxford University Press.

Hamm, Keith. 1983. "Patterns of Influence Among Committees, Agencies, and Interest Groups." *Legislative Studies Quarterly* 8: 379–426.

Hanushek, Erik. 1997. "Assessing the Effects of School Resources on Student Performance: An Update." *Educational Evaluation and Policy Analysis* 19: 141–164.

Haveman, Robert. 1987. "Policy Evaluation Research After Twenty Years." *Policy Studies Journal* 16: 191–218.

Heaney, Michael, and John Mark Hansen. 2006. "Building the Chicago School." *American Political Science Review* 100: 589–596.

Heclo, Hugh. 1977. *A Government of Strangers: Executive Politics in Washington*. Washington, DC: Brookings Institution Press.

———. 1978. "Issue Networks and the Executive Establishment." In *The New American Political System*, ed. Anthony King, 87–124. Washington, DC: American Enterprise Institute.

Henrich, Joseph, Robert Boyd, Samuel Bowles, Colin Camerer, Ernst Fehr, Herbert Gintis, and Richard McElreath. 2001. "In Search of Homo-Economicus: Behavioral Experiments in 15 Small-Scale Societies." *American Economic Review* 91: 73–78.

Hibbing, John R., and Elizabeth Theiss-Morse. 1995. *Congress as Public Enemy*. Cambridge, MA: Cambridge University Press.

———. 2002. *Stealth Democracy: Americans' Belief About How Government Should Work*. Cambridge, MA: Cambridge University Press.

———. 2005. "Citizenship and Civic Engagement." *Annual Review of Political Science* 8: 227–249.

Hicks, J. R. 1939. "The Foundations of Welfare Economics." *Economic Journal* 49: 696–712.

Hill, Kim Quaile. 1997. "In Search of Policy Theory." *Policy Currents* 7 (April): 1–9.

Hjern, Benny. 1982. "Implementation Research: The Link Gone Missing." *Journal of Public Policy* 2: 301–308.

Hjern, Benny, and Chriss Hull. 1983. "Implementation Research as Empirical Constitutionalism." *European Journal of Political Research* 10: 105–115.

Hogwood, Brian, and Lewis Gunn. 1984. *Policy Analysis for the Real World*. New York: Oxford University Press.

Howell-Moroney, Michael. 2008. "The Tiebout Hypothesis 50 Years Later: Lessons and Lingering Challenges for Metropolitan Governance in the 21st Century." *Public Administration Review* (January/February): 97–109.

Huckfeldt, Robert, and John Sprague. 1987. "Networks in Context: The Social Flow of Political Information." *American Political Science Review* 81: 1197–1216.

Ingram, Helen. 1990. "Implementation: A Review and Suggested Framework." In *Public Administration: The State of the Art*, ed. Naomi Lynn and Aaron Wildavsky. Chatham, NJ: Chatham House.

Ingram, Helen M., and Anne L. Schneider. 2005a. *Deserving and Entitled: Social Constructions and Target Populations*. Albany, NY: SUNY Press.

———. 2005b. "Public Policy and the Social Construction of Deservedness." In *Deserving and Entitled: Social Constructions and Target Populations*, ed. Anne L. Schneider and Helen M. Ingram, 1–28. Albany, NY: SUNY Press.

———. 2006. "Policy Analysis for Democracy." In *The Oxford Handbook of Public Policy*, ed. Michael Moran, Martin Rein, and Robert E. Goodin, 169–189. New York: Oxford University Press.

Ingram, Helen, Anne L. Schneider, and Peter deLeon. 2007. "Social Construction and Policy Design." In *Theories of the Policy Process.* 2nd ed., ed. Paul A. Sabatier, 93–126. Boulder, CO: Westview Press.

Jenkins-Smith, Hank C., and Paul A. Sabatier. 1993. "The Study of the Public Policy Process." In *Policy Change and Learning: An Advocacy Coalition Approach,* ed. Paul A. Sabatier and Hank C. Jenkins-Smith, 1–12. Boulder, CO: Westview Press.

Jones, Bryan D. 2001. *Politics and the Architecture of Choice: Bounded Rationality and Governance.* Chicago: University of Chicago Press.

———. 2003. "Bounded Rationality and Political Science: Lessons from Public Administration and Public Policy." *Journal of Public Administration Research and Theory* 13: 395–412.

Jones, Bryan D., and Frank R. Baumgartner. 2005. *The Politics of Attention: How Government Prioritizes Problems.* Chicago: University of Chicago Press.

Jones, Bryan D., Frank R. Baumgartner, and James L. True. 1998. "Policy Punctuations: U.S. Budget Authority, 1947–1995." *Journal of Politics* 60(1): 1–33.

Jones, Bryan D., Tracy Sulkin, and Heather A. Larsen. 2003. "Policy Punctuations in American Political Institutions." *American Political Science Review* 97(1): 151–169.

Jones, Bryan D., and Walter Williams. 2007. *The Politics of Bad Ideas.* New York: Longman.

Jones, Charles O. 1970. *An Introduction to the Study of Public Policy.* Belmont, CA: Wadsworth.

———. 1976. "Why Congress Can't Do Policy Analysis (Or Words to That Effect)." *Policy Analysis* 2: 251–264.

Just, R. E., D. L. Hueth, and A. Schmitz. 2004. *Welfare Economics of Public Policy: A Practical Approach to Project and Policy Evaluation.* Cheltenham: Edward Elgar.

Kahneman, Daniel, and Amos Tversky. 1978. "Prospect Theory: An Analysis of Decision Under Risk." *Econometrica* 47: 263–291.

Kahneman, Daniel, and Robert Sugden. 2005. "Experienced Utility as a Standard of Policy Evaluation." *Environmental and Resource Economics* 32: 161–181.

Kahneman, Daniel, and Richard H. Thaler. 2006. "Anomalies: Utility Maximization and Experienced Utility." *Journal of Economic Perspectives* 20(1): 221–234.

Kaldor, N. 1939. "Welfare Propositions of Economics and Interpersonal Comparison of Utility." *Economic Journal* 39: 549–552.

Kathlene, Lyn, and John Martin. 1991. "Enhancing Citizen Participation: Panel Designs, Perspectives, and Policy Formulation." *Journal of Policy Analysis and Management* 10: 46–63.

Kellow, Aynsley. 1988. "Promoting Elegance in Policy Theory: Simplifying Lowi's Arenas of Power." *Policy Studies Journal* 16 (Summer): 713–724.

————. 1989. "Taking the Long Way Home? A Reply to Spitzer on the Arenas of Power." *Policy Studies Journal* 17 (Spring): 537–546.

Kenny, Christopher B. 1992. "Political Participation and Effects from the Social Environment." *American Journal of Political Science* 36: 259–267.

Kerwin, Cornelius. 1999. *Rulemaking: How Government Agencies Write Law and Make Policy.* Washington, DC: CQ Press.

King, Gary, R. Keohane, and S. Verba. 1994. *Designing Social Inquiry: Scientific Inference in Qualitative Research.* Princeton, NJ: Princeton University Press.

Kingdon, John W. 1995. *Agendas, Alternatives, and Public Policies.* 2nd ed. Boston: Little, Brown.

Kirp, D. 1992. "The End of Policy Analysis." *Journal of Policy Analysis and Management* 11: 693–696.

Kjellberg, Francesco. 1977. "Do Policies (Really) Determine Politics? And Eventually How?" *Policy Studies Journal* (Special Issue): 554–570.

Kluver, L. 1995. "Consensus Conferences at the Danish Board of Technology." In *Public Participation in Science,* ed. S. Joss and J. Durant. London: Science Museum.

Kuhn, Thomas. 1970. *The Structure of Scientific Revolutions.* Chicago: University of Chicago Press.

Kuran, Timur. 1995. *Private Truths, Public Lies: The Social Consequences of Preference Falsification.* Cambridge, MA: Harvard University Press.

Ladd, Helen F. 2002. "School Vouchers: A Critical View." *Journal of Economic Perspectives* 16: 3–24.

Lasswell, Harold. 1936. *Who Gets What, When, and How?* New York: McGraw Hill.

————. 1951a. "The Immediate Future of Research Policy and Method in Political Science." *American Political Science Review* 45: 133–142.

————. 1951b. "The Policy Orientation." In *The Policy Sciences: Recent Developments in Scope and Method,* ed. Daniel Lerner and Harold Lasswell, 3–15. Stanford: Stanford University Press.

————. 1956. "The Political Science of Science: An Inquiry into the Possible Reconciliation of Mastery and Freedom." *American Political Science Review* 50: 961–979.

————. 1971. *A Pre-View of the Policy Sciences.* New York: American Elsevier.

Leach, William D., and Paul A. Sabatier. 2005. "To Trust an Adversary: Integrating Rational and Psychological Models of Collaborative Policymaking." *American Political Science Review* 99(4): 491–503.

LeDoux, Joseph. 1996. *The Emotional Brain: The Mysterious Underpinnings of Emotional Life.* New York: Simon & Schuster.

————. 2002. *Synaptic Self: How Our Brains Become Who We Are.* New York: Penguin Books.

Lemann, Nicholas. 1995. "The Great Sorting." *The Atlantic Monthly* 276(3): 84–97.

Lester, James. 1990. "A New Federalism? Environmental Policy in the States." In *Environmental Policy in the 1990s*, ed. Norman Vig and Michael Kraft. Washington, DC: Congressional Quarterly Press.

Lester, James, and Malcolm Goggin. 1998. "Back to the Future: The Rediscovery of Implementation Studies. *Policy Currents* (September): 1–7.

Lester, James, and Joseph Stewart Jr. 2000. *Public Policy: An Evolutionary Approach.* Belmont, CA: Wadsworth.

Levin, Henry, and Patrick McEwan. 2001. *Cost-Effectiveness Analysis.* 2nd ed. Thousand Oaks, CA: Sage.

Lin, Ann Chih. 1996. "When Failure Is Better than Success: Subverted, Aborted, and Non-Implementation." Paper presented at the 1996 Annual Meeting of the American Political Science Association.

Lindblom, Charles E. 1959. "The Science of Muddling Through." *Public Administration Review* 19: 79–88.

———. 1979. "Still Muddling: Not Yet Through." *Public Administration Review* 39: 517–526.

Lipsky, Michael. 1971. "Street Level Bureaucracy and the Analysis of Urban Reform." *Urban Affairs Quarterly* 6: 391–409.

———. 1980. *Street-Level Bureaucracy.* New York: Russell Sage Foundation.

Lowery, David, W. E. Lyons, and Ruth Hoogland DeHoog. 1995. "The Empirical Evidence for Citizen Information and a Market for Public Goods." *American Political Science Review* 89(3): 705–707.

Lowi, Theodore J. 1964. "American Business, Public Policy, Case Studies, and Political Theory." *World Politics* 16(4): 677–715.

———. 1970. "Decision Making vs. Policy Making: Toward an Antidote for Technocracy." *Public Administration Review* (May/June): 314–325.

———. 1972. "Four Systems of Policy, Politics, and Choice." *Public Administration Review* 33 (July–August): 298–310.

———. 1988. "Comment." *Policy Studies Journal* 16 (Summer): 725–728.

Lyons, W. E., David Lowery, and Ruth Hoogland DeHoog. 1992. *The Politics of Dissatisfaction: Citizens, Services, and Urban Institutions.* New York: M. E. Sharpe.

Macedo, Stephen. 2005. *Democracy at Risk: How Political Choices Undermine Citizen Participation and What We Can Do About It.* Washington, DC: Brookings Institution Press.

Majone, Giandomenico. 2006. "Agenda Setting." In *The Oxford Handbook of Public Policy*, ed. Michael Moran, Martin Rein, and Robert E. Goodin, 228–250. New York: Oxford University Press.

Majone, Giandomenico, and Aaron Wildavsky. 1979. "Implementation as Evolution." In *Implementation*, ed. Jeffrey Pressman and Aaron Wildavsky. Berkeley: University of California Press.

March, James G. 1994. *A Primer on Decision Making: How Decisions Happen.* New York: Free Press.

March, James G., and Johan P. Olsen. 2006. "The Logic of Appropriateness." In *The Oxford Handbook of Public Policy*, ed. Michael Moran, Martin Rein, and Robert E. Goodin, 689–708. New York: Oxford University Press.

Marcus, George E., W. Russell Neuman, and Michael MacKuen. 2000. *Affective Intelligence and Political Judgment*. Chicago: University of Chicago Press.

Mark, M. M., G. T. Henry, and G. Julnes. 1999. "Toward an Integrative Framework for Evaluation Practice." *American Journal of Evaluation* 20: 177–198.

Matland, Richard. 1995. "Synthesizing the Implementation Literature: The Ambiguity-Conflict Model of Policy Implementation." *Journal of Public Administration Research and Theory* 5: 145–174.

May, Peter J. 1991. "Reconsidering Policy Design: Policies and Publics." *Journal of Public Policy* 11(2): 187–206.

———. 1992. "Policy Learning and Failure." *Journal of Public Policy* 12(4): 331–354.

Mayhew, David R. 1974. *The Electoral Connection*. New Haven: Yale University Press.

Mazmanian, Daniel, and Paul Sabatier. 1983. *Implementation and Public Policy*. Glendale, IL: Scott, Foresman.

McCool, Daniel C. 1995a. "Policy Subsystems." In *Public Policy Theories, Models, and Concepts: An Anthology*, ed. Daniel C. McCool, 251–255. Englewood Cliffs, NJ: Prentice Hall.

———. 1995b. *Public Policy Theories, Models and Concepts: An Anthology*. Englewood Cliffs, NJ: Prentice Hall.

———. 1995c. "The Theoretical Foundations of Policy Studies." In *Public Policy Theories, Models, and Concepts: An Anthology*, ed. Daniel C. McCool, 1–27. Englewood Cliffs, NJ: Prentice Hall.

———. 1995d. "Discussion." In *Public Policy Theories, Models, and Concepts: An Anthology*, ed. Daniel C. McCool, 380–389. Englewood Cliffs, NJ: Prentice Hall.

McDermott, Rose. 2004. "The Feeling of Rationality: The Meaning of Neuroscientific Advances for Political Science." *Perspectives on Politics* 2: 691–706.

McDermott, Rose, James Fowler, and Oleg Smirnov. 2008. "On the Evolutionary Origins of Prospect Theory." *Journal of Politics* 70(2): forthcoming.

McFarlane, Deborah. 1989. "Test the Statutory Coherence Hypothesis: The Implementation of Federal Family Planning Policy in the States." *Administration & Society* 20: 395–422.

Meier, Kenneth. 1994. *The Politics of Sin*. New York: M. E. Sharpe.

———. 1999. "Drugs, Sex, Rock, and Roll: A Theory of Morality Politics." *Policy Studies Journal* 27: 681–695.

Meier, Kenneth, and Jeff Gill, eds. 2000. *What Works: A New Approach to Program and Policy Analysis*. Boulder, CO: Westview Press.

Meier, Kenneth, and Deborah McFarlane. 1996. "Statutory Coherence and Policy Implementation: The Case of Family Planning." *Journal of Public Policy* 15(3): 281–298.

Meier, Kenneth, J. L. Polinard, and Robert D. Wrinkle. 2000. "Bureaucracy and Organizational Performance: Causality Arguments About Public Schools." *American Journal of Political Science* 44(3): 590–602.

Melnick, R. Shep. 1994. "Separation of Powers and the Strategy of Rights: The Expansion of Special Education." In *The New Politics of Public Policy*, ed. Marc K. Landy and Martin A. Levin, 23–46. Baltimore: Johns Hopkins University Press.

Meltsner, A. 1976. *Policy Analysts in the Bureaucracy.* Berkeley: University of California Press.

Metcalf, Kim, Ronald Beghetto, and Natalie Legan. 2002. "Interpreting Voucher Research: The Influence of Multiple Comparison Groups and Types." Paper presented at The Promise and Reality of School Choice: The Milwaukee Experience. October 17–18, 2002, Milwaukee, WI.

Moe, Terry. 2001. *Schools, Vouchers, and the American Public.* Washington, DC: Brookings Institution Press.

Mohr, Lawrence. 1995. *Impact Analysis for Program Evaluation.* 2nd ed. Thousand Oaks, CA: Sage.

———. 1999. "The Qualitative Method of Impact Analysis." *American Journal of Evaluation* 99: 69–85.

Mooney, Christopher. 1991. "Information in State Legislative Decision Making." *Legislative Studies Quarterly* 16: 445–455.

———, ed. 2000. *The Public Clash of Private Values: The Politics of Morality Policy.* Chatham, NJ: Chatham House.

Mooney, Christopher, and Mei-Hsien Lee. 1999. "Morality Policy Reinvention: State Death Penalties." *Annals of the American Academy of Political and Social Sciences* 566 (November): 80–92.

Munger, Michael. 2000. *Analyzing Policy: Choices, Conflicts, and Practices.* New York: W. W. Norton.

Nakamura, Robert, and Frank Smallwood. 1980. *The Politics of Policy Implementation.* New York: St. Martin's.

Nas, T. F. 1996. *Cost-Benefit Analysis: Theory and Application.* Thousand Oaks, CA: Sage.

Nelson, Barbara J. 1984. *Making an Issue of Child Abuse: Political Agenda Setting for Social Problems.* Chicago: University of Chicago Press.

Newell, Allen, and Herbert A. Simon. 1972. *Human Problem Solving.* Englewood Cliffs, NJ: Prentice Hall.

Nicholson-Crotty, Sean, and Kenneth Meier. 2005. "From Perception to Public Policy: Translating Social Constructions into Policy Designs." In *Deserving and Entitled: Social Constructions and Target Populations*, ed. Anne L. Schneider and Helen M. Ingram, 223–242. Albany, NY: SUNY Press.

Niskanen, William. 1971. *Bureaucracy and Representative Government.* Hawthorne, NY: Aldine de Gruyter.

Nowak, Martin A., Karen M. Page, and Karl Sigmund. 2000. "Fairness Versus Reason in the Ultimatum Game." *Science* 289: 1773–1775.

Orbell, John, Tomonori Morikawa, Jason Hartwig, James Hanley, and Nicholas Allen. 2004. "Machiavellian Intelligence as a Basis for the Evolution of Cooperative Dispositions." *American Political Science Review* 98: 1–16.

Ostrom, Elinor. 1998. "A Behavioral Approach to the Rational Theory of Collective Action, Presidential Address, American Political Science Association, 1997." *American Political Science Review* 92(1): 1–22.

———. 2005. "Toward a Behavioral Theory Linking Trust, Reciprocity, and Reputation." In *Trust and Reciprocity: Interdisciplinary Lessons from Experimental Research*, ed. Elinor Ostrom and James Walker, 19–79. New York: Russell Sage.

———. 2007. "Institutional Rational Choice: An Assessment of the Institutional Analysis." In *Theories of the Policy Process*, ed. Paul A. Sabatier, 21–64. Boulder, CO: Westview Press.

Ostrom, Elinor, Roy Gardner, and James Walker. 1994. *Rules, Games, and Common-Pool Resources*. Ann Arbor, MI: University of Michigan Press.

Ostrom, Elinor, James Walker, and Roy Gardner. 1992. "Covenants with and Without a Sword: Self-Governance Is Possible." *American Political Science Review* 86(2): 404–417.

Ostrom, Vincent. 1973. *The Intellectual Crisis in Public Administration*. Tuscaloosa, AL: University of Alabama Press.

O'Toole, Laurence J., Jr. 1986. "Policy Recommendations for Multi-Actor Implementation: An Assessment of the Field." *Journal of Public Policy* 6(2): 181–210.

———. 1995. "Rational Choice and Policy Implementation: Implications for Interorganizational Network Management." *American Review of Public Administration* 25: 43–57.

———. 2000. "Research on Policy Implementation: Assessments and Prospects." *Journal of Public Administration Research and Theory* 20: 263–288.

Page, Edward C. 2006. "The Origins of Policy." In *The Oxford Handbook of Public Policy*, ed. Michael Moran, Martin Rein, and Robert E. Goodin, 207–227. New York: Oxford University Press.

Palumbo, Dennis. 1981. "The State of Policy Studies Research and the Policy of the New Policy Studies Review." *Policy Studies Review* 1: 5–10.

Panksepp, Jaak. 2003. "Feeling the Pain of Social Loss." *Science* 302: 237–239.

Patton, M. Q. 2000. "Overview: Language Matters." *New Directions for Evaluation* 86: 5–16.

Pressman, Jeffrey, and Aaron Wildavsky. 1973. *Implementation: How Great Expectations in Washington Are Dashed in Oakland*. Berkeley: University of California Press.

Quade, E. S. 1989. *Analysis for Public Decisions*. 3rd ed. New York: North-Holland.

Radin, Beryl. 1997. "Presidential Address: The Evolution of the Policy Analysis Field: From Conversations To Conversations." *Journal of Policy Analysis and Management* 2: 204–218.

———. 2000. *Beyond Machiavelli: Policy Analysis Comes of Age.* Washington, DC: Georgetown University Press.

Rebell, Michael. 1998. "Fiscal Equity Litigation and the Democratic Imperative." *Journal of Education Review* 24: 23–50.

Redford, Emmette S. 1969. *Democracy in the Administrative State.* New York: Oxford University Press.

Renn, Ortwin, Thomas Webber, Horst Rakel, Peter Dienel, and Brenda Johnson. 1993. "Public Participation in Decision Making: A Three-Step Procedure." *Policy Sciences* 26: 189–214.

Rich, Andrew. 2001. "The Politics of Expertise in Congress and the News Media." *Social Science Quarterly* 82: 583–601.

Richardson, H. S. 2000. "The Stupidity of the Cost-Benefit Standard." *Journal of Legal Studies* 29: 971–1003.

Ripley, Randall B. 1985. *Policy Analysis in Political Science.* Chicago: Nelson-Hall.

Robinson, Scott E., Floun'say Caver, Kenneth J. Meier, and Laurence J. O'Toole Jr. 2007. "Explaining Policy Punctuations: Bureaucratization and Budget Change." *American Journal of Political Science* 51 (January): 140–150.

Rose, Richard. 1993. *Lesson-Drawing in Public Policy.* Chatham, NJ: Chatham House.

Rosenbaum, R. 1981. "Statutory Structure and Policy Implementation: The Case of Wetlands Regulation." In *Effective Policy Implementation*, ed. Daniel Mazmanian and Paul Sabatier, 63–85. Lexington, MA: D.C. Heath.

Rossi, Peter H., and Howard E. Freeman. 1993. *Evaluation: A Systematic Approach.* 5th ed. Thousand Oaks, CA: Sage Publications.

Rothstein, Richard. 1997. *What Do We Know About Declining (or Rising) Student Achievement?* Arlington, VA: Educational Research Service.

Rubin, Paul H. 2002. *Darwinian Politics: The Evolutionary Origin of Freedom.* New Brunswick, NJ: Rutgers University Press.

Sabatier, Paul A. 1988. "An Advocacy Coalition Framework of Policy Change and the Role of Policy-Oriented Learning Therein." *Policy Sciences* 21: 129–168.

———. 1991a. "Political Science and Public Policy." *PS: Political Science and Politics* 24: 144–147.

———. 1991b. "Toward Better Theories of the Policy Process." *PS: Political Science and Politics* 24: 147–156.

———. 1997. "The Status and Development of Policy Theory: A Reply to Hill." *Policy Currents* 7 (December): 1–10.

———. 1999a. "The Need for Better Theories." In *Theories of the Policy Process*, ed. Paul Sabatier, 3–18. Boulder, CO: Westview Press.

————, ed. 1999b. *Theories of the Policy Process*. Boulder, CO: Westview Press.

————. 2007. "Fostering the Development of Policy Theory." In *Theories of the Policy Process*. 2nd ed., ed. Paul A. Sabatier, 321–336. Boulder, CO: Westview Press.

Sabatier, Paul A., and Hank C. Jenkins-Smith. 1999. "The Advocacy Coalition Framework: An Assessment." In *Theories of the Policy Process*, ed. Paul A. Sabatier, 117–166. Boulder, CO: Westview Press.

Saetren, Harald. 2005. "Fact and Myths About Research on Public Policy Implementation: Out-of-Fashion, Allegedly Dead, but Still Very Much Alive and Relevant." *The Policy Studies Journal* 33: 559–582.

Sanfey, Alan G., James Billing, Jessica A. Aronson, Leigh E. Nystrom, and Jonathan D. Cohen. 2003. "The Neural Basis of Economic Decision-Making in the Ultimatum Game." *Science* 300: 1755–1758.

Schachter, Hindy Lauer. 2007. "Does Frederick Taylor's Ghost Still Haunt the Halls of Government? A Look at the Concept of Governmental Efficiency in Our Time." *Public Administration Review* (September/October): 800–810.

Schattschneider, E. E. 1965. *The Semi-Sovereign People*. New York: Wadsworth.

Scheberle, Denise. 1997. *Federalism and Environmental Policy: Trust and the Politics of Implementation*. Washington, DC: Georgetown University Press.

Schneider, Anne, and Helen Ingram. 1993. "Social Constructions of Target Populations: Implications for Politics and Policy." *American Political Science Review* (June): 334–347.

————. 1997. *Policy Design for Democracy*. Lawrence, KS: University of Kansas Press.

Schneider, Mark, and Jack Buckley. 2002. "What Do Parents Want from Schools? Evidence from the Internet." *Educational Evaluation and Policy Analysis* 24(2): 133–144.

Schneider, Mark, Paul Teske, Melissa Marschall, and Christine Roch. 1998. "Shopping for Schools: In the Land of the Blind, the One-Eyed Parent May Be Enough." *American Journal of Political Science* 42(3): 769–793.

Scholz, John T. 1998. "Trust, Taxes, and Compliance." In *Trust and Governance*, ed. Valerie Braithwaite and Margaret Levi, 135–166. New York: Russell Sage Foundation.

Schram, Arthur, and Joep Sonnemans. 1996. "Why People Vote: Experimental Evidence." *Journal of Economic Psychology* 17: 417–442.

Schram, Sanford. 2005. "Putting a Black Face on Welfare: The Good and the Bad." In *Deserving and Entitled: Social Constructions and Target Populations*, ed. Anne L. Schneider and Helen M. Ingram, 261–289. Albany, NY: SUNY Press.

Scriven, Michael. 1967. "The Methodology of Evaluation." In *Perspectives of Curriculum Evaluation*, ed. Ralph Tyler, Robert Gagane, and Michael

Scriven. AERA Monograph Series on Curriculum Evaluation. Chicago: Rand McNally.

——. 1991. *Evaluation Thesaurus*. Newbury Park, CA: Sage.

Shadish, William, Thomas Cook, and Donald Campbell. 2002. *Experimental and Quasi-Experimental Designs for Generalized Causal Inference*. Boston: Houghton Mifflin.

Shadish, William, Thomas Cook, and Laura Leviton. 1991. *Foundations of Program Evaluation: Theories of Practice*. Newbury Park, CA: Sage.

Shulock, Nancy. 1997. "The Paradox of Policy Analysis: If It Is Not Used, Why Do We Produce So Much of It?" *Journal of Policy Analysis and Management* 18: 226–244.

Simon, Herbert A. 1947. *Administrative Behavior*. New York: Free Press.

——. 1955. "A Behavioral Model of Rational Choice." *The Quarterly Journal of Economics* 69(1): 99–118.

——. 1997. *Administrative Behavior*. 4th ed. New York: Free Press.

——. 1985. "Human Nature in Politics: The Dialogue with Psychology and Political Science." *Political Psychology* 16: 45–61.

Smirnov, Oleg. 2007. "Altruistic Punishment in Politics and Life Sciences." *Perspectives on Politics* 5(3): 489–501.

Smith, Kevin B. 2002. "Typologies, Taxonomies and the Benefits of Policy Classification." *Policy Studies Journal* 30: 379–395.

——. 2003. *The Ideology of Education*. Albany, NY: SUNY Press.

——. 2005. "Data Don't Matter? Academic Research and School Choice." *Perspectives on Politics* 3(2): 285–299.

——. 2006a. "Economic Techniques." In *The Oxford Handbook of Public Policy*, ed. Michael Moran, Martin Rein, and Robert E. Goodin, 729–745. New York: Oxford University Press.

——. 2006b. "Representational Altruism: The Wary Cooperator as Authoritative Decision Maker." *American Journal of Political Science* 50(4): 1013–1022.

Smith, Kevin B., and Scott Granberg-Rademacker. 2003. "Money Only Matters If You Want It To? Exposing the Normative Implications of Empirical Research." *Political Research Quarterly* 56: 223–232.

Smith, Kevin B., and Christopher W. Larimer. 2004. "A Mixed Relationship: Bureaucracy and School Performance." *Public Administration Review* (November/December): 728–736.

Smith, Kevin B., and Michael J. Licari. 2007. *Public Administration: Power and Politics in the Fourth Branch of Government*. New York: Oxford University Press.

Smith, Kevin B., and Kenneth Meier. 1995. *The Case Against School Choice*. New York: M. E. Sharpe.

Soss, Joe. 1999. "Lessons of Welfare: Policy Design, Political Learning, and Political Action." *American Political Science Review* 93: 363–380.

———. 2005. "Making Clients and Citizens: Welfare Policy as a Source of Status, Belief, and Action." In *Deserving and Entitled: Social Constructions and Target Populations*, ed. Anne L. Schneider and Helen M. Ingram, 291–328. Albany, NY: SUNY Press.

Spitzer, Robert J. 1987. "Promoting Policy Theory: Revising the Arenas of Power." *Policy Studies Journal* (June): 675–689.

———. 1989. "From Complexity to Simplicity: More on Policy Theory and the Arenas of Power." *Policy Studies Journal* 17 (Spring): 529–536.

Steinberger, Peter J. 1980. "Typologies of Public Policy: Meaning Construction and the Policy Process." *Social Science Quarterly* (September): 185–197.

Stone, Deborah. 1988. *Policy Paradox and Political Reason.* Glenview, IL: Scott, Foresman.

———. 2002. *Policy Paradox: The Art of Political Decision Making.* New York: W. W. Norton.

———. 2005. "Foreword." In *Deserving and Entitled: Social Constructions and Target Populations*, ed. Anne L. Schneider and Helen M. Ingram, xi. Albany, NY: SUNY Press.

Talmage, H. 1982. "Evaluation of Programs." In *Encyclopedia of Educational Research.* 5th ed., ed. H. E. Mitzel, 592–611. New York: Free Press.

Tatalovich, R., and B. W. Daynes, eds. 1998. *Moral Controversies in American Politics.* New York: M. E. Sharpe.

Teske, Paul, Mark Schneider, Michael Mintrom, and Samuel Best. 1993. "Establishing the Micro Foundations of a Macro Theory: Information, Movers, and the Competitive Local Market for Public Goods." *American Political Science Review* 87: 702–713.

Thacher, D., and M. Rein. 2004. "Managing Value Conflict in Public Policy." *Governance* 17: 457–486.

Theodoulou, Stella. 1995. "The Contemporary Language of Public Policy: A Starting Point." In *Public Policy: The Essential Readings*, ed. Stella Theodoulou and Matthew Cahn, 1–9. Englewood Cliffs, NJ: Prentice Hall.

Tiebout, Charles M. 1956. "A Pure Theory of Local Expenditures." *The Journal of Political Economy* 64: 416–424.

Trisko, Karen Sue, and V. C. League. 1978. *Developing Successful Programs.* Oakland, CA: Awareness House.

True, James L., Bryan D. Jones, and Frank R. Baumgartner. 1999. "Punctuated-Equilibrium Theory: Explaining Stability and Change in American Policymaking." In *Theories of Policy Process*, ed. Paul A. Sabatier, 97–116. Boulder, CO: Westview Press.

Truman, David. 1951. *The Governmental Process: Political Interests and Public Opinion.* New York: Knopf.

Turnbull, H. Rutherford, III. 1986. *Free Appropriate Public Education: The Law and Children with Disabilities.* Denver, CO: Love Publishing Company.

Tversky, Amos, and Daniel Kahneman. 1981. "The Framing of Decisions and the Psychology of Choice." *Science* 211: 453–458.

Tyler, Tom R. 1990. *Why People Obey the Law*. New Haven: Yale University Press.

———. 2001. "The Psychology of Public Dissatisfaction with Government." In *What Is It About Government That Americans Dislike?*, ed. John R. Hibbing and Elizabeth Theiss-Morse, 227–242. Cambridge: Cambridge University Press.

Unnever, James, Allan Kerckhoff, and Timothy Robinson. 2000. "District Variations in Educational Resources and Student Outcomes." *Economics of Education Review* 19: 245–259.

Verstegen, Deborah, and Richard King. 1998. "The Relationship Between School Spending and Student Achievement: A Review and Analysis of 35 Years of Production Function Research." *Journal of Education Economics* 24: 243–262.

Waldo, Dwight. 1946. *The Administrative State*. San Francisco: Chandler.

Walsh, Anthony. 2006. "Evolutionary Psychology and Criminal Behavior." In *Missing the Revolution: Darwinism for Social Scientists*, ed. Jerome H. Barkow, 225–268. New York: Oxford University Press.

Wanat, John. 1974. "Bases of Budgetary Incrementalism." *American Political Science Review* 68: 1221–1228.

Weber, J. Mark, Shirli Kopelman, and David M. Messick. 2004. "A Conceptual Review of Decision Making in Social Dilemmas: Applying a Logic of Appropriateness." *Personality and Social Psychology Review* 8(3): 281–307.

Weimer, David, and Aidan Vining. 2005. *Policy Analysis: Concepts and Practice*. Upper Saddle River, NJ: Prentice Hall.

Weiss, Carol H. 1998. *Evaluation*. Upper Saddle River, NJ: Prentice Hall.

Wenger, Jennie. 2000. "What Do Schools Produce? Implications of Multiple Outputs in Education." *Contemporary Economic Policy* 18(1): 27–36.

Weston, Drew. 2007. *The Political Brain: The Role of Emotion in Deciding the Fate of the Nation*. New York: PublicAffairs.

Whiten, Andrew, and Richard B. Byrne, eds. 1997. *Machiavellian Intelligence II: Extensions and Applications*. Cambridge: Cambridge University Press.

Wholey, Joseph S., et al. 1970. *Federal Evaluation Policy*. Washington, DC: The Urban Institute.

Wildavsky, Aaron. 1964. *The Politics of the Budgetary Process*. Boston: Little, Brown.

Williams, Walter. 1971. *Social Policy Research and Analysis*. New York: American Elsevier.

———. 1998. *Honest Numbers and Democracy*. Washington, DC: Georgetown University Press.

Wilson, James Q. 1973a. "On Pettigrew and Armor." *The Public Interest* 30: 132–134.

————. 1973b. *Political Organizations*. New York: Basic Books.

Wilson, Richard. 2006. "Policy Analysis as Policy Advice." In *The Oxford Handbook of Public Policy*, ed. Michael Moran, Martin Rein, and Robert E. Goodin, 152–168. New York: Oxford University Press.

Winter, Søren. 1999. "New Directions for Implementation Research." *Policy Currents* 8(4): 1–5.

Wolff, Jonathan, and Dirk Haubrich. 2006. "Economism and Its Limits." In *The Oxford Handbook of Public Policy*, ed. Michael Moran, Martin Rein, and Robert E. Goodin, 746–770. New York: Oxford University Press.

Wood, B. Dan, and Alesha Doan. 2003. "The Politics of Problem Definition: Applying and Testing Threshold Models." *American Journal of Political Science* 47(4): 640–653.

Wood, B. Dan, and Arnold Vedlitz. 2007. "Issue Definition, Information Processing, and the Politics of Global Warming." *American Journal of Political Science* 51(3): 552–568.

Yanow, D. 2000. *Conducting Interpretive Policy Analysis*. Newbury Park, CA: Sage.

Zahariadis, Nikolaos. 1999. "Ambiguity, Time, and Multiple Streams." In *Theories of the Policy Process*, ed. Paul A. Sabatier. Boulder, CO: Westview Press.

Zeckhauser, R., and E. Schaefer. 1968. "Public Policy and Normative Economic Theory." In *The Study of Policy Formation*, ed. R. Bauer and K. J. Gergen, 27–101. Glencoe, IL: Free Press.

INDEX

Accountability, 191–192
Activity element: impact analysis,
    137–140
Adaptive rationality, 210–211, 218–221
Administrative Behavior (1947), 50–53
Administrative implementation,
    173–174
Adoption, policy: stages and fields of
    public policy, 236 (fig.)
Advantaged groups, 194–196, 204
Advocacy groups, 195
African Americans, 195
Agenda setting, 6
    evolution of stages theory, 30 (table)
    irrationality of policy process, 188
    policy change and social utility,
        211–212
    role of emotions in decision making,
        216
    stages and fields of public policy,
        236 (fig.)
    stages heuristic, 34
Aid to Families with Dependent
    Children (AFDC), 196–197
AIDS, 220
Ambiguity, implementation studies
    and, 173–174
American Journal of Evaluation (AJE),
    153n1
Anderson, Charles, 185–186
Anderson, James E., 3–4, 30 (table), 32
Antidemocratic nature of rationalism,
    116–117
Assessment of policy. *See* Impact
    analysis
Auditing: process evaluations, 135
Axelrod, Robert, 228

Bardach, Eugene, 162–163, 173
Before-and-after comparison, 149–150
Behavioral economics, 220–221, 229n4
Biology, 223
Bottom-up implementation theory, 56,
    166–168, 173, 177. *See also*
    Rationalist approach to policy
Bounded rationality, 21 (table), 23
    (table), 50–56, 211, 222–223, 236
Branch method of decision making,
    53–54
Brewer, Gerry D., 30 (table)
Buckley, Jack, 65
Budget game, 163
Budget processes, 54–55
Burden/benefit analysis, 195–197, 203
Bureaucracy, policy implementation
    and, 155–156
Bush, George W., 191–192, 221

Categorization driving policy design,
    42–43, 193–194, 203
Causality
    complexity of implementation, 172
    diagnostic and counterfactual
        approaches, 140–144
    impact analysis, 132, 152–153
    perspective approach to
        implementation, 166
    program theory, 144–147
    statutory coherence hypothesis of
        implementation,
        171–172
Center perspective of implementation,
    164–166, 168
Characteristics of public policy, 3–4
Charitable giving, 219–220

Cheaters, 217–218, 221
Child abuse, 220
Choices, 237
Chubb, John, 24n1
Citizen participation
　democratic goals of policy design,
　　189–193, 200
　institutional rational choice, 66–73
　participatory policy analysis, 122–123,
　　201–203, 243–244
　policy design, 182–183, 203–206
　public choice, 60–65
　role in policy sciences, 11–12
　shaping policy implementation,
　　167–168
　Tiebout model, 57–59
Classification of policy types, 33, 41,
　46–47, 234–236
Client orientation of rationalist policy
　analysis, 113–114
Clinton administration, 188–189
Coalitional strength, 174
Coercive power, 37–41, 183, 240
Cognitive psychology, 52, 223–224
Collective-action problems, 69–73
Common-pool resource dilemmas,
　69–70, 218–219, 226
Community, 60–65, 189–191
Comparison group, 149–151
Complexity of implementation, 166, 169
Compliance: process evaluations, 135
Conceptual challenges to policy studies,
　239–241
Conceptual frameworks, 21–23 (table),
　24n2, 231–233. *See also* Stages
　heuristic; Typologies, policy
Conflict, 39, 173–174, 235
Conforming, social, 219–220
Congressional Budget Office, 2
Consensus: participatory policy analysis,
　244
Consensus conference, 122–123
Consequences, 129–133. *See also*
　Outcomes
Consistent preferences, 52, 229n4
Constituent policy, 37–38, 40–42
Constructing the Political Spectacle
　(Edelman), 183–184
Constructionism, 204

Consumer surplus, 112, 128n5
Contenders, 194–197, 204
Control, policy implementation and,
　160, 162–163
Control group, 149–151
Co-occurrence, 141
Cooperative behavior, 210, 217–219,
　226–227
Coordination, failed implementation
　through, 160–161
Correlation design, 147–148, 150–151
Cost-benefit analysis (CBA), 8, 13
　as impact analysis, 130–131
　democratic values in policy design,
　　202
　policy design, 183–185, 188–189
　rationalist approach to policy analysis,
　　119–120
　removing emotion from decision
　　making, 215–216
　science in policy research, 13
　social construction of target groups in
　　policy design, 194–197
　social welfare economics,
　　108–112
　typologies theory, 39, 48n3
　unseen consequences of policy
　　implementation, 130
Counterfactual approach to causality,
　141–143, 147
　correlation design, 150–151
　experimental design, 148
　impact analysis, 152–153
　quasi-experimental design, 150
　regression discontinuity design, 153n4
Co-variation, 141
Criminal justice policy, 24n1, 150, 199,
　225–227
Crystal-ball gazing, policy analysis as,
　129–130

Danish Board of Technology, 122–123
Data gathering: normative bias of
　program evaluation, 139
Deadweight loss, 112
Death penalty, 226
Decision making
　bounded rationality, 50–56
　cognitive shortcuts, 210

human behavior explaining, 221–224
incrementalism, 52–56
irrationality of policy process, 188
origins of rationalism, 103–104
public policy as study of, 49–50
role of emotions in, 214–216
Decision points in policy
implementation, 160
Declaration of intent, 155–157
Deconstructionism, 200–201
Defining public policy, 3–4
deLeon, Linda, 174
deLeon, Peter, 30 (table), 174, 176–177,
195, 200–201, 204
Deliberative democracy, 121, 243–244
Deliberative polling, 123, 128n10
Democracy
deliberative democracy, 121, 243–244
democratic values in policy design,
197–203
education promoting, 119
inefficiency of, 61
policy sciences, 11–15
public choice equating democracy
with free markets, 59–60
reconciling with political
implementation, 178–179
values used in policy design, 189–192
Dependents, 194–197, 204
Descriptive evaluation, 136–137
Deviants, 194–197, 204
Diagnostic approach to causality,
141–143
Diffusion theory: fields of policy study,
21 (table)
Discourse theory, 22 (table), 121–122
Dispersed decision-making system, 160
Distributive policy, 234
adaptive welfare economics to public
policy study, 108–110
democratic goals of policy design,
189–193
Kaldor-Hicks compensation principle,
120
social construction and target groups
in policy design, 194–197
typologies theory, 37–39, 41–42, 48n3
Drug-treatment program, 142–143
Drunk driving, 136

Economic Development Agency (EDA),
159, 163
Economic rationality, 222
Economics
alternatives to public policy studies,
209–210
behavioral, 229n4
central, unifying conceptual
framework, 19
fields of policy study, 23 (table)
policy theory, 233–234
public choice, 57
rationalist approach to policy analysis,
102–103
welfare economics paradigm,
107–112
Economies of scope, 192
Edelman, Murray, 183–184, 188,
192–193, 199, 205–206
Education
accountability, 191–192
children with disabilities, 220
disadvantages of experimental design
in policy evaluation, 148–149
education production model
correlating monetary inputs with
education outputs, 117–119
impact analysis, 132
implementation study, 179
outcome lines linking policy to
objectives, 144–147
outcomes representing problems,
138–139
program evaluation, 133–134
public policy as academic discipline,
1–2
school choice, 58, 64–65, 67–69, 119,
148–149, 215–216
Effectiveness of policy design, 6,
151–152, 206
Efficiency of policy design, 6
cost-benefit analysis, 120
democratic goals of policy design,
189–193
Kaldor-Hicks compensation principle
measuring, 110–112, 124
social framing impairing policy
efficiency, 221
social surplus measuring, 128n5

Efficiency of policy design *(continued)*
  social welfare paradigm, 108
  Tiebout hypothesis, 61
Elites, 63
Emotional intelligence, 229n2
Emotional rationality, 215–216,
  218–219, 224
Emotions
  emotional dimensions of policy
    design, 182–183, 188
  policy decision making, 214–216
  unfair behavior and punishment,
    225–226
  wary cooperator, 217–220
Energy crisis, 115
Environment of Evolutionary
  Adaptation (EEA), 217, 219, 224,
  226
Epistemology, 231–233, 241–245. *See
  also* Post-positivist approach to
  policy; Rationalist approach to
  policy
Equity: democratic goals of policy
  design, 189–193, 200
Evaluation, policy, 5–7
  American Journal of Evaluation, 153n1
  consistent preferences, 229n4
  emergence of, 12–13
  evolution of stages theory, 30 (table)
  fields of policy study, 22 (table)
  formative and summative, 134–135
  implementation studies and, 157
  intersubjective framework, 186
  objectivity in, 192
  policy design, 184
  policy theory, 237–238
  process and outcome evaluations,
    135–137
  program evaluation, 132–137
  social constructions in policy design,
    193–199
  stages and fields of public policy,
    236 (fig.)
Evaluation, program, 135
  diagnostic approach to causality,
    141–143
  impact analysis and, 132–137
  normative bias, 139

Evolutionary process, implementation
  as, 163–164
Evolutionary psychology
  alternative approaches to policy study,
    209–211
  criminal justice policy, 225–227
  decision-making process, 221–224
  merging policy studies with, 217–221
  prospect theory, 220–221
  See also Human behavior
Expectations, wary cooperator and, 219
Expected payoffs, rationalist approach to
  estimating, 113
Experienced utility, 229n4
Experimental design, 147–149, 153n4
Expressive utility, 213–214

Fact-value dichotomy, 11–15, 127n4
Failed policy: implementation studies,
  158–160
Failure. *See* Outcomes
"Fast and frugal" decision-making
  heuristic, 218
Fields of public policy, 20–23 (table),
  236 (fig.)
Fischer, Frank, 184–186, 188, 193, 199,
  205–206
Fishkin, James, 121, 128n10
Focusing illusion, 229n4
Food resources, 217
Forester, John, 184–185
Formative evaluations, 134–136
The Foundation of Policy Analysis
  (Brewer and deLeon), 30 (table)
Fox, Michael J., 220
Franklin, Benjamin, 103–106, 110
Frederickson, H. George, 191

Game theory, 69–70, 162–163,
  171–173
Garbage can model of organizational
  behavior, 21 (table), 236
Goals
  defining policy, 240
  deflection of goals leading to policy
    failure, 162–163
  descriptive evaluation,
    136–137

statutory coherence hypothesis of implementation, 171–172
See also Objectives, policy
Goggin, Malcolm, 170–171, 174–177
Gore, Al, 221
Government Accountability Office (GAO), 2
Government agencies
  defining public policy in terms of, 3–4
  multiple-level coordination leading to policy failure, 159–160
  policy implementation, 155–156
  policy sciences, 9
  policy typologies and resulting politics, 38 (table), 39–40
Group dynamics, 210
Group preferences, decision making based on, 216

Happiness, 213
Health care, 13–14
Hermeneutics, 22 (table), 204
Heuristic reasoning, 210–211
Hospital utilization study, 138
Housing project, 160–161
Human behavior
  adaptive rationality, 210–211
  bottom-up implementation theory, 168
  explaining the decision-making process, 221–224
  implementation as evolutionary process, 164
  implementation studies, 175–176
  preference falsification, 213–214
  research design and impact analysis, 143–144
  role of emotions in decision making, 214–216
  wary cooperator, 217–220
  See also Evolutionary psychology

Identifiable individuals, 220–221, 226–227
Identity, group, 219
Image, policy, 211–214, 220–221
Impact analysis, 152–153
  cost-benefit analysis, 130–131

identifying the problem and measuring the outcome, 137–140
logic and theory of, 140–144
necessity of, 130
outcome evaluation, 135
program evaluation, 132–137
program theory, 144–147
research design, 147–152
Implementation: How Great Expectations in Washington Are Dashed in Oakland (Pressman and Wildavsky), 158–160
Implementation, policy, 129–130
  as evolutionary process, 163–164
  as key to policy failure, 161–162
  bureaucratic path of, 155–156
  case studies method, 16
  center perspective theory, 164–166
  complexity of, 166, 170–171
  defining the problem, 156–158
  evolution of stages theory, 30 (table)
  fields of policy study, 23 (table)
  games approach to, 162–163
  impact analysis, 130
  importance of understanding, 158–162
  job creation failure, 158–160
  lack of explanatory framework, 17
  matrix approach, 173–175
  model community failure, 160–161
  origins and future of implementation research, 178–179
  periphery perspective, 166–168
  policy studies and, 172–173
  policy theory, 233, 237
  post-positivism, 245
  process and outcome evaluations, 135–136
  reformers, skeptics, terminators, and testers, 175–177
  stages and fields of public policy, 236 (fig.)
  statutory coherence hypothesis of implementation, 171–172
  systematic study of, 156
  theory construction, 162–169, 231–232
Implementation and Public Policy (Mazmanian and Sabatier), 164–166

The Implementation Game (Bardach), 162–163
Incentives, 39
Incrementalism, 23 (table), 52–56, 210
Individual preferences, 217
Individual welfare, 108
Informed decision making, 60–64
Ingram, Helen, 194–196, 199–204
"Institutional analysis and development" or IAD, 69–73
Institutional design correcting for cognitive limitations, 210
Institutional rational choice, 66–73
Institutional reform, 118, 143–144
Instrumental learning, 198
Interpretive analysis, post-positivist approach using, 121–122
Interrupted time series design, 149–150, 153n4
Interventions, 139
Intrinsic utility, 213
An Introduction to the Study of Public Policy (Jones), 30 (table)
Intuitive nature of public policy, 3

Jacobellis v. Ohio, 3
Job-creation project, 158–160, 163
Johnson administration, 160–161
Jones, Bryan, 223
Jones, Charles O., 30 (table), 31–32
Jury trials, 226–227

Kaldor-Hicks compensation principle, 110–112, 120, 124

Language shaping policy, 183–185, 188
Lasswell, Harold, 8–10, 12–13, 20, 24n1, 239–240
  evolution of stages theory, 30 (table)
  policy process, 29
  policy process model, 29–32
Lester, James, 174–177
Liberal-rationalism, 200
Liberty: democratic goals of policy design, 189–191, 200
Lindblom, Charles, 52–56
Linear problem-solving paradigm, 104–107
Lipsky, Michael, 166–168

Local factors, 65
Local level implementation, 161
Localities, 57–58
Logic of appropriateness, 219
"Logic of appropriateness," 71–72
"Looking at the Efficiency Concept in Our Time" (Schachter), 192
Lowi, Theodore, 28, 36–42, 45–46

Machiavelli, Niccolo, 7–8
Machiavellian intelligence, 226
Madison, James, 8
Majone, Giandomenico, 163–164
Mann, Horace, 133–134
Marginal groups, 198–199
Market analysis
  education production, 119
  public choice equating democracy with free markets, 59–60
  welfare economics, 107–112
Matland, Richard, 173–175, 177
Matrix approach to implementation, 173–175
Max Planck Institute for Human Development, 211
May, Peter, 193, 198
Mazmanian, Daniel, 164–166, 170, 178
McFarlane, Deborah, 171
Means, political, 159–160
Methodology
  academic characteristics of public policy study, 231–233
  fields of policy study, 21–23 (table)
  methodological individualism, 108
  methodological sophistication of policy sciences, 9
  public policy fields, 13
  rationalist and post-positivist approaches to policy analysis, 102–103
Military applications, rationalist approach and, 114–115
Mixed policy cases, 43–44
Mobility, 64
Model communities project, 160–161
Moe, Terry, 24n1
Moral algebra method of decision making, 103–106, 110
Moral entrepreneurs, 198–199

Morality policy, 234–235
Multidisciplinary nature of policy sciences, 9
Multijurisdictional communities, 57–60
Multimethodological approach to policy design, 186
Multiple actors problem, 42–43
Multiple outcomes, 138
Multiple streams, 21 (table), 211–212, 234

Narrative crafting public policy, 183–185, 188
National mood, 214
National Public Radio (NPR), 219
Neuroscience, 209–210, 212, 214–216
New institutionalism, 210
No Child Left Behind Act, 191–192
Normative theory, 13, 131–133, 137, 238
Nuclear science, 213–214

Oakland, California, 158–160, 163
Objectives, policy
  impact analysis, 131–132
  implementation studies, 157–158
  outcome lines linking policy to, 144–147
  ranking policy alternatives, 106–107
  statutory coherence hypothesis of implementation, 171–172
  welfare economics paradigm, 108
Operations research, 114–115
Orbell, John, 222–223
Organizational process, 236–237
Orientations, policy, 20–23 (table)
Ostracism behavior, 219
Ostrom, Elinor, 66, 69–70, 218–219
Outcomes
  correlation design, 150–151
  education policy, 68
  failure of policy studies, 238–239
  impact analysis, 130–132, 137–140
  implementation studies and policy evaluation, 157, 174
  multiple outcomes and single outcomes with multiple elements, 138
  outcome evaluations, 135–137
  outcome line, 144–147

perspective approach to implementation, 165
program evaluation, 137
quasi-experimental design, 150
rationalist approach to estimating, 105, 113
subjectivity of policy design, 185
typology theory and, 42
See also Impact analysis; Implementation
Outputs
  decision making based on, 216
  democratic goals of policy design, 190
  education production model, 119
  policy typologies theory, 36–41
  typologies and, 42, 47
The Oxford Handbook of Public Policy, 1

Pareto principle, 108–110, 109 (fig.), 120
Parking space problem, 111–112
Parkinson's disease, 220
Participatory policy analysis (PPA), 122–123, 201–203, 243–244
Peer pressure, 219–220
Perception, 12
Periphery perspective of implementation, 164–168
Personal testimony, 220
Perspective, implementation and, 164–168
Philosophy of policy. *See* Post-positivist approach; Rationalist approach
"Piling on" game, 163
Plato, 7–8
Policy analysis
  deliberative democracy, 243–244
  emergence of, 12–13
  fields of policy study, 2, 5–7, 22 (table)
  history of policy studies, 8
  policy design and, 185–186
  policy theory, 237–238
  rationalist and post-positivist approaches, 102–103
  role of emotions in decision making, 216
See also Cost-benefit analysis
Policy Analysis in Political Science (Ripley), 30 (table)
Policy change, 211–214

Policy design
    allocation and distribution of values,
        181–183
    democratic values, 199–203
    design-process paradox, 187–193
    fields of policy study, 22–23 (table)
    multimethodological approach to, 186
    social constructions and target
        populations, 193–199
    stages and fields of public policy,
        236 (fig.)
    subjective nature of, 183–187
    testing design theories, 203–205
Policy Design for Democracy (Schneider
    and Ingram), 201–202
Policy entrepreneurs, 199
Policy evaluation. *See* Evaluation, policy
Policy implementation. *See*
    Implementation, policy
Policy learning, 198
"The Policy Orientation" (Lasswell), 9
Policy Paradox (Stone), 189
Policy process. *See* Process, policy
Policy research. *See* Research design;
    Research question
Policy sciences
    as policy studies, 241
    democratic values in policy design,
        200
    fracturing of, 11–15
    history of policy studies, 8–10
    policy orientations, 20
    public choice, 62–63
    rationalist approach, 104–105, 113
Policy streams, 21 (table), 211–212, 234
Policy studies
    characteristics of, 231–233
    failure to produce unified theory,
        16–17
    fractured nature of policy sciences,
        11–15
    implementation studies, 172–173
    origins of program evaluation, 134
    public policy as study of decision
        making, 49–50
    theoretical contributions, 233–239
Policy Studies Journal, 43
Polis model, 187–188, 238

Political entrepreneurs, 199
Political learning, 198
Political science, 8, 17–18, 21 (table)
Political spectacle, 183–184
Politics
    allocation of values, 181–183
    defining, 239–240, 247n3
    design policy, 186
    fields of policy study, 21–23 (table)
    implementation as extension of, 163
    importance of perception in, 12
    policy causing, 25n4, 28, 37–41, 45
    policy typologies and resulting
        politics, 38 (table)
    political power of target groups,
        194–197
    post-positivist critique of rationalism,
        120–121
Politics, Values, and Public Policy
    (Fischer), 184
Positivism, 122–123, 126–127
Post-positivist approach to policy,
    102–103
    decision-making process, 223
    democratic values in policy design,
        200–201
    diagnostic approach to causality, 143
    education production, 117–119
    impact analysis, 131–132, 139
    implementation theory, 168–169
    interpretive nature of, 121
    policy design, 206
    policy theory, 233, 238
    positivism and, 126–127
    program theory, 146–147
    rationalist approach and, 116–117
    rejecting public choice, 59
    strengths and weaknesses of, 241–245
Preference falsification, 213–214
Pressman, Jeffrey, 16–17, 158–160, 178
A Pre-View of the Policy Sciences
    (Lasswell), 30 (table)
Priestly, Joseph, 103–104
The Prince (Machiavelli), 7–8
Procedural rationality, 51–52
Process, policy
    constructing a unified policy theory,
        29–32

defining public policy fields, 5–7
design-process paradox, 187–188
emergence of, 12–13
implementation studies and policy
    evaluation, 157
policy process model, 31–32
policy sciences, 9
Process evaluations, 135–137
Production, education as, 117–119
Program evaluation. *See* Evaluation,
    program
Program theory, 22 (table), 144–147,
    237–238
Prohibition, 166
Propaganda, 8–9
Prospect theory, 220–221
Psychological mechanisms, 217–218
Public administration, 18, 127n4. *See
    also* Implementation
Public Administration Review, 192
Public choice, 23 (table), 24n3, 56–61,
    66–73
Public good, 13–14, 57–58
Public interest, 5, 107
Public policy
    causing politics, 25n4, 28, 37–41, 45
    characteristics of good policy theory,
        28–29, 36, 43–44
    defining, 3–4
    See also Evaluation, policy;
        Implementation, policy; Policy
        analysis; Policy design
Public policy studies
    academic and professional areas of,
        1–2
    defining the fields of, 5–7
    history of, 7–11
Public Policy-Making (Anderson), 30
    (table)
Punctuated equilibrium, 21 (table), 56,
    210–214, 224
Punishment, 69–70, 225–226
Pure policy cases, 43–44
Purposive nature of policy, 181–182, 240

Qualitative methodology, 137, 141–143
Quantitative methodology, 13–14,
    105–107, 133

Quantitative program evaluation. *See*
    Impact analysis
Quasi-experimental design, 147–150,
    153n4

Randomization of subjects, 147–149,
    153n4
Ranking system, 103–107, 119–120
Rational actor model, 66, 223
Rationalism
    adaptive rationality, 210–211
    decision making, 49–50
    decision-making process, 222–224
    emotions overriding, 214–216
    explaining human behavior, 209–210
    institutional rational choice, 66–73
    rational comprehensive model of
        decision making, 53
    social exclusion, 211–213
Rationalist approach to policy
    antidemocratic nature of, 116–117
    cost-benefit analysis, 119–120
    critique of post-positivism, 123–124
    decision-making process, 224–225
    design-process paradox, 187–188
    impact analysis, 131–132
    implementation theory, 168–169
    origins of, 103–107
    policy design, 181–183, 187–188
    policy theory, 233, 237–238
    positivism and, 126–127
    strengths and weaknesses of, 241–245
    successful and failed applications of,
        112–116
    welfare economics paradigm, 107–112
Rationality, bounded, 21 (table), 23
    (table), 50–56, 211, 222–223, 236
Reality, 242
Reason, political, 187–188
Redistributive policy, 37–38, 41–42,
    48n3, 109–110, 234
Reformers of implementation studies,
    175–176
Regression discontinuity design, 153n4
Regulative policy, 37–39, 41–42, 48n3,
    144, 234
The Republic (Plato), 7–8
Reputational utility, 213–214

Research design
  impact analysis, 143–144, 147–153
  program theory, 147
Research question
  characterizing public policy study, 20
  defining, 104
  fields of policy study, 21–23 (table)
  impact analysis, 137–140
Resource allocation
  adaptive welfare economics to public
    policy study, 109–110
  administrative implementation, 174
  common-pool resource dilemmas,
    69–70, 218–219, 226
  democratic goals of policy design,
    189–193
  diversion of resources leading to
    policy failure, 162–163
  economies of scope, 192
  efficiency of policy, 123–124
  perspective approach to
    implementation, 166
  post-positivism, 117–119
  social construction of target groups,
    194–197
  statutory coherence hypothesis of
    implementation, 171–172
Results-driven management, 191
Ripley, Randall B., 30 (table)
Risk, 221
Root method of decision making, 53–54

Sabatier, Paul, 15–16, 33–35, 47–48,
    164–166, 169–170, 178, 223–224
Sanctions, 39
"Satisficing," 54
Schattschneider, E. E., 37
Schneider, Anne L., 194–196, 199–204
Schneider, Mark, 65
School choice, 58, 64–69, 119, 148–149,
    215–216
Scientific method, 17–18, 242–243
Security: democratic goals of policy
    design, 189–191
Self-selection, correlational design and,
    150–151
Signature, 142
Simon, Herbert, 50–53

Simplicity characterizing good theory,
    43–44
Single outcomes with multiple elements,
    138
Skeptics of implementation studies,
    175–177
Small business, 195
Small pox eradication, 174
Smith, Adam, 8
Social choice, 108, 112, 125–127
Social constructions, policy design and,
    193–203, 206
Social exclusion, 211–213
Social learning, 198, 204
Social outcomes, 191
Social pressure, 217, 229n1
Social problems, 5–7, 165–166
Social psychology, 212, 223–224
Social science
  centralized theory, 16–17
  program evaluation, 134
  rationalist approach to policy analysis,
    102–103
  theoretical failings of, 18–19
Social security, 110, 221
Social support, 213
Social surplus, 128n5
Social utility, 213
Social values. *See* Values
Social welfare
  common-pool resource dilemmas,
    218–219
  policy effectiveness, 188–190
  quantifying, 107
  social construction of recipients,
    194–197
  wary cooperator model, 217–218
  welfare economics paradigm, 109 (fig.)
  welfare to work, 218
Soss, Joe, 196–197, 201
Sovereignty, 58–59
Stages heuristic, 235–236, 236 (fig.)
  as theoretical failure, 27–28
  contribution to policy theory, 46–47
  criticism of, 32–36
  evolution of, 30 (table)
  fields of policy study, 21 (table)
  policy process model, 29–32

Standard Social Science Model, 224
Status-seeking, 226
Statutory coherence hypothesis of
  implementation, 166, 171–172
Stewart, Potter, 3
Stone, Deborah, 17–18, 187–194,
  199–200, 204–206
Streams, 21 (table), 211–212, 234
Street-level bureaucrats, 167–168
Subjective nature of policy design,
  183–187, 200
Subobjectives, 145–146
Substance of policy, 181–182
Substantive rationality, 51–53
Success. *See* Outcomes
Summative evaluations, 134–136
Surplus, 128n5
Symbolic elements of policy, 182–185,
  188, 205
The Symbolic Uses of Politics (Edelman),
  184
Systems theory: fields of policy study,
  21 (table)

Target population
  periphery theory of implementation,
    168
  social constructions in policy design,
    193–199, 201–203
  statutory coherence hypothesis of
    implementation, 171–172
  subjective nature of policy design,
    183–187
  use of narrative in policy design, 188
Task environment, 222–223
Tax policy: wary cooperator model,
  217–218
Taxonomic policy classification, 46–47
Technocracy, policy sciences as, 11–15
Technocratic elite, 56, 121
Temporal precedence, 141
Tenacity game, 163
Terminators of implementation studies,
  175–176
Teske, Paul, 61–62
Testers of implementation studies,
  175–176
Theoretical framework, 233

Theory construction, 14–19, 28–29, 36,
  43–44, 231–232
Three Mile Island, 214
Tiebout, Charles, 57–59
Tiebout hypothesis, 57–60, 67, 72,
  215–216
Tokenism game, 163
Top-down implementation theory,
  164–166, 168–169, 173, 177
Tractability of a problem, 165–166
Transmission of objectives, 165–166
Typologies, policy, 234–236
  as theoretical failure, 27–28
  criticism of, 41–46
  elements of, 36–41

Unambiguous model of rational
  decision making, 193
Urban model communities project,
  160–161
Utilitarianism, 22 (table), 110–111, 124,
  200

Values
  allocation and distribution of,
    181–183, 240–241
  democratic values in policy design,
    189–192, 199–203
  driving policy analysis, 117–118
  driving rationalism, 114, 126–127
  fact-value dichotomy in public
    administration, 127n4
  monetary values of cost-benefit
    analysis, 120
  policy analysis addressing, 102
  policy design addressing, 183–187,
    203–205
  policy sciences, 11–15
  post-positivist critique of rationalism,
    120–121
  rationalist view of, 105, 242, 244–245
  symbolic and emotional dimensions
    of policy design, 182–183
Vietnam War, 13, 115
Vouchers, school. *See* School choice

Waldo, Dwight, 178
War on Poverty, 13, 115

Wary cooperator model, 217–220
Wealth distribution, 108–110
Welfare, social. *See* Social welfare
Welfare economics paradigm, 22 (table),
    107–112, 124, 215–216
White, Ryan, 220

Wildavsky, Aaron, 16–17, 158–160,
    163–164, 178
Wilson, James Q., 24n1, 139, 199
Wilson's Laws, 139
Windows, policy, 236
World War II, 114–115

Made in the USA
Lexington, KY
14 January 2013